"No other guid[e]  a pleasure to re[ad]..."

"... Excellently organized for the casual traveler who is looking for a mix of recreation and cultural insight."
Washington Post

★ ★ ★ ★ ★ (5-star rating) "Crisply written and remarkably personable. Cleverly organized so you can pluck out the minutest fact in a moment. Satisfyingly thorough."
Réalités

"The information they offer is up-to-date, crisply presented but far from exhaustive, the judgments knowledgeable but not opinionated." *New York Times*

"The individual volumes are compact, the prose succinct, and the coverage up-to-date and knowledgeable . . . The format is portable and the index admirably detailed."
John Barkham Syndicate

"... An abundance of excellent directions, diversions, and facts, including perspectives and getting-ready-to-go advice — succinct, detailed, and well organized in an easy-to-follow style." *Los Angeles Times*

"They contain an amount of information that is truly staggering, besides being surprisingly current."
Detroit News

"These guides address themselves to the needs of the modern traveler demanding precise, qualitative information . . . Upbeat, slick, and well put together."
Dallas Morning News

"... Attractive to look at, refreshingly easy to read, and generously packed with information." *Miami Herald*

"These guides are as good as any published, and much better than most." *Louisville* (Kentucky) *Times*

Stephen Birnbaum Travel Guides

Acapulco
Bahamas, and Turks & Caicos
Barcelona
Bermuda
Boston
Canada
Cancun, Cozumel, & Isla Mujeres
Caribbean
Chicago
Disneyland
Eastern Europe
Europe
Europe for Business Travelers
Florence
France
Great Britain
Hawaii
Honolulu
Ireland
Italy
Ixtapa & Zihuatanejo
Las Vegas
London
Los Angeles
Mexico
Miami & Ft. Lauderdale
Montreal & Quebec City
New Orleans
New York
Paris
Portugal
Puerto Vallarta
Rome
San Francisco
South America
Spain
Toronto
United States
USA for Business Travelers
Vancouver
Venice
Walt Disney World
Washington, DC
Western Europe

CONTRIBUTING EDITORS

Neva Allen
Stephen Allen
Joseph Chassler
Elliot S. Krane

MAPS   Mark Carlson
       Susan Carlson

SYMBOLS   Gloria McKeown

A Stephen Birnbaum Travel Guide

Birnbaum's LAS VEGAS 1993

Alexandra Mayes Birnbaum
EDITOR

Lois Spritzer
EXECUTIVE EDITOR

Laura L. Brengelman
Managing Editor

Mary Callahan
Jill Kadetsky
Susan McClung
Beth Schlau
Dana Margaret Schwartz
Associate Editors

Gene Gold
Assistant Editor

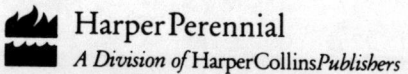

HarperPerennial
A Division of HarperCollins*Publishers*

To Stephen, who merely made all this possible.

BIRNBAUM'S LAS VEGAS 1993. Copyright © 1993 by HarperCollins Publishers. All rights reserved. Printed in the United States of America. No part of this book may be used or reproduced in any manner whatsoever without written permission except in the case of brief quotations embodied in critical articles and reviews. For information address HarperCollins*Publishers,* 10 East 53rd Street, New York, NY 10022.

FIRST EDITION

ISSN 0749-2561 (Stephen Birnbaum Travel Guides)
ISSN 1061-5423 (Las Vegas)
ISBN 0-06-278057-3 (pbk.)

93 94 95 96 97 CC/WP 10 9 8 7 6 5 4 3 2 1

Contents

ix   **A Word from the Editor**
1   **How to Use This Guide**

GETTING READY TO GO

All the practical travel data you need to plan your vacation down to the final detail.

When and How to Go

- 9   When to Go
- 10   Traveling by Plane
- 26   On Arrival
- 30   Package Tours

Preparing

- 35   Calculating Costs
- 35   Planning a Trip
- 37   How to Use a Travel Agent
- 38   Insurance
- 42   Hints for Handicapped Travelers
- 49   Hints for Single Travelers
- 50   Hints for Older Travelers
- 53   Hints for Traveling with Children

On the Road

- 57   Credit Cards and Traveler's Checks
- 60   Time Zone and Business Hours
- 60   Mail, Telephone, and Electricity
- 62   Staying Healthy
- 66   Legal Aid
- 66   Drinking and Drugs
- 67   Tipping
- 68   Religion on the Road

Sources and Resources

- 69 Tourist Information Offices
- 69 Books, Magazines, and Newsletters
- 71 Cameras and Equipment

THE CITY

A thorough, qualitative guide to Las Vegas. Each section offers a comprehensive report on the city's most compelling attractions and amenities, designed to be used on the spot.

- 75 Specific Data About Las Vegas

DIVERSIONS

A selective guide to more than a dozen active and/or cerebral vacation themes, including the best places to pursue them.

For the Experience

- 99 Quintessential Las Vegas
- 102 High-Rollin' Hotels
- 105 Vegas Victuals
- 106 Best in Shows
- 108 Luck Be A Lady: Gambling
- 120 Vegas Vows: Winning Weddings
- 122 A Shutterbug's Las Vegas

For the Body

- 127 Great Golf
- 128 Tennis
- 129 Sailing and fishing

DIRECTIONS

A walk along the Strip and six drives that explore nearby areas and venture farther, to California's Death Valley and Utah's Zion and Bryce Canyon national parks.

- 133 **Introduction**

- 135 Tour 1: The Strip
- 144 Tour 2: Red Rock Canyon, Pahrump Winery

- 148 Tour 3: Mt. Charleston
- 152 Tour 4: Boulder City, Hoover Dam, Lake Mead, Valley of Fire
- 158 Tour 5: Laughlin
- 162 Tour 6: Death Valley National Monument, Rhyolite
- 167 Tour 7: Zion and Bryce Canyon

173 **Index**

A Word from the Editor

My husband Steve Birnbaum's memory of this city in the desert dated back to an almost once-upon-a-time era. Birnbaum family legend had it that my father-in-law was involved in building the *Thunderbird* hotel (now closed), one of Las Vegas's original gambling oases. On telling me the tale, there were numerous and amusing allusions to an "Uncle Benny." It came as something of a shock when many years later, Warren Beatty portrayed this purported relative on the silver screen — but used the name by which Uncle Benny was known to his non-intimates: Bugsy (né Siegel).

Part of the family lore included Steve's being sent to the *Thunderbird* by his father one summer, ostensibly to take the hotel's inventory. As I recall the story, he began by counting the number of broom closets and sets of cutlery, when he discovered (and meticulously recorded) the hotel's most valuable inventory: showgirls. But I digress.

My first view of Vegas came some years later when I was sent out to attend a ski equipment convention (Steve declined to join me on *that* trip). The sound of slot machines greeted me as I stepped into McCarran International Airport; I was whisked to the Strip, and found myself ensconced in a high roller's suite that was wallpapered in what looked like not-at-all-fabulous-fake orange fur, complete with a mirror over a very round bed. But I soon discovered that just beyond the glitz and glitter of the casinos lay elegant residential areas and the real, honest-to-goodness desert.

And although the one-armed bandits are still on patrol from your moment of arrival, and you ain't seen nothing until you've seen a mega-star Las Vegas headliner show, it is a city: of the only-in-America variety.

My own evolution as a traveler (which happily continues) is mirrored by the evolution of our guidebook series. When we began our series of modern travel guides, we logically began with "area" books, attempting to publish guides that would include the widest possible number of attractive destinations. When the public seemed to accept our new way of delivering travel data, we added titles covering only a single country, and when these became popular we began our newest expansion phase, which centers on a group of books that deal with only a single city. Now we can not only highlight our favorite urban destinations, but really describe how to get the very most out of a visit.

Such treatment of travel information only mirrors an increasingly pervasive trend among travelers — the frequent return to a treasured travel spot. Once upon a time, even the most dedicated travelers would visit distant parts of the world no more than once in a lifetime — usually as part of some sort of Grand

x A WORD FROM THE EDITOR

Tour. But greater numbers of would-be sojourners are now availing themselves of the opportunity to visit a favored part of the world over and over again.

So where once it was routine to say you'd "seen" a particular city or country after a very superficial, once-over-lightly encounter, the more perceptive travelers of today recognize that it's entirely possible to have only skimmed the surface of a specific travel destination even after having visited that place more than a dozen times. Similarly, repeated visits to a single site permit true exploration of special interests, whether they be sporting, artistic, or intellectual.

For those of us who now have spent the last several years working out the special system under which we present information in this series, the luxury of being able to devote nearly as much space as we'd like to just a single city is as close to paradise for guide writers and editors as any of us expects to come. But clearly this is not the first guide to the glitter of Las Vegas — one suspects that guides of one sort or another have existed at least since the day when the visionary Mr. Siegel made an offer that couldn't be refused — so a traveler might logically ask why a new one is suddenly necessary.

Our answer is that the nature of travel to Las Vegas — and even of the travelers who now routinely make the trip — has changed dramatically of late. For the past 200 years or so, travel to even a town within our own country was considered an elaborate undertaking, one that required extensive advance planning. But with the advent of jet air travel in the late 1950s and of increased-capacity, wide-body aircraft during the late 1960s, travel to and around once distant destinations became extremely common. Attitudes as well as costs have changed significantly in the last couple of decades.

Obviously, any new guidebook to Las Vegas must keep pace with and answer the real needs of today's travelers. That's why we've tried to create a guide that's specifically organized, written, and edited for the more demanding modern traveler, one for whom qualitative information is infinitely more desirable than mere quantities of unappraised data. We think that this book, along with all the other guides in our series, represents a new generation of travel guides — one that is especially responsive to modern needs and interests.

For years, dating back as far as Herr Baedeker, travel guides have tended to be encyclopedic, seemingly much more concerned with demonstrating expertise in geography and history than with a real analysis of the sorts of things that actually concern a typical modern tourist. But today, when it is hardly necessary to tell a traveler where Las Vegas is (in many cases, the traveler has been there nearly as often as the guidebook editors), it becomes the responsibility of those editors to provide new perspectives and to suggest new directions in order to make the guide genuinely valuable.

That's exactly what we've tried to do in this series. I think you'll notice a different, more contemporary tone to the text, as well as an organization and focus that are distinctive and more functional. And even a random reading of what follows will demonstrate a substantial departure from the standard guidebook orientation, for we've not only attempted to provide information of a more compelling sort, but we also have tried to present the data in a format that makes it particularly accessible.

A WORD FROM THE EDITOR xi

Needless to say, it's difficult to decide just what to include in a guidebook of this size — and what to omit. Early on, we realized that giving up the encyclopedic approach precluded our listing every single route and restaurant, a realization that helped define our overall editorial focus. Similarly, when we discussed the possibility of presenting certain information in other than strict geographic order, we found that the new format enabled us to arrange data in a way that we feel best answers the questions travelers typically ask.

Large numbers of specific questions have provided the real editorial skeleton for this book. The volume of mail we regularly receive emphasizes that modern travelers want very precise information, so we've tried to organize our material in the most responsive way possible. Readers who want to know the best hotel or the best place to get a free lunch in Las Vegas will have no trouble extracting that data from this guide.

Travel guides are, understandably, reflections of personal taste, and putting one's name on a title page obviously puts one's preferences on the line. But I think I ought to amplify just what "personal" means. Like Steve, I don't believe in the sort of personal guidebook that's a palpable misrepresentation on its face. It is, for example, hardly possible for any single travel writer to visit thousands of restaurants (and nearly as many hotels) in any given year and provide accurate appraisals of each. And even if it were physically possible for one human being to survive such an itinerary, it would of necessity have to be done at a dead sprint, and the perceptions derived therefrom would probably be less valid than those of any other intelligent individual visiting the same establishments. It is, therefore, impossible (especially in a large, annually revised and updated guidebook *series* such as we offer) to have only one person provide all the data on the entire world.

I also happen to think that such individual orientation is of substantially less value to readers. Visiting a single hotel for just one night or eating one hasty meal in a random restaurant hardly equips anyone to provide appraisals that are of more than passing interest. No amount of doggedly alliterative or oppressively onomatopoeic text can camouflage a technique that is essentially specious. We have, therefore, chosen what I like to describe as the "thee and me" approach to restaurant and hotel evaluation and, to a somewhat more limited degree, to the sites and sights we have included in the other sections of our text. What this really reflects is a personal sampling tempered by intelligent counsel from informed local sources, and these additional friends-of-the-editor are almost always residents of the city and/or area about which they are consulted.

Despite the presence of several editors, writers, researchers, and local contributors, very precise editing and tailoring keep our text fiercely subjective. So what follows is the gospel according to Birnbaum, and it represents as much of our own taste and instincts as we can manage. It is probable, therefore, that if you like your cities stylish and prefer small hotels with personality to huge high-rise anonymities, we're likely to have a long and meaningful relationship. Readers with dissimilar tastes may be less enraptured.

I also should point out something about the person to whom this guidebook is directed. Above all, he or she is a "visitor." This means that such elements as restaurants have been specifically picked to provide the visitor with a representative, enlightening, stimulating, and above all pleasant experience. Since so many extraneous considerations can affect the reception and service accorded a regular restaurant patron, our choices can in no way be construed as an exhaustive guide to resident dining. We think we've listed all the best places, in various price ranges, but they were chosen with a visitor's enjoyment in mind.

Other evidence of how we've tried to tailor our text to reflect modern travel habits is most apparent in the section we call DIVERSIONS. Where once it was common for travelers to spend an urban visit in a determinedly passive state, the emphasis is far more active today. So we've organized every activity we could reasonably evaluate and arranged the material in a way that is especially accessible to activists of either athletic or cerebral bent. It is no longer necessary, therefore, to wade through a pound or two of superfluous prose just to find the hotel with the most spectacular show or the casino with the biggest payoff in the city.

If there is a single thing that best characterizes the revolution in and evolution of current holiday habits, it is that most travelers now consider travel a right rather than a privilege. No longer is a family trip to the far corners of the world necessarily a once-in-a-lifetime thing; nor is the idea of visiting exotic, faraway places in the least worrisome. Travel today translates as the enthusiastic desire to sample all of the world's opportunities, to find that elusive quality of experience that is not only enriching but comfortable. For that reason, we've tried to make what follows not only helpful and enlightening, but the sort of welcome companion of which every traveler dreams.

Finally, I also should point out that every good travel guide is a living enterprise; that is, no part of this text is carved in stone. In our annual revisions, we refine, expand, and further hone all our material to serve your travel needs better. To this end, no contribution is of greater value to us than your personal reaction to what we have written, as well as information reflecting your own experiences while using the book. We earnestly and enthusiastically solicit your comments about this guide *and* your opinions and perceptions about places you have recently visited. In this way, we will be able to provide the most current information — including the actual experiences of recent travelers — and to make those experiences more readily available to others. Please write to us at 10 E. 53rd St., New York, NY 10022.

We sincerely hope to hear from you.

ALEXANDRA MAYES BIRNBAUM

How to Use This Guide

A great deal of care has gone into the special organization of this guidebook, and we believe it represents a real breakthrough in the presentation of travel material. Our aim is to create a new, more modern generation of travel books, and to make this guide the most useful and practical travel tool available today.

Our text is divided into four basic sections in order to present information in the best way on every possible aspect of a vacation to Las Vegas. This organization itself should alert you to the vast and varied opportunities available, as well as indicate all the specific data necessary to plan a successful visit. You won't find much of the conventional "swaying palms and shimmering sand" text here; we've chosen instead to deliver more useful and practical information. Prospective itineraries tend to speak for themselves, and with so many diverse travel opportunities, we feel our main job is to highlight what's where and to provide basic information — how, when, where, how much, and what's best — to assist you in making the most intelligent choices possible.

Here is a brief summary of the four basic sections of this book, and what you can expect to find in each. We believe that you will find both your travel planning and en route enjoyment enhanced by having this book at your side.

GETTING READY TO GO

This mini-encyclopedia of practical travel facts is a sort of know-it-all companion with all the precise information necessary to create a successful trip to Las Vegas. There are entries on more than 25 separate topics, including how to get where you're going, what preparations to make before leaving, what to expect, what your trip is likely to cost, and how to avoid prospective problems. The individual entries are specific, realistic, and where appropriate, cost-oriented.

We expect you to use this section most in the course of planning your trip, for its ideas and suggestions are intended to simplify this often confusing period. Entries are intentionally concise, in an effort to get to the meat of the matter with the least extraneous prose. These entries are augmented by extensive lists of specific sources from which to obtain even more specialized data, plus some suggestions for obtaining travel information on your own.

THE CITY

The individual report on Las Vegas has been created with the assistance of researchers, contributors, professional journalists, and experts who live in the city. Although useful at the planning stage, THE CITY is really designed to be taken along and used on the spot. The reports offer a short-stay guide,

2 HOW TO USE THIS GUIDE

including an essay introducing the city as a historic entity and as a contemporary place to visit. *At-a-Glance* material is actually a site-by-site survey of the most important, interesting, and sometimes most eclectic sights to see, and things to do. *Sources and Resources* is a concise listing of pertinent tourist information meant to answer myriad potentially pressing questions as they arise — from simple things such as the address of the local tourism office, how to get around, which sightseeing tours to take, and when special events occur, to something more difficult, like where to find the best hotel extravaganzas, or hail a taxi, which are the chic places to shop, and where the best casinos are to be found. *Best in Town* lists our collection of cost-and-quality choices of the best places to eat and sleep on a variety of budgets.

DIVERSIONS

This section is designed to help travelers find the best places in which to engage in a wide range of physical and cerebral activities, without having to wade through endless pages of unrelated text. This very selective guide lists the broadest possible range of activities, including all the best places to pursue them.

We start with a list of special places to stay and eat, and move to activities that require some perspiration — sports preferences and other rigorous pursuits — as well as a number of more spiritual vacation opportunities. In every case, our suggestions of a particular location — and often our recommendation of a specific hotel — is intended to guide you to that special place where the quality of experience is likely to be highest. Whether you seek a historic hotel or museum or the best place to shop or sail, each category is the equivalent of a comprehensive checklist of the absolute best in Las Vegas.

DIRECTIONS

Here are seven tours, including a walk along the city's famed Strip, three day trips to nearby sites, and three longer routes that take you to the picturesque boomtown of Laughlin and into California's Death Valley and Utah's Bryce Canyon and Zion National Parks. This is the only section of the book that is organized geographically; some itineraries can be "connected" for longer sojourns or used individually for short, intensive explorations.

Although each of the book's sections has a distinct format and a special function, they have all been designed to be used together to provide a complete inventory of travel information. To use this book to full advantage, take a few minutes to read the table of contents and random entries in each section to get a firsthand feel for how it all fits together.

Pick and choose needed information. Assume, for example, that you have always wanted to visit Las Vegas and partake of its spectacular mega-shows and casinos — but you never really knew how to organize it or where to go. Choose specific nightspots from the selections offered in "Nightclubs and Nightlife" in THE CITY, add some of the shows and casinos noted in the walking tour of the Strip in DIRECTIONS, and cross-reference with those in

HOW TO USE THIS GUIDE 3

the roundup of the best in the city in the *Best in Shows* and *Luck Be a Lady* sections in DIVERSIONS.

In other words, the sections of this book are building blocks designed to help you put together the best possible trip. Use them selectively as a tool, a source of ideas, a reference work for accurate facts, and a guidebook to the best buys, the most exciting sights, the most pleasant accommodations, the tastiest food — *the best travel experience* that you can possibly have.

Las Vegas

Downtown

- Lions Memorial Park
- Fantasy Park
- Washington Ave.
- McWilliams Ave.
- Whipple Park
- Cashman Field Center
- Bonanza Rd.
- I-15
- Harris Ave.
- Las Vegas Transit Terminal
- Wilson Ave.
- Oran K. Gragson Expy.
- US 95
- Bonanza Rd.
- Maryland Pkwy.
- Post Office
- City Hall
- Union Plaza
- Las Vegas Club
- Golden Nugget
- Greyhound Bus Depot
- Court House
- 1st St.
- Main St.
- Casino Center Blvd.
- 3rd St.
- 4th St.
- Las Vegas Blvd.
- Fremont St.
- 6th St.
- Carson Ave.
- Bridger Ave.
- 7th St.
- Ogden Ave.
- Stewart St.
- 8th St.
- Federal Bldg.
- Clark Ave.
- 9th St.
- Lewis Ave.
- 10th St.
- 11th St.
- Bonneville St.
- Hoover Ave.
- Coolidge Ave.
- Garces Ave.
- Gass St.
- 13th St.
- 14th St.
- 15th St.
- 16th St.
- Charleston Blvd.
- Dutton Park
- 9th St.
- Huntridge Circle Park
- Discovery Dr.
- Colorado Ave.
- 3rd St.
- 4th St.
- Rexford Pl.
- 5th St.
- Norman Ave.
- Franklin Ave.
- Industrial Blvd.
- Utah Ave.
- 6th St.
- 7th St.
- 8th St.
- Bracken Ave.
- Wyoming Ave.
- Oakey Blvd.
- New York St.
- Chicago St.
- Main St.
- Casino Center Blvd.
- Las Vegas Blvd.
- Canosa Ave.
- 11th St.
- 15th St.
- St. Louis St.
- Boston St.
- Baltimore St.
- Fairfield Ave.
- Paradise Rd.
- Beverly Way
- Baker Park
- Maryland Pkwy.
- Bonita Ave.
- St. Louis Ave.
- Phillips Ave.
- Exley Ave.
- 589
- Sahara Ave.
- Sahara

0 mile 3/4

This map continues on ↓ facing page

N

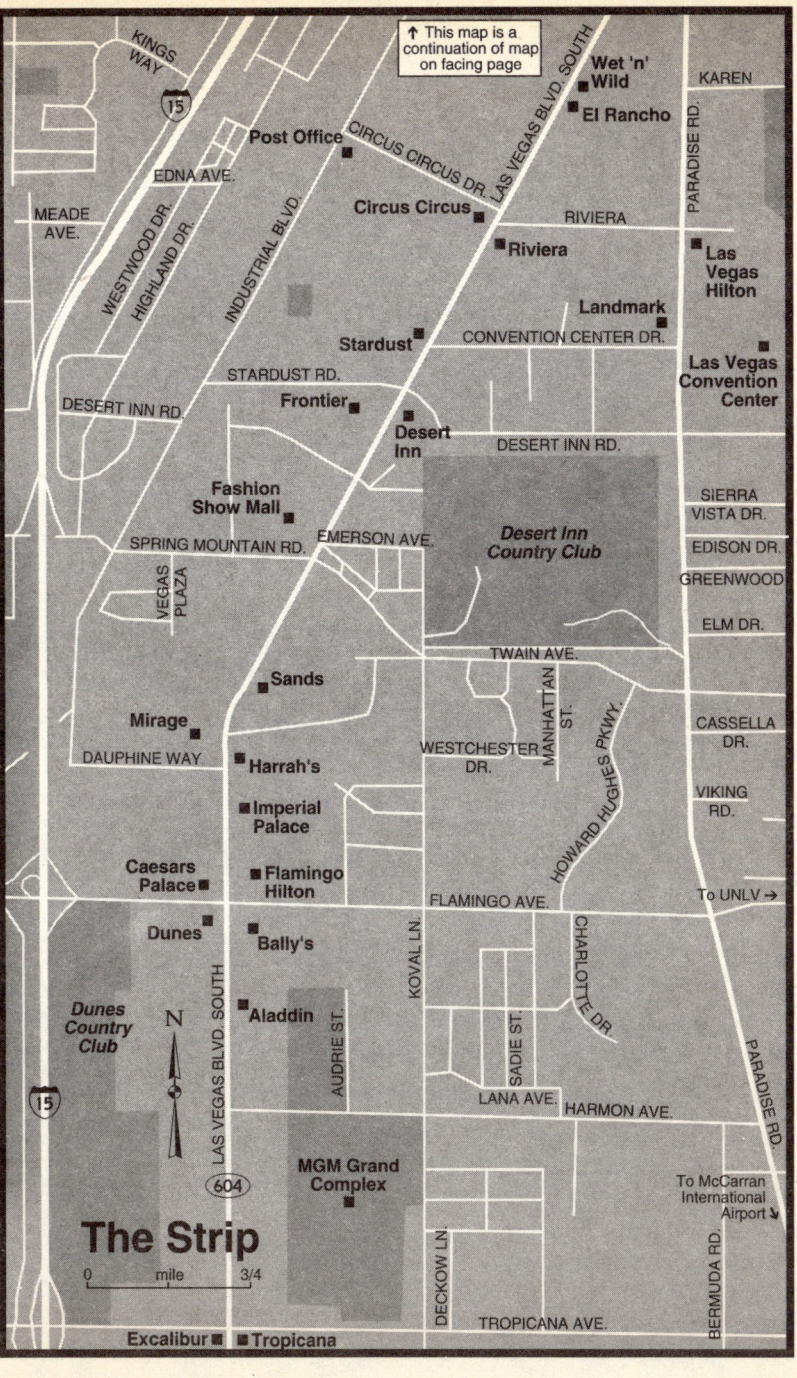

GETTING READY TO GO

When and How to Go

When to Go

 There isn't really a best time to visit Las Vegas; the desert city is popular year-round. Since it *is* in the middle of the desert, summers are hot and dry, with 100-degree-plus temperatures not uncommon. Winters are pleasant and mild, often in the low 60s (but cold at night), and outdoor activity takes place throughout the year.

There are good reasons for visiting Las Vegas any time of the year. There are no real off-season periods when attractions are closed, so you aren't risking the disappointment of arriving at an attraction and finding the gates locked. The only slow "seasons" usually are the weeks between December 10 and *Christmas,* and the first 2 weeks in June. You won't necessarily find bargains then, but hotel prices in general are so low in Las Vegas because of the fierce competition that you won't need them.

■**Note:** When planning the timing of your visit, there is one period during which you must be particularly careful. The city is packed the week between *Christmas* and *New Year's,* and reservations should be made for that time by the previous September. In addition, it is a good idea to check with your travel agent or the Las Vegas Convention and Visitors Authority (phone: 702-892-0711) to find out if any large conventions will be in town at the time you are thinking of going. Some of the big meetings can use up 3,000 or 4,000 hotel rooms. It is also advised never to arrive in the city without a confirmed hotel reservation. Las Vegas does fill up its thousands of hotel rooms regularly.

WEATHER: Travelers can get current readings and extended forecasts through the *Weather Channel Connection,* the worldwide weather report center of the *Weather Channel,* a cable TV station. By dialing 900-WEATHER and punching in either the first four letters of the city name or the area code (LASV or 702 for Las Vegas) for over 600 cities in the US (including Puerto Rico and the US Virgin Islands), an up-to-date recording will provide such information as current temperature, barometric pressure, relative humidity, and wind speed, as well as a general 2-day forecast. Beach, boating, and highway reports are also provided for some locations. This 24-hour service can be accessed from any touch-tone phone in the US, and costs 95¢ per minute. The charge will show up on your phone bill. For additional information, write to the *Weather Channel Connection,* 2600 Cumberland Pkwy., Atlanta, GA 30339 (phone: 404-434-6800).

CULTURAL EVENTS: Symphony concerts, opera, and jazz are featured throughout the year at the *Artemus W. Ham Concert Hall* and the *Judy Bayley Theatre* on the University of Nevada at Las Vegas campus. Also available are performances at a variety of theaters, such as the *New West Stage Company,* which presents its season at the *Charleston Heights Arts Center,* and the *Actor's Repertory Theater.* But people usually come to Las Vegas for the entertainment at the hotel showrooms. Big-name entertainment is a trademark of *Caesars Palace,* the *Mirage,* the *Las Vegas Hilton,* and the *Aladdin.* Production spectaculars are produced nightly at *Bally's,* the *Excalibur,* the *Riviera,* the *Tropicana,* and the *Flamingo Hilton.*

As for museums, the *Las Vegas Natural History Museum* has a collection of animated dinosaurs, and the University of Nevada at Las Vegas has a *Museum of Natural History* with collections of Indian artifacts and live desert reptiles. Other museums worth visiting are the *Las Vegas Art Museum,* the *Liberace Museum, Guinness World of Records Museum, Ripley's Believe It or Not Odditorium,* the *Lost City Museum of Archaeology* (in the Valley of Fire area), and the *Imperial Palace Auto Collection.*

FESTIVALS: The *Las Vegas International Marathon* will be held February 6 this year. During the *Helldorado Days* festival, held for 10 days in May, the city celebrates its western heritage with rodeos, parades, beauty contests, and, for those who want some slower-paced action, a beard-growing contest. The *Desert Inn LPGA International Golf Tournament* takes place in March or April, the *Las Vegas Senior Classic* is in late April or May, and the *Las Vegas Invitational Golf Tournament* is in October. The *Jaycees State Fair* is also in October at the *Convention Center* and has carnival acts, magic shows, rides, livestock, and craft exhibits. The *National Finals Rodeo* opens in early December at the *Thomas and Mack Center* for 10 days. And *New Year's Eve* is the time for a enormous downtown street festival drawing thousands of people and culminating in a giant fireworks display.

Traveling by Plane

Flying is the quickest, most convenient means of travel between different parts of the country. It *sounds* expensive to travel across the US by air, but when all costs are taken into account for traveling any substantial distance, plane travel usually is less expensive per mile than traveling by car. It also is the most economical way to go in terms of time. Although touring by car, bus, or train certainly is a more scenic way to travel, air travel is far faster and more direct — and the less time spent in transit, the more time spent in Las Vegas.

SCHEDULED FLIGHTS: Numerous airlines offer regularly scheduled flights to McCarran International Airport, which handles domestic scheduled flights and domestic and international charters.

Listed below are the major national air carriers serving Las Vegas and their toll-free telephone numbers:

American and American Eagle: 800-433-7300.
America West: 800-247-5692.
Continental: 800-525-0280.
Delta and Delta Connection: 800-221-1212.
Northwest and NW Airlink: 800-225-2525.
Southwest Airlines: 800-531-5601.
TWA: 800-221-2000.
United: 800-241-6522.
USAir: 800-428-4322.

Tickets – A full-fare ticket provides maximum flexibility for travel on regularly scheduled flights. There are no advance booking or other ticketing requirements — except seat availability — although cancellation restrictions vary. It pays to check *before* booking your flight. It also is advisable to reserve well in advance during popular vacation periods and around holiday times.

Fares – Full-fare tickets are followed by a wide variety of discount fares, which even

GETTING READY / Traveling by Plane

experts find hard to keep current. With these fares, the less you pay for your ticket, the more restrictions and qualifications are likely to be attached to the ticket purchase, including the months (and the days of the week) during which you must travel, how far in advance you must purchase your ticket, the minimum and maximum amount of time you may or must remain away, and your willingness to decide on and stick with a return date at the time of booking. It is not uncommon for passengers sitting side by side on the same plane to have paid fares varying by hundreds of dollars, and all too often the traveler paying more would have been equally willing (and able) to accept the terms of the far less expensive ticket.

Perhaps the most common misconception about fares on scheduled airlines is that the cost of the ticket determines how much service will be provided on the flight. This is true only to a certain extent. A far more realistic rule of thumb is that the less you pay for your ticket, the more restrictions and qualifications are likely to come into play before you board the plane (as well as after you get off).

In general, domestic airfares break down to four basic categories — first class, business class, coach (also called economy or tourist class), and excursion or discount fares. In addition, Advance Purchase Excursion (APEX) fares offer savings under certain conditions.

A **first class** ticket admits you to the special section of the aircraft with larger seats, more legroom, better (or more elaborately served) food, free drinks, free headsets for movies and music channels, and above all, personal attention. First class fares cost about twice those of full-fare (often called "regular") economy.

Behind first class often lies **business class**, usually a separate cabin or cabins. While standards of comfort and service are not as high as in first class, they represent a considerable improvement over conditions in the rear of the plane, with roomier seats, more leg and shoulder space between passengers, and fewer seats abreast. Free liquor and headsets, a choice of meal entrées, and a separate counter for speedier check-in are other inducements. Note that airlines often have their own names for their business class service — such as Ambassador Class on *TWA* and Medallion Class on *Delta*.

The terms of the **coach** or **economy** fare may vary slightly from airline to airline, and in fact from time to time airlines may be selling more than one type of economy fare. Coach or economy passengers sit more snugly, as many as 10 in a single row on a wide-body jet, behind the first class and business class sections. Normally, alcoholic drinks are not free, nor are the headsets.

In first, business class, and regular economy, passengers are entitled to reserve seats and are sold tickets on an open reservation system. They may travel on any scheduled flight they wish, buy a one-way or round-trip ticket, and have the ticket remain valid for a year. There are no requirements for a minimum or maximum stay or for advance booking and (often) no cancellation penalties — but beware, the rules regarding cancellation vary from carrier to carrier. The fare also allows free stopover privileges, although these can be limited in economy.

Excursion and other **discount** fares are the airlines' equivalent of a special sale and usually apply to round-trip bookings only. These fares generally differ according to the season and the number of travel days permitted. They are only a bit less flexible than full-fare economy tickets, and are, therefore, often useful for both business and holiday travelers. Most round-trip excursion tickets include strict minimum and maximum stay requirements and reservations and can be changed only within the specified time limits. So don't count on extending a ticket beyond the specified time of return or staying less time than required. Different airlines may have different regulations concerning the number of stopovers permitted, and sometimes excursion fares are less expensive during midweek. The availability of these reduced-rate seats is most limited at busy times such as holidays. Discount or excursion fare ticket holders sit with the coach passengers and, for all intents and purposes, are indistinguishable from them. They receive all the same basic services, even though they may have paid anywhere between 30% and 55% less for the trip. Obviously, it's wise to make plans early enough to qualify for this less expensive transportation if possible.

These discount or excursion fares may masquerade under a variety of names and invariably have strings attached. A common requirement is that the ticket be purchased a certain number of days — usually between 7 and 21 days — in advance of departure, though it may be booked weeks or months in advance (it has to be "ticketed," or paid for, shortly after booking, however). The return reservation usually has to be made at the time of the original ticketing and often cannot be changed later than a certain number of days (again, usually 7 to 21 days) before the return flight. If events force a change in the return reservation after the date allowed, the passenger may have to pay the difference between the round-trip excursion rate and the round-trip coach rate, although some carriers permit such scheduling changes for a nominal fee. In addition, some airlines may allow passengers to use their discounted fares by standing by for an empty seat, even if the carrier doesn't otherwise have standby fares. Another common condition is the minimum and maximum stay requirement; for example, 1 to 6 days or 6 to 14 days (but including at least a Saturday night). Last, cancellation penalties of up to 50% of the full price of the ticket have been assessed — if a refund is offered at all — so check the specific penalty in effect when you purchase your discount/excursion ticket.

On some airlines, the ticket bearing the lowest price of all the current discount fares is the ticket where no change at all in departure and/or return flights is permitted, and where the ticket price is totally nonrefundable. If you do buy such a nonrefundable ticket, you should be aware of a policy followed by some airlines that may make it easier to change your plans if necessary. For a fee — set by each airline and payable at the airport when checking in — you *may* be able to change the time or date of a return flight on a nonrefundable ticket. However, if the nonrefundable ticket price for the replacement flight is higher than that of the original (as often is the case when trading in a weekday for a weekend flight), you also will have to pay the difference. Any such change must be made a certain number of days in advance — in some cases as little as 2 days — of either the original or the replacement flight, whichever is earlier; restrictions are set by the individual carrier. (Travelers holding a nonrefundable or other restricted ticket who must change their plans due to a family emergency should know that some carriers may make special allowances in such situations.)

■ **Note:** Due to recent changes in many US airlines' policies, nonrefundable tickets are now available that carry none of the above restrictions. Although passengers still may *not* be able to obtain a refund for the price paid, the time or date of a departing or return flight may be changed at any time (assuming seats are available) for a nominal service charge.

There also is a newer, often less expensive, type of excursion fare, the **APEX**, or **Advanced Purchase Excursion** fare. As with traditional excursion fares, passengers paying an APEX fare sit with and receive the same basic services as any other coach or economy passengers, even though they may have paid 50% less for their seats. In return, they are subject to certain restrictions. In the case of domestic flights, the ticket usually is good for a minimum of 7 days away and a maximum, currently, of 1 to 6 months (depending on the airline and the destination); and as its name implies, it must be "ticketed," or paid for in its entirety, a certain period of time before departure — usually 21 days.

The drawback to some APEX fares is that they penalize travelers who change their minds — and travel plans. Usually, the return reservation must be made at the time of the original ticketing, and if for some reason you change your schedule, you will have to pay a penalty of $100 or 10% of the ticket value, whichever is greater, as long as you travel within the valid period of your ticket. More flexible APEX fares recently have been introduced, which allow travelers to make changes in the date or time of their flights for a nominal charge (as low as $25).

With either type of APEX, if you change your return to a date less than the minimum stay or more than the maximum stay, the difference between the round-trip APEX fare and the full round-trip coach rate will have to be paid. There also is a penalty of anywhere from $50 to $100 or more for canceling or changing a reservation *before* travel begins — check the specific penalty in effect when you purchase your ticket. No stopovers are allowed on an APEX ticket, but it is possible to create an open-jaw effect by buying an APEX ticket on a split-ticket basis. Depending on the destination, domestic APEX tickets may be sold at basic and peak rates (the peak season will vary) and may include surcharges for weekend flights.

Standby fares, at one time the rock-bottom price at which a traveler could fly to different parts of the US, have become elusive. At the time of this writing, most major scheduled airlines did not regularly offer standby fares on US domestic flights. Because airline fares and their conditions constantly change, however, bargain hunters should not hesitate to ask if such a fare exists at the time they plan to travel.

Something else to check is the possibility of qualifying for a **GIT** (Group Inclusive Travel) fare, which requires that a specific dollar amount of ground arrangements be purchased, in advance, along with the ticket. The requirements vary as to the number of travel days and stopovers permitted, and the minimum number of passengers required for a group. The actual fares also vary, but the cost will be spelled out in brochures distributed by the tour operators handling the ground arrangements. In the past, GIT fares were among the least expensive available from the established carriers, but the prevalence of discount fares has caused group fares to all but disappear from some air routes. Travelers reading brochures on group package tours to San Francisco will find that, in almost all cases, the applicable airfare given as a sample (to be added to the price of the land package to obtain the total tour price) is an APEX fare, the same discount fare available to the independent traveler.

The major airlines serving US domestic routes also may offer individual fare excursion rates similar to GIT fares, which are sold in conjunction with ground accommodation packages. Previously called ITX, and sometimes referred to as individual tour-basing fares, these fares generally are offered as part of "air/hotel/car/transfer packages," and can reduce the cost of an economy fare by more than a third. The packages are booked for a specific amount of time, with return dates specified; rescheduling and cancellation restrictions and penalties vary from carrier to carrier. At the time of this writing, these fares were offered by *American, Delta, Northwest, TWA,* and *USAir*. Note that their offerings may or may not represent substantial savings over standard economy fares, so check at the time you plan to travel. (For further information on package options, see *Package Tours,* in this section.)

Travelers looking for the least expensive possible airfares should, finally, scan the pages of their hometown newspapers (especially the Sunday travel section) for announcements of special promotional fares. Most airlines offer their most attractive special fares to encourage travel during slow seasons and to inaugurate and publicize new routes. Even if none of these factors applies, prospective passengers can be fairly sure that the number of discount seats per flight at the lowest price is strictly limited, or that the fare offering includes a set expiration date — which means it's absolutely necessary to move fast to enjoy the lowest possible price.

Among other special airline promotional deals for which you should be on the lookout are discount or upgrade coupons sometimes offered by the major carriers and found in mail-order merchandise catalogues. For instance, airlines sometimes issue coupons that typically cost around $25 each and are good for a percentage discount or an upgrade on a domestic airline ticket. The only requirement beyond the fee generally is that a coupon purchaser must buy at least one item from the catalogue. There usually are some minimum airfare restrictions before the coupon is redeemable, but in general these are worthwhile offers. Restrictions often include certain blackout days (when the coupon cannot be used at all), usually imposed during peak travel periods. These coupons are particularly valuable to business travelers who tend to buy full-fare tickets, and while the coupons are issued in the buyer's name, they can be used by others who are traveling on the same itinerary.

It's always wise to ask about discount or promotional fares and about any conditions that might restrict booking, payment, cancellation, and changes in plans. Check the prices from neighboring cities. A special rate may be offered in a nearby city but not in yours, and it may be enough of a bargain to warrant your leaving from that city. Ask if there is a difference in price for midweek versus weekend travel, or if there is a further discount for traveling early in the morning or late at night. Also be sure to investigate package deals, which are offered by virtually every airline. These may include car rental, accommodations, and dining and/or sightseeing features, in addition to the basic airfare, and the combined cost of packaged elements usually is considerably less than the cost of the exact same elements when purchased separately.

If in the course of your research you come across a deal that seems too good to be true, keep in mind that logic may not be a component of deeply discounted airfares — there's not always any sane relationship between miles to be flown and the price to get there. More often than not, the level of competition on a given route dictates the degree of discount, so don't be dissuaded from accepting an offer that sounds irresistible just because it also sounds illogical. Better to buy that inexpensive fare while it's being offered and worry about the sense — or absence thereof — while you're flying to your desired destination.

When you're satisfied that you've found the lowest possible price for which you can conveniently qualify (you may have to call the airline more than once, because different airline reservations clerks have been known to quote different prices), make your booking. Then, to protect yourself against fare increases, purchase and pay for your ticket as soon as possible after you've received a confirmed reservation. Airlines generally will honor their tickets, even if the operative price at the time of your flight is higher than the price you paid; if fares go up between the time you *reserve* a flight and the time you *pay* for it, you likely will be out of luck. Finally, with excursion or discount fares, it is important to remember that when a reservations clerk says that you must purchase a ticket by a specific date, this is an absolute deadline. Miss the deadline and the airline may automatically cancel your reservation without telling you.

■**Note:** Another wrinkle in the airfare scene is that if the fares go *down* after you purchase your ticket, you *may* be entitled to a refund of the difference. However, this is only possible in certain situations — availability and advance purchase restrictions pertaining to the lower rate are set by the airline. If you suspect that you may be able to qualify for such a refund, check with your travel agent or the airline.

Frequent Flyers – Most of the leading carriers serving Las Vegas — including *American, Delta, Northwest, United,* and *USAir* — offer a bonus system to frequent travelers. After the first 10,000 miles, for example, a passenger might be eligible for a first class seat for the coach fare; after another 10,000 miles, he or she might receive a discount on his or her next ticket purchase. The value of the bonuses continues to increase as more miles are logged.

Bonus miles also may be earned by patronizing affiliated car rental companies or hotel chains, or by using one of the credit cards that now offer this reward. In deciding whether to accept such a credit card from one of the issuing organizations that tempt you with frequent flyer mileage bonuses on a specific airline, first determine whether

GETTING READY / Traveling by Plane 15

the interest rate charged on the unpaid balance is the same as (or less than) possible alternate credit cards, and whether the annual "membership" fee also is equal or lower. If these charges are slightly higher than those of competing cards, weigh the difference against the potential value in airfare savings. Also ask about any bonus miles awarded just for signing up — 1,000 is common, 5,000 generally the maximum.

For the most up-to-date information on frequent flyer bonus options, you may want to send for the monthly newsletter *Frequent.* Issued by Frequent Publications, it provides current information about frequent flyer plans in general, as well as specific data about promotions, awards, and combination deals to help you keep track of the profusion — and confusion — of current and upcoming availabilities. For a year's subscription, send $33 to Frequent Publications, 4715-C Town Center Dr., Colorado Springs, CO 80916 (phone: 800-333-5937).

There also is a monthly magazine called *Frequent Flyer,* but unlike the newsletter mentioned above, its focus is primarily on newsy articles of interest to business travelers and other frequent flyers. Published by Official Airline Guides (PO Box 58543, Boulder, CO 80322-8543; phone: 800-323-3537), *Frequent Flyer* is available for $24 for a 1-year subscription.

Low-Fare Airlines – Increasingly, the stimulus for special fares is the appearance of airlines associated with bargain rates. On these airlines, all seats generally sell for the same price, which tends to be somewhat below the lowest discount fare offered by the larger, more established airlines. It is important to note that tickets offered by these smaller companies frequently are not subject to the same restrictions as some of the discounted fares offered by the more established carriers. They may not require advance purchase or minimum and maximum stays, may involve no cancellation penalties, and may be available one way or round trip. A disadvantage to some low-fare airlines, however, is that when something goes wrong, such as delayed baggage or a flight cancellation due to equipment breakdown, their smaller fleets and fewer flights mean that passengers may have to wait longer for a solution than they would on one of the equipment-rich major carriers.

Taxes and Other Fees – Travelers who have shopped for the best possible flight at the lowest possible price should be warned that a number of extras will be added to that price and collected by the airline or travel agent who issues the ticket. The 10% federal US Transportation Tax applies to travel within the US or US territories. Another fee is charged by some airlines to cover more stringent security procedures, prompted by recent terrorist incidents. Note that these taxes *usually* (but not always) are included in advertised fares and in the prices quoted by airlines reservations clerks.

Reservations – For those who don't have the time or patience to investigate personally all possible air departures and connections for a proposed trip, a travel agent can be of inestimable help. A good agent should have all the information on which flights go where and when, and which categories of tickets are available on each. Most have computerized reservation links with the major carriers, so that a seat can be reserved and confirmed in minutes. An increasing number of agents also possess fare-comparison computer programs, so they often are very reliable sources of detailed competitive price data. (For more information, see *How to Use a Travel Agent,* in this section.)

When making plane reservations through a travel agent, ask the agent to give the airline your home phone number, as well as your daytime business phone number. All too often the agent uses the agency number as the official contact for changes in flight plans. Especially during the winter, weather conditions hundreds or even thousands of miles away can wreak havoc with flight schedules. Aircraft are constantly in use, and a plane delayed in the Orient or on the West Coast can miss its scheduled flight from the East Coast the next morning. The airlines are fairly reliable about getting this sort of information to passengers if they can reach them; diligence does little good at 10 PM if the airline has only the agency's or an office number.

Reconfirmation is not generally required on domestic flights. However, it always is

16 GETTING READY / Traveling by Plane

wise to call ahead to make sure that the airline did not slip up in entering your original reservation, or in registering any changes you may have made since, and that it has your seat reservation and/or special meal request in the computer. If you look at the printed information on your ticket, you'll see the airline's reconfirmation policy stated explicitly. Don't be lulled into a false sense of security by the "OK" on your ticket next to the number and time of the flight. This only means that a reservation has been entered; a reconfirmation still may be necessary. If in doubt — call.

If you plan not to take a flight on which you hold a confirmed reservation, by all means inform the airline. Because the problem of "no-shows" is a constant expense for airlines, they are allowed to overbook flights, a practice that often contributes to the threat of denied boarding for a certain number of passengers (see "Getting Bumped," below).

Seating – For most types of tickets, airline seats usually are assigned on a first-come, first-served basis at check-in, although some airlines make it possible to reserve a seat at the time of ticket purchase. Always check in early for your flight, even with advance seat assignments. A good rule of thumb for domestic flights is to arrive at the airport *at least* 1 hour before the scheduled departure to give yourself plenty of time in case there are long lines.

Most airlines furnish seating charts, which make choosing a seat much easier, but there are a few basics to consider. You must decide whether you prefer a window, aisle, or middle seat. On those few domestic flights where smoking is permitted (see "Smoking," below), you also should indicate if you prefer the smoking or nonsmoking section.

The amount of legroom provided (as well as chest room, especially when the seat in front of you is in a reclining position) is determined by something called "pitch," a measure of the distance between the back of the seat in front of you and the front of the back of your seat. The amount of pitch is a matter of airline policy, not the type of plane you fly. First class and business class seats have the greatest pitch, a fact that figures prominently in airline advertising. In economy class or coach, the standard pitch ranges from 33 to as little as 31 inches — downright cramped.

The number of seats abreast, another factor determining comfort, depends on a combination of airline policy and airplane dimensions. First class and business class have the fewest seats per row. Economy generally has 9 seats per row on a DC-10 or an L-1011, making either one slightly more comfortable than a 747, on which there normally are 10 seats per row. A 727 has 6 seats per row.

Airline representatives claim that most aircraft are more stable toward the front and midsection, while the seats farthest from the engines are quietest. Passengers who have long legs and are traveling on a wide-body aircraft might request a seat directly behind a door or emergency exit, since these seats often have greater than average pitch, or a seat in the first row of a given section, which offers extra legroom — although these seats are increasingly being reserved for passengers who are willing (and able) to perform certain tasks in the event of emergency evacuation. It often is impossible, however, to see the movie from seats that are directly behind the plane's exits. Be aware that the first row of the economy section (called a "bulkhead" seat) on a conventional aircraft (not a widebody) does *not* offer extra legroom, since the fixed partition will not permit passengers to slide their feet under it, and that watching a movie from this first-row seat also can be difficult and uncomfortable. These bulkhead seats do, however, provide ample room to use a bassinet or safety seat and often are reserved for families traveling with small children.

A window seat protects you from aisle traffic and clumsy serving carts and also provides a view, while an aisle seat enables you to get up and stretch your legs without disturbing your fellow travelers. Middle seats are the least desirable, and seats in the last row are the worst of all, since they seldom recline fully. If you wish to avoid children on your flight or if you find that you are sitting in an especially noisy section, you usually are free to move to any unoccupied seat — if there is one.

If you are large, you may face the prospect of a long flight with special trepidation. Center seats in the alignments of wide-body 747s, L-1011s, and DC-10s are about 1½ inches wider than those on either side, so larger travelers tend to be more comfortable there.

Despite all these rules of thumb, finding out which specific rows are near emergency exits or at the front of a wide-body cabin can be difficult because seating arrangements on any two identical planes vary from airline to airline. There is, however, a quarterly publication called the *Airline Seating Guide* that publishes seating charts for most major US airlines and many foreign carriers as well. Your travel agent should have a copy, or you can buy the US edition for $39.95 per year. Order from Carlson Publishing Co., Box 888, Los Alamitos, CA 90720 (phone: 800-728-4877 or 310-493-4877).

Simply reserving an airline seat in advance, however, actually may guarantee very little. Most airlines require that passengers arrive at the departure gate at least 45 minutes (sometimes more) ahead of time to hold a seat reservation. Some carriers may cancel seat assignments and may not honor reservations of passengers who have not checked in some period of time — usually around 30 minutes, depending on the airport — before the scheduled departure time, and they ask travelers to check in at least 1 hour before all domestic flights. It pays to read the fine print on your ticket carefully and follow its requirements.

A far better strategy is to visit an airline ticket office (or one of a select group of travel agents) to secure an actual boarding pass for your specific flight. Once this has been issued, airline computers show you as checked in, and you effectively own the seat you have selected (although some carriers may not honor boarding passes of passengers arriving at the gate less than 10 minutes before departure). This also is good — but not foolproof — insurance against getting bumped from an overbooked flight and is, therefore, an especially valuable tactic at peak travel times.

Smoking – One decision regarding choosing a seat has been taken out of the hands of most domestic travelers who smoke. Effective February 25, 1990, the US government imposed a ban that prohibits smoking on all flights scheduled for 6 hours or less within the US and its territories. The new regulation applies to both domestic and international carriers serving these routes.

Only flights with a *continuous* flying time of over 6 hours between stops in the US or its territories are exempt. Even if the total flying time is longer, smoking is not permitted on segments of domestic flights where the time between US landings is under 6 hours — for instance, flights that include a stopover (even with no change of plane), or connecting flights. To further complicate the situation, several individual carriers ban smoking altogether on certain routes.

On those flights that do permit smoking, the US Department of Transportation has determined that nonsmoking sections must be enlarged to accommodate all passengers who wish to sit in one. The airline does not, however, have to shift seating to accommodate nonsmokers who arrive late for a flight or travelers flying standby. Cigar and pipe smoking are prohibited on all flights, even in the smoking sections.

For a wallet-size guide that notes in detail the rights of nonsmokers according to these regulations, send a self-addressed, stamped envelope to ASH (Action on Smoking and Health), Airline Card, 2013 H St. NW, Washington, DC 20006 (phone: 202-659-4310).

Meals – If you have specific dietary requirements, be sure to let the airline know well before departure time. The available meals include vegetarian, seafood, kosher, Muslim, Hindu, high-protein, low-calorie, low-cholesterol, low-fat, low-sodium, diabetic, bland, and children's menus (not all of these may be available on every carrier). There is no extra charge for this option. It usually is necessary to request special meals when you make your reservations — check-in time is too late. It's also wise to reconfirm that your request for a special meal has made its way into the airline's computer — the time to do this is 24 hours before departure. (Note that special meals generally are not

18 GETTING READY / Traveling by Plane

available on shorter domestic flights, particularly on small local carriers. If this poses a problem, try to eat before you board, or bring a snack with you.)

Baggage – Though airline baggage allowances vary slightly, in general, all passengers are allowed to carry on board, without charge, one piece of luggage that will fit easily under a seat of the plane or in an overhead bin, and whose combined dimensions (length, width, and depth) do not exceed 45 inches. A reasonable amount of reading material, camera equipment, and a handbag also are allowed. In addition, all passengers are allowed to check two bags in the cargo hold: one usually not to exceed 62 inches when length, width, and depth are combined, the other not to exceed 55 inches in combined dimensions. Generally no single bag may weigh more than 70 pounds.

Charges for additional, oversize, or overweight bags usually are made at a flat rate; the actual dollar amount varies from carrier to carrier. If you plan to travel with any special equipment or sporting gear, be sure to check with the airline beforehand. Most have specific procedures for handling such baggage, and you may have to pay for transport regardless of how much other baggage you have checked. Golf clubs and skis may be checked through as luggage (most airlines are accustomed to handling them), but tennis rackets should be carried onto the plane.

To reduce the chances of your luggage going astray, remove all airline tags from previous trips, and label each bag inside and out — with your business address, rather than your home address, on the outside, to prevent thieves from knowing whose house might be unguarded. Lock everything and double-check the tag that the airline attaches to make sure that it is correctly coded LAS for Las Vegas.

If your bags are not in the baggage claim area after your flight or if they're damaged, report the problem to airline personnel immediately. Keep in mind that policies regarding the specific time limit within which you have to make your claim vary from carrier to carrier. Fill out a report form on your lost or damaged luggage and keep a copy of it and your original baggage claim check. If you must surrender the check to claim a damaged bag, get a receipt for it to prove that you did, indeed, check your baggage on the flight. If luggage is missing, be sure to give the airline your destination and/or a telephone number where you can be reached. Also take the name and number of the person in charge of recovering lost luggage.

Most airlines have emergency funds for passengers stranded away from home without their luggage, but if it turns out that your bags are truly lost and not simply delayed, do not then and there sign any paper indicating you'll accept an offered settlement. Since the airline is responsible for the value of your bags within certain statutory limits ($1,250 per passenger for lost baggage on a US domestic flight), you should take the time to assess the extent of your loss (see *Insurance,* in this section). It's a good idea to keep records indicating the value of the contents of your luggage. A wise alternative is to take a Polaroid picture of the most valuable of your packed items just after putting them in your suitcase.

Considering the increased incidence of damage to baggage, now more than ever it's advisable to keep the sales slips that confirm how much you paid for your bags. These are invaluable in establishing the value of damaged luggage and eliminate any arguments. A better way to protect your precious gear from the luggage-eating conveyers is to try to carry it on board whenever possible.

Airline Clubs – US carriers often have clubs for travelers who pay for membership. These clubs are not solely for first class passengers, although a first class ticket *may* entitle a passenger to lounge privileges. Membership entitles the traveler use of the private lounges at airports along their route, to refreshments served in those lounges, and to check-cashing privileges at most of their counters. Extras include special telephone numbers for individual reservations, embossed luggage tags, and a membership card for identification. Airlines serving Las Vegas that offer membership in such clubs include the following:

American: The *Admiral's Club.* Single yearly membership $225 for the first year; $125 yearly thereafter; spouse an additional $70 per year.

Delta: The *Crown Club.* Single yearly membership $150; spouse an additional $50 per year; 3-year and lifetime memberships also available.

Northwest: The *World Club.* Single yearly membership $140 (plus a onetime $50 initiation fee); spouse an additional $50 per year; 3-year and lifetime memberships also available.

TWA: The *Ambassador Club.* Single yearly membership $150; spouse an additional $25 per year; 3-year and lifetime memberships also available.

United: The *Red Carpet Club.* Single yearly membership $125 (plus a onetime $100 initiation fee); spouse an additional $70; 3-year and lifetime memberships also available.

USAir: The *USAir Club.* Single yearly membership $125; spouse an additional $25 per year; 3-year and lifetime memberships also available.

Note that the companies above do not have club facilities in all airports. Other airlines also may offer a variety of special services in many airports.

Getting Bumped – A special air travel problem is the possibility that an airline will accept more reservations (and sell more tickets) than there are seats on a given flight. This is entirely legal and is done to make up for "no-shows," passengers who don't show up for a flight for which they have made reservations and bought tickets. If the airline has oversold the flight and everyone does show up, there simply aren't enough seats. When this happens, the airline is subject to stringent rules designed to protect travelers.

In such cases, the airline first seeks ticket holders willing to give up their seats voluntarily in return for a negotiable sum of money or some other inducement, such as an offer of upgraded seating on the next flight or a voucher for a free trip at some other time. If there are not enough volunteers, the airline may bump passengers against their wishes.

Anyone inconvenienced in this way, however, is entitled to an explanation of the criteria used to determine who does and does not get on the flight, as well as compensation if the resulting delay exceeds certain limits. If the airline can put the bumped passengers on an alternate flight that is *scheduled to arrive* at their original destination within 1 hour of their originally scheduled arrival time, no compensation is owed. If the delay is more than 1 hour but less than 2 hours on a domestic US flight, they must be paid denied-boarding compensation equivalent to the one-way fare to their destination (but not more than $200). If the delay is more than 2 hours after the original arrival time on a domestic flight, the compensation must be doubled (not more than $400). The airline also may offer bumped travelers a voucher for a free flight instead of the denied-boarding compensation. The passenger may be given the choice of either the money or the voucher, the dollar value of which may be no less than the monetary compensation to which the passenger would be entitled. The voucher is not a substitute for the bumped passenger's original ticket; the airline continues to honor that as well. Keep in mind that the above regulations and policies are for US flights only.

To protect yourself as best you can against getting bumped, arrive at the airport early, allowing plenty of time to check in and get to the gate. If the flight is oversold, ask immediately for the written statement explaining the airline's policy on denied-boarding compensation and its boarding priorities. If the airline refuses to give you this information, or if you feel they have not handled the situation properly, file a complaint with both the airline and the appropriate government agency (see "Consumer Protection," below).

Delays and Cancellations – The above compensation rules also do not apply if the flight is canceled or delayed, or if a smaller aircraft is substituted due to mechanical problems. Each airline has its own policy for assisting passengers whose flights are delayed or canceled or who must wait for another flight because their original one was overbooked. Most airline personnel will make new travel arrangements if necessary. If the delay is longer than 4 hours, the airline may pay for a phone call or telegram, a meal, and in some cases, a hotel room and transportation to it.

■ **Caution:** If you are bumped or miss a flight, be sure to ask the airline to notify other airlines on which you have reservations or connecting flights. When your name is taken off the passenger list of your initial flight, the computer usually cancels all of your reservations automatically, unless *you* take steps to preserve them.

CHARTER FLIGHTS: By booking a block of seats on a specially arranged flight, charter tour operators offer travelers air transportation for a substantial reduction over the full coach or economy fare. These operators may offer air-only charters (selling transportation alone) or charter packages (the flight plus a combination of land arrangements such as accommodations, meals, tours, or car rentals). Charters are especially attractive to people living in smaller cities or out-of-the-way places, because they frequently leave from nearby airports, saving travelers the inconvenience and expense of getting to a major gateway.

From the consumer's standpoint, charters differ from scheduled airlines in two main respects: You generally need to book and pay in advance, and you can't change the itinerary or the departure and return dates once you've booked the flight. In practice, however, these restrictions don't always apply. Today, although most domestic charter flights still require advance reservations, some permit last-minute bookings (when there are unsold seats available), and some even offer seats on a standby basis. Though charters almost always are round-trip, and it is unlikely that you would be sold a one-way seat on a round-trip flight, on rare occasions one-way tickets on charters are offered.

Things to keep in mind about the charter game:

1. It cannot be repeated often enough that if you are forced to cancel your trip, you can lose much (and possibly all) of your money unless you have cancellation insurance, which is a *must* (see *Insurance*, in this section). Frequently, if the cancellation occurs far enough in advance (often 6 weeks or more), you may forfeit only a $25 or $50 penalty. If you cancel only 2 or 3 weeks before the flight, there may be no refund at all unless you or the operator can provide a substitute passenger.
2. Charter flights may be canceled by the operator up to 10 days before departure for any reason, usually underbooking. Your money is returned in this event, but there may be too little time for you to make new arrangements.
3. Most charters have little of the flexibility of some regularly scheduled flights regarding refunds and the changing of flight dates; if you book a return flight, you must be on it or lose your money.
4. Charter operators are permitted to assess a surcharge, if fuel or other costs warrant it, of up to 10% of the airfare up to 10 days before departure.
5. Because of the economics of charter flights, your plane almost always will be full, so you will be crowded, though not necessarily uncomfortable. (There is, however, a new movement among charter airlines to provide flight accommodations that are more comfort-oriented, so this situation may change in the near future.)

To avoid problems, *always* choose charter flights with care. When you consider a charter, ask your travel agent who runs it and carefully check the company. The Better Business Bureau in the company's home city can report on how many complaints, if any, have been lodged against it in the past. Protect yourself with trip cancellation and interruption insurance, which can help safeguard your investment if you, or a traveling companion, are unable to make the trip and must cancel too late to receive a full refund from the company providing your travel services. (This is advisable whether you're buying a charter flight alone or a tour package for which the airfare is provided by charter or scheduled flight.)

Bookings – If you do fly on a charter, read the contract's fine print carefully and pay particular attention to the following:

Instructions concerning the payment of the deposit and its balance and to whom the check is to be made payable. Ordinarily, checks are made out to an escrow account, which means the charter company can't spend your money until your flight has safely returned. This provides some protection for you. To ensure the safe handling of your money, make out your check to the escrow account, the number of which must appear by law on the brochure, though all too often it is on the back in fine print. Write the details of the charter, including the destination and dates, on the face of the check; on the back, print "For Deposit Only." Your travel agent may prefer that you make out your check to the agency, saying that it will then pay the tour operator the fee minus commission. It is perfectly legal to write the check as we suggest, however, and if your agent objects too vociferously (he or she should trust the tour operator to send the proper commission), consider taking your business elsewhere. If you don't make your check out to the escrow account, you lose the protection of that escrow should the trip be canceled. Furthermore, recent bankruptcies in the travel industry have served to point out that even the protection of escrow may not be enough to safeguard a traveler's investment. More and more, insurance is becoming a necessity. The charter company should be bonded (usually by an insurance company), and if you want to file a claim against it, the claim should be sent to the bonding agent. The contract will set a time limit within which a claim must be filed.

Specific stipulations and penalties for cancellations. Most charters allow you to cancel up to 45 days in advance without major penalty, but some cancellation dates are 50 to 60 days before departure.

Stipulations regarding cancellation and major changes made by the charterer. US rules say that charter flights may not be canceled within 10 days of departure except when circumstances — such as natural disasters or political upheavals — make it physically impossible to fly. Charterers may make "major changes," however, such as in the date or place of departure or return, but you are entitled to cancel and receive a full refund if you don't wish to accept these changes. A price increase of more than 10% at any time up to 10 days before departure is considered a major change; no price increase at all is allowed during the last 10 days immediately before departure.

At the time of this writing, the following companies regularly offered charter flights within the US. As indicated, some of these companies sell charter flights directly to clients, while others are wholesalers and must be contacted through a travel agent.

Amber Tours (7337 W. Washington St., Indianapolis, IN 46251; phone: 800-225-9920). Offers Las Vegas charters. Retails to the general public.

Apple Vacations West (25 NW Point Blvd., Elk Grove Village, IL 60007; phone: 800-365-2775). Operates Las Vegas charters out of Chicago. This agency is a wholesaler, so use a travel agent.

Funway Holidays/Funjet (PO Box 1460, Milwaukee, WI 53201-1460; phone: 800-558-3050). This agency is a wholesaler, so use a travel agent.

Las Vegas Connection (11010 Spring Hill Dr., Spring Hill, FL 34608; phone: 800-628-3427) Operates Las Vegas charters from Florida. Retails to the general public.

MLT Vacations (5130 Hwy. 101, Minnetonka, MN 55345; phone: 800-328-0025). Offers packages including accommodations and transportation, as well as air seats only. This agency is a wholesaler, so use a travel agent.

Morris Air Service (260 E. Morris Ave., Salt Lake City, UT 84115-3200; phone: 800-444-5660). Retails to the general public.

MTI Vacations (1220 Kensington Ct., Oak Brook, IL 60521; phone: 800-323-7285). This agency is a wholesaler, so use a travel agent.

Suntrips (2350 Paragon Dr., San Jose, CA 95131; phone: 800-SUNTRIP in California; 408-432-0700 elsewhere in the US). Retails to the general public.

You also may want to subscribe to the travel newsletter *Jax Fax,* which regularly features a list of charter companies and packagers offering seats on US charter flights. For a year's subscription send a check or money order for $12 to *Jax Fax,* 397 Post Rd., Darien, CT 06820 (phone: 203-655-8746).

DISCOUNTS ON SCHEDULED FLIGHTS: Promotional fares often are called discount fares because they cost less than what used to be the standard airline fare — full-fare economy. Nevertheless, they cost the traveler the same whether they are bought through a travel agent or directly from the airline. Tickets that cost less if bought from some outlet other than the airline do exist, however. While it is likely that the vast majority of travelers flying within the US in the near future will be doing so on a promotional fare or charter rather than on a "discount" air ticket of this sort, it still is a good idea for cost-conscious consumers to be aware of the latest developments in the budget airfare scene. Note that the following discussion makes clear-cut distinctions among the types of discounts available based on how they reach the consumer; in actual practice, the distinctions are not nearly so precise.

Net Fare Sources – The newest notion for reducing the costs of travel services comes from travel agents who offer individual travelers "net" fares. Defined simply, a net fare is the bare minimum amount at which an airline or tour operator will carry a prospective traveler. It doesn't include the amount that normally would be paid to the travel agent as a commission. Traditionally, such commissions amount to about 10% on domestic fares — not counting significant additions to these commission levels that are paid retroactively when agents sell more than a specific volume of tickets or trips for a single supplier. At press time, at least one travel agency in the US was offering travelers the opportunity to purchase tickets and/or tours for a net price. Instead of earning its income from individual commissions, this agency assesses a fixed fee that may or may not provide a bargain for travelers; it requires a little arithmetic to determine whether to use the services of a net travel agent or those of one who accepts conventional commissions. One of the potential drawbacks of buying from agencies selling travel services at net fares is that some airlines refuse to do business with them, thus possibly limiting your flight options.

Travel Avenue is a fee-based agency that rebates its ordinary agency commission to the customer. For domestic flights, they will find the lowest retail fare, then rebate 7% to 10% (depending on the airline selected) of that price minus a $25 ticket-writing charge. If the ticket includes more than eight separate flights, an additional $10 fee is charged. Customers using free flight coupons pay the ticket-writing charge, plus an additional $5 coupon-processing fee.

Travel Avenue will rebate its commissions on all tickets, including heavily discounted fares and senior citizen passes. Available 7 days a week, reservations should be made far enough in advance to allow the tickets to be sent by first class mail, since extra charges accrue for special handling. It's possible to economize further by making your own airline reservation, then asking *Travel Avenue* only to write/issue your ticket. For travelers outside the Chicago area, business may be transacted by phone and purchases charged to a credit card. For information, contact *Travel Avenue* at 641 W. Lake St., Suite 201, Chicago, IL 60606-1012 (phone: 312-876-1116 in Illinois; 800-333-3335 elsewhere in the US).

Consolidators and Bucket Shops – Other vendors of travel services can afford to sell tickets to their customers at an even greater discount because the airline has sold the tickets to them at a substantial discount (usually accomplished by sharply increasing commissions to that vendor), a practice in which many airlines indulge, albeit discreetly, preferring that the general public not know they are undercutting their own "list" prices. Airlines anticipating a slow period on a particular route sometimes sell off a certain portion of their capacity at a very great discount to a wholesaler, or consolidator. The wholesaler sometimes is a charter operator who resells the seats to the public as though they were charter seats, which is why prospective travelers perusing the brochures of charter operators with large programs frequently see a number of flights designated as "scheduled service." As often as not, however, the consolidator, in turn, sells the seats to a travel agency specializing in discounting. Airlines also can sell seats directly to such an agency, which thus acts as its own consolidator. The airline offers the seats either at a net wholesale price, but without the volume-purchase requirement that would be difficult for a modest retail travel agency to fulfill, or at the standard price, but with a commission override large enough (as high as 50%) to allow both a profit and a price reduction to the public.

Travel agencies specializing in discounting sometimes are called "bucket shops," a term once fraught with connotations of unreliability in this country. But in today's highly competitive travel marketplace, more and more conventional travel agencies are selling consolidator-supplied tickets, and the old bucket shops' image is becoming respectable. Agencies that specialize in discounted tickets exist in most large cities, and usually can be found by studying the smaller ads in the travel sections of local Sunday newspapers.

Before buying a discounted ticket, whether from a bucket shop or a conventional, full-service travel agency, keep the following considerations in mind: To be in a position to judge how much you'll be saving, first find out the "list" prices of tickets to your destination. Then do some comparison shopping among agencies. Also bear in mind that a ticket that may not differ much in price from one available directly from the airline may, however, allow the circumvention of such things as the advance-purchase requirement. If your plans are less than final, be sure to find out about any other restrictions, such as penalties for canceling a flight or changing a reservation. Most discount tickets are non-endorsable, meaning that they can be used only on the airline that issued them, and they usually are marked "nonrefundable" to prevent their being cashed in for a list-price refund.

A great many few bucket shops are small businesses operating on a thin margin, so it's a good idea to check the local Better Business Bureau for any complaints registered against the one with which you're dealing — before parting with any money. If you still do not feel reassured, consider buying discounted tickets only through a conventional travel agency, which can be expected to have found its own reliable source of consolidator tickets — some of the largest consolidators, in fact, sell only to travel agencies.

A few bucket shops require payment in cash or by certified check or money order, but if credit cards are accepted, use that option. Note, however, if buying from a charter operator selling both scheduled and charter flights, that the scheduled seats are not protected by the regulations — including the use of escrow accounts — governing the charter seats. Well-established charter operators, nevertheless, may extend the same protections to their scheduled flights, and when this is the case, consumers should be sure that the payment option selected directs their money into the escrow account.

Listed below are some of the consolidators frequently offering discounted domestic fares:

Bargain Air (655 Deep Valley Dr., Suite 355, Rolling Hills, CA 90274; phone: 800-347-2345 or 213-377-2919).

Maharaja/Consumer Wholesale Travel (34 W. 33rd St., Suite 1014, New York, NY 10001; phone: 212-213-2020 in New York; 800-223-6862 elsewhere in the US).

TFI Tours International (34 W. 37th St., 12th Floor, New York, NY 10001; phone: 212-736-1140 in New York State; 800-825-3834 elsewhere in the US).

25 West Tours (2490 Coral Way, Miami, FL 33145; phone: 305-856-0810 in Florida; 800-925-0250 elsewhere in the US).

Unitravel (1177 N. Warson Rd., St. Louis, MO 63132; phone: 314-569-0900 in Missouri; 800-325-2222 elsewhere in the US).

Check with your travel agent for other sources of consolidator-supplied tickets.

■ **Note:** Although rebating and discounting are becoming increasingly common, there is some legal ambiguity concerning them. Strictly speaking, it is legal to discount domestic tickets but not international tickets. On the other hand, the law that prohibits discounting, the Federal Aviation Act of 1958, is consistently ignored these days, in part because consumers benefit from the practice and in part because many illegal arrangements are indistinguishable from legal ones. Since the line separating the two is so fine that even the authorities can't always tell the difference, it is unlikely that most consumers would be able to do so, and in fact it is not illegal to *buy* a discounted ticket. If the issue of legality bothers you, ask the agency whether any ticket you're about to buy would be permissible under the above-mentioned act.

Last-Minute Travel Clubs – Still another way to take advantage of bargain airfares is open to those who have a flexible schedule. A number of organizations, usually set up as last-minute travel clubs and functioning on a membership basis, routinely keep in touch with travel suppliers to help them dispose of unsold inventory at discounts of between 15% and 60%. A great deal of the inventory consists of complete package tours and cruises, but some clubs offer air-only charter seats and, occasionally, seats on scheduled flights.

Members generally pay an annual fee and receive a toll-free hotline telephone number to call for information on imminent trips. In some cases, they also receive periodic mailings with information on bargain travel opportunities for which there is more advance notice. Despite the suggestive names of the clubs providing these services, last-minute travel does not necessarily mean that you cannot make plans until literally the last minute. Trips can be announced as little as a few days or as much as 2 months before departure, but the average is from 1 to 4 weeks' notice.

Among the organizations regularly offering such discounted travel opportunities in the US are the following:

Discount Travel International (152 W. 72nd St., Suite 223, New York, NY 10023; phone: 212-362-3636). Annual fee: $45 per household.

Encore/Short Notice (4501 Forbes Blvd., Lanham, MD 20706; phone: 301-459-8020; 800-638-0930 for customer service). Annual fee: $36 per family for Encore (main discount travel program), $48 per family for Short Notice program.

Last Minute Travel (1249 Boylston St., Boston MA 02215; phone: 800-LAST-MIN or 617-267-9800). No fee.

Moment's Notice (425 Madison Ave., New York, NY 10017; phone: 212-486-0503). Annual fee: $45 per family.

Traveler's Advantage (3033 S. Parker Rd., Suite 1000, Aurora, CO 80014; phone: 800-548-1116). Annual fee: $49 per family.

Vacations to Go (2411 Fountain View, Suite 201, Houston, TX 77057; phone: 800-338-4962). Annual fee: $19.95 per family.

Worldwide Discount Travel Club (1674 Meridian Ave., Miami Beach, FL 33139; phone: 305-534-2082). Annual fee: $40 per person; $50 per family.

■ **Note:** For additional information on last-minute travel discounts, a new "900" number telephone service called *Last Minute Travel Connection* (phone: 900-446-8292) provides recorded advertisements (including contact information) for discount offerings on airfares, package tours, cruises, and other travel opportunities.

Since companies update their advertisements as often as every hour, listings are current. This 24-hour service is available to callers using touch-tone phones; the cost is $1 per minute (the charge will show up on your phone bill). For more information, contact *La Onda, Ltd.*, 601 Skokie Blvd., Suite 224, Northbrook, IL 60062 (phone: 708-498-9216).

Generic Air Travel – Organizations that apply the same flexible-schedule idea to air travel only and arrange for flights at literally the last minute also exist. Their service sometimes is known as "generic" air travel, and it operates somewhat like an ordinary airline standby service, except that the organizations running it do not guarantee flights to a specific destination, but only to a general region, and offer seats on not one but several scheduled and charter airlines.

One pioneer of generic flights is *Airhitch* (2790 Broadway, Suite 100, New York, NY 10025; phone: 212-864-2000), which had offered its Calhitch program, now temporarily discontinued, for East Coast–West Coast flights that could be useful in connecting for Las Vegas. When making travel plans, call to find out if the service has resumed. When Calhitch is operating, prospective travelers stipulate a range of at least 5 consecutive departure dates and their desired destination, along with alternate choices, and pay the fare in advance. They are then sent a voucher good for travel *on a space-available basis* on flights to their destination region (not necessarily the first city requested). The week before this range of departure dates begins, travelers must contact *Airhitch* for specific information about flights on which seats may be available and instructions on how to proceed for check-in. (Return fights are arranged in the same manner as the outbound flights — a specified period of travel is decided upon, and a few days before this date range begins, prospective passengers contact *Airhitch* for details about flights that may be available.) If the client does not accept any of the suggested flights or cancels his or her travel plans after selecting a flight, the amount paid may be applied toward a future fare or the flight arrangements can be transferred to another individual (although, in both cases, an additional fee may be charged). No refunds are offered unless the prospective passenger does not ultimately get on any flight in the specified date range; in such a case, the full fare is refunded. (Note that *Airhitch*'s slightly more expensive Target program, which provides confirmed reservations on specific dates to specific destinations, offers passengers greater — but not guaranteed — certainty regarding destinations and other flight arrangements.)

Bartered Travel Sources – Suppose a hotel buys advertising space in a newspaper. As payment, the hotel gives the publishing company the use of a number of hotel rooms in lieu of cash. This is barter, a common means of exchange among hotels, airlines, car rental companies, cruise lines, tour operators, restaurants, and other travel service companies. When a bartering company finds itself with empty airline seats (or excess hotel rooms, or cruise ship cabin space, and so on) and offers them to the public, considerable savings can be enjoyed.

Bartered travel clubs offer discounts of up to 50% to members, who pay an annual fee (approximately $50 at press time) which entitles them to select from the flights, cruises, hotel rooms, or other travel services that the club obtained by barter. Members usually present a voucher, club credit card, or scrip (a dollar-denomination voucher negotiable only for the bartered product) to the hotel, which in turn subtracts the dollar amount from the bartering company's account.

Selling bartered travel is a perfectly legitimate means of retailing. One advantage to club members is that they don't have to wait until the last minute to obtain flight or room reservations.

Among the companies specializing in bartered travel, the following frequently offer members travel services throughout the US:

Travel Guild (18210 Redmond Way, Redmond, WA 98052; phone: 206-861-1900). Annual fee: $48 per family.

Travel World Leisure Club (225 W. 34th St., Suite 2203, New York, NY 10122; phone: 800-444-TWLC or 212-239-4855). Annual fee: $50 per person; $20 for each additional member of a family.

OTHER DISCOUNT TRAVEL SOURCES: An excellent source of information on economical travel opportunities is the *Consumer Reports Travel Letter,* published monthly by Consumers Union. It keeps abreast of the scene on a wide variety of fronts, including package tours, rental cars, insurance, and more, but it is especially helpful for its comprehensive coverage of airfares, offering guidance on all the options, from scheduled flights on major or low-fare airlines to charters and discount sources. For a year's subscription, send $37 ($57 for 2 years) to *Consumer Reports Travel Letter* (PO Box 53629, Boulder, CO 80322-3629; phone: 800-999-7959). For information on other travel newsletters, see *Books, Magazines, and Newsletters,* in this section.

CONSUMER PROTECTION: Consumers who feel that they have not been dealt with fairly by an airline should make their complaints known. Begin with the customer service representative at the airport where the problem occurred. If your complaint cannot be resolved there to your satisfaction, write to the airline's consumer office. In a businesslike, typed letter, explain what reservations you held, what happened, the names of the employees involved, and what you expect the airline to do to remedy the situation. Send copies (never the originals) of the tickets, receipts, and other documents that back your claims. Ideally, all correspondence should be sent via certified mail, return receipt requested. This provides proof that your complaint was received.

Passengers with consumer complaints — lost baggage, compensation for getting bumped, violation of smoking and nonsmoking rules, deceptive practices by an airline — who are not satisfied with the airline's response should contact the Department of Transportation (DOT), Consumer Affairs Division (400 Seventh St. SW, Room 10405, Washington, DC 20590; phone: 202-366-2220). DOT personnel stress, however, that consumers initially should direct their complaints to the airline that provoked them.

Remember, too, that the federal Fair Credit Billing Act permits purchasers to refuse to pay for credit card charges for services which have not been delivered, so the onus of dealing with the receiver for a bankrupt airline, for example, falls on the credit card company. Do not rely on another airline to honor any ticket you're holding from a failed airline, since the days when virtually all major carriers subscribed to a default protection program that bound them to do so are long gone. Some airlines may voluntarily step forward to accommodate the stranded passengers of a fellow carrier, but this is now an entirely altruistic act.

The deregulation of US airlines has meant that travelers must find out for themselves what they are entitled to receive. The Department of Transportation's informative consumer booklet *Fly Rights* is a good place to start. To receive a copy, send $1 to the Superintendent of Documents (US Government Printing Office, Washington, DC 20402-9325; phone: 202-783-3238). Specify its stock number, 050-000-00513-5, and allow 3 to 4 weeks for delivery.

On Arrival

FROM THE AIRPORT TO THE CITY: McCarran International Airport is located 5 miles south of Las Vegas. The ride from the airport to the Strip usually takes from 15 to 20 minutes, depending on traffic and time of day, and 10 or so minutes more to the downtown area. The taxi fare to the Strip runs about $7 to $10, $10 to $15 to downtown. A number of bus services operate from the airport for about $3.50 to the Strip and $4.50 downtown. You can get one up at the airport, but must make a reservation for the return trip. Among the companies are *Bell Trans* (phone: 702-739-7990), *Gray Line of Southern Nevada* (phone: 702-739-5700), and *Lucky 7* (phone: 702-739-6177). They each run regularly, every 10 to 15 minutes.

CAR RENTAL: Unless planning to drive round trip from home, most travelers who want to drive while on vacation simply rent a car. They can rent a car through a travel agent or national rental firm before leaving home, or from a local company once they arrive in Las Vegas. Another possibility, also arranged before departure, is to rent the car as part of a larger travel package.

It's tempting to wait until arrival to scout out the lowest-priced rental from the company located the farthest from the airport high-rent district and offering no pick-up services. But if your arrival coincides with a holiday or a peak travel period, you may be disappointed to find that even the most expensive car in the city was reserved months ago. Whenever possible, it is best to reserve in advance, anywhere from a few days ahead in slack periods to a month or more during the busier seasons.

Often, the easiest place to rent (or at least pick up) the car is at the airport on arrival. The majority of the national car rental companies have locations at McCarran International Airport, where shuttle buses from each company pick up clients from the terminals and take them to the car rental locations. Travel agents can arrange rentals for clients, but it is just as easy to call and rent a car yourself. Listed below are the major national rental companies that have locations in Las Vegas and offer nationwide, toll-free telephone numbers:

Alamo: 800-327-9633.
American International Rent-A-Car: 800-527-0202.
Avis: 800-331-1212.
Budget Rent-A-Car: 800-527-0700.
Dollar Rent A Car: 800-800-4000.
Hertz: 800-654-3131.
National Car Rental: 800-CAR-RENT.
Sears Rent-A-Car: 800-527-0770.
Thrifty Rent-A-Car: 800-367-2277.

Often, less expensive car rentals may be obtained from the lesser-known national and regional chains that in many cases limit their advertising to the yellow pages. These companies frequently do most of their business in insurance replacement but are happy to accommodate any tourists who come their way. Following is a list of such firms doing business in Las Vegas, most with nationwide 800 numbers. For the companies that do not have a nationwide reservations service, the number provided is that of the most convenient location for visitors, and they will provide details on other locations if desired.

Action Car Rental: 702-365-1766.
Agency Rent-A-Car: 800-321-1972.
Airways Rent A Car: 800-952-9200.
Enterprise Rent-A-Car: 800-325-8007.
Lloyd's International Rent A Car: 800-654-7037.
Payless Car Rental: 800-PAYLESS.
Reserve Rent-A-Car: 800-346-6556.
Snappy Car Rental: 702-739-0220.

If you decide to wait until after you arrive, you'll find a surprising number of small companies listed in the local yellow pages. One such company is *Rebel Rent-A-Car* (5466 Paradise Rd.; phone: 800-372-1981 or 702-597-0427). Others include *Executive Rent-A-Car* (2855 Las Vegas Blvd. S.; phone: 702-732-1991), *Abbey Rent-A-Car* (3751 Las Vegas Blvd. S.; phone: 800-631-8909 or 702-736-4988), *US Rent A Car* (4920

Paradise Rd.; phone: 800-777-9377 or 702-798-6100), and *Allstate Car Rental* (5175 Rent A Car Rd.; phone: 800-634-6186 or 702-798-8589) near the airport. *Freedom Free Day Rent-A-Car* (4920 Paradise Rd.; phone: 702-733-9221) provides a free day for every 4 days' rental. All of these companies pick up at the airport.

To economize on a car rental, also consider one of the firms that rents 3- to 5-year-old cars that are well worn but (presumably) mechanically sound; one such company is *Rent-a-Wreck* (5506 S. Paradise Rd.; phone: 702-736-0040), and another is *Kut-Rate Used Car Rentals* (517 Park Paseo; phone: 702-384-8885). While these companies do not make airport pick-ups and it would be advisable to call ahead to see what cars they have available, it might well be worth the taxi ride.

At the other extreme, for those who feel like splurging, *Showcase Rent-A-Car* near the airport (1521 Swenson St.; phone: 702-736-2592) offers a Rolls-Royce, Jaguars, Mercedes, BMWs, and Corvettes. One week's notice is required. *Rent A Vette Classic Car Rental*, a division of *Rebel Rent-A-Car* (phone: 702-736-2592; see above for address), offers Corvettes, Mercedes, BMWs, Porsches, and Mustangs. Both companies pick up at the airport.

Requirements – Whether you decide to rent a car in advance from a large national rental company or wait to rent from a local company, you should know that renting a car is rarely as simple as signing on the dotted line and roaring off into the night. If you are renting for personal use, you must have a valid driver's license and will have to convince the renting agency that (1) you are personally creditworthy, and (2) you will bring the car back at the stated time. This will be easy if you have a major credit card; most rental companies accept credit cards in lieu of a cash deposit, as well as for payment of your final bill. If you prefer to pay in cash, leave your credit card imprint as a "deposit," then pay your bill in cash when you return the car.

Note that *Avis, Budget, Hertz,* and other national companies usually *will* rent to travelers paying in cash and leaving either a credit card imprint or a substantial amount of cash as a deposit. This is not necessarily standard policy, however, as other national chains and a number of local companies will *not* rent to an individual who doesn't have a valid credit card. In this case, you will have to call around to find a company that accepts cash.

Also keep in mind that although the minimum age to drive in most states is 16, the minimum age to rent a car is set by the rental company. (Restrictions vary from company to company, as well as at different locations.) Many firms have a minimum age requirement of 21 years, some raise that to 23 and 25 years, and for some models of cars it rises to 30 years. The upper age limit at many companies is between 69 and 75; others have no upper limit or may make drivers above a certain age subject to special conditions.

Costs – Finding the most economical car rental will require some telephone shopping on your part. As a *general* rule, expect to hear lower prices quoted by the smaller, strictly local companies than by the well-known international names.

Comparison shopping always is advisable, however. Even the international giants offer discount plans whose conditions are easy for most travelers to fulfill. For instance, *Budget* and *National* sometimes offer discounts of anywhere from 10% to 30% off their usual rates (according to the size of the car and the duration of the rental), provided that the car is reserved a certain number of days before departure (usually 7 to 14 days, but it can be less), is rented for a minimum period (5 days or, more often, a week), is paid for at the time of booking, and, in most cases, is returned to the same location that supplied it or to another in the same area. Similar discount plans include *Hertz*'s Leisure Rates and *Avis*'s Supervalue Rates.

If driving short distances for only a day or two, the best deal may be a per-day, per-mile rate: You pay a flat fee for each day you keep the car, plus a per-mile charge. An increasingly common alternative is to be granted a certain number of free miles each day and then be charged on a per-mile basis over that number.

GETTING READY / On Arrival 29

Most companies also offer a flat per-day rate with unlimited free mileage; this certainly is the most economical rate if you plan to drive over 100 miles. Make sure that the low, flat daily rate that catches your eye, however, is indeed a per-day rate: Often the lowest price advertised by a company turns out to be available only with a minimum 3-day rental — fine if you want the car that long, but not the bargain it appears if you really intend to use it no more than 24 hours. Flat weekly rates also are available, as are some flat monthly rates that represent a further saving over the daily rate.

Another factor influencing cost is the type of car you rent. Rentals are based on a tiered price system, with different sizes of cars — variations of budget, economy, regular, and luxury — often listed as A (the smallest and least expensive) through F, G, or H, and sometimes even higher. Charges may increase by only a few dollars a day through several categories of subcompact and compact cars — where most of the competition is — then increase by great leaps through the remaining classes of full-size and luxury cars and passenger vans. The larger the car, the more it costs to rent and the more gas it consumes, but for some people the greater comfort and extra luggage space of a larger car (in which bags and sporting gear can be safely locked out of sight) may make it worth the additional expense. Also more expensive are sleek sports cars, but again, for some people the thrill of driving such a car — for a week or a day — may be worth it.

Electing to pay for collision damage waiver (CDW) protection — often called loss damage waiver (LDW) in the US — will add considerably to the cost of renting a car. You may be responsible for the *full value* of the vehicle being rented if it is damaged or stolen, but you can dispense with all of the possible liability by buying the offered waiver at a cost of around $10 to $13 a day (although in some states, it may cost as little as $5). Before making any decisions about optional collision damage waivers, however, check with your own insurance agent and determine whether your personal automobile insurance policy covers rented vehicles; if it does, you probably won't need to pay for the waiver. Be aware, too, that increasing numbers of credit cards automatically provide CDW coverage if the car rental is charged to the appropriate credit card. However, the specific terms of such credit card coverage differ sharply among individual card companies, so check with the credit card company for information on the nature and amount of coverage provided. Business travelers also should be aware that, at the time of this writing, *American Express* had withdrawn its automatic CDW coverage from some corporate *Green* card accounts and limited the length of coverage — watch for similar cutbacks by other credit card companies.

When inquiring about CDW coverage and costs, be aware that a number of car rental companies now are automatically including the cost of this waiver in their quoted prices. This does not mean that they are absorbing this cost and you are receiving free coverage — in many cases total rental prices have increased to include the former CDW charge. The disadvantage of this inclusion is that you probably will not have the option to refuse this coverage, and will end up paying the added charge — even if you already are adequately covered by your own insurance policy or through a credit card company.

Additional costs to be added to the price tag include drop-off charges or one-way service fees. The lowest price quoted by any given company may apply only to a car that is returned to the same location from which it was rented. A slightly higher rate may be charged if the car is to be returned to a different location (even within the same city).

Also, don't forget to factor in the price of gas. Rental cars usually are delivered with a full tak of gas. (This is not always the case, however, so check the gas gauge when picking up the car, and have the amount of gas noted on your rental agreement if the tank is not full.) Remember to fill the tank before you return the car or you will have to pay to refill it, and gasoline at the car rental company's pump always is much more expensive then at a service station. This policy may vary for smaller local and regional companies; ask when picking up the vehicle. Before leaving the lot, also check that the rental car has a spare tire and jack in the trunk.

Package Tours

If the mere thought of buying a package for your visit to Las Vegas conjures up visions of a trip spent marching in lockstep through the city's attractions with a horde of frazzled fellow travelers, remember that packages have come a long way. For one thing, not all packages necessarily are escorted tours, and the one you buy does not have to include any organized touring at all — nor will it necessarily include traveling companions. If it does, however, you'll find that people of all sorts — many just like yourself — are taking advantage of packages today because they are economical and convenient and save an immense amount of planning time. Given the high cost of travel these days, packages have emerged as a particularly wise buy.

In essence, a package is just an amalgam of travel services that can be purchased in a single transaction. A package (tour or otherwise) may include any or all of the following: round-trip transportation, local transportation (and/or car rentals), accommodations, some or all meals, sightseeing, entertainment, transfers to and from the hotel, taxes, tips, escort service, and a variety of incidental features that might be offered as options at additional cost. In other words, a package can be any combination of travel elements, from a fully escorted tour offered at an all-inclusive price to a simple fly/drive booking that allows you to move about totally on your own. Its principal advantage is that it saves money: The cost of the combined arrangements invariably is well below the price of all of the same elements if bought separately, and, particularly if transportation is provided by discount flight, the whole package could cost less than just a round-trip economy airline ticket on a regularly scheduled flight. A package provides more than economy and convenience: It releases the traveler from having to make individual arrangements for each separate element of a trip.

Tour programs generally can be divided into two categories — "escorted" (or locally hosted) and "independent." An escorted tour means that a guide will accompany the group from the beginning of the tour through to the return flight; a locally hosted tour means that the group will be met upon arrival at each location by a different local host. On independent tours, there generally is a choice of hotels, meal plans, and sightseeing trips, as well as a variety of special excursions. The independent plan is for travelers who do not want a totally set itinerary, but who do prefer confirmed hotel reservations. Whether choosing an escorted or an independent tour, always bring along complete contact information for your tour operator in case a problem arises, although tour operators often have local affiliates who can give additional assistance or make other arrangements on the spot.

To determine whether a package — or more specifically, *which* package — fits your travel plans, start by evaluating your interests and needs, deciding how much and what you want to spend, see, and do. Gather brochures on Las Vegas tours. Be sure that you take the time to read each brochure *carefully* to determine precisely what is included. Keep in mind that they are written to entice you into signing up for a package tour. Often the language is deceptive and devious. For example, a brochure may quote the lowest prices for a package tour based on facilities that are unavailable during the off-season, undesirable at any season, or just plain nonexistent. Information such as "breakfast included" or "plus tax" (which can add up) should be taken into account. Note, too, that the prices quoted in brochures almost always are based on double

GETTING READY / Package Tours

occupancy: The rate listed is for each of two people sharing a double room, and if you travel alone, the supplement for single accommodations can raise the price considerably (see *Hints for Single Travelers,* in this section).

In this age of erratic airfares, the brochure most often will *not* include the price of an airline ticket in the price of the package, though sample fares from various gateway cities usually will be listed separately, as extras to be added to the price of the ground arrangements. Before figuring your actual costs, check the latest fares with the airlines, because the samples invariably are out of date by the time you read them. If the brochure gives more than one category of sample fares per gateway city — such as an individual tour-basing fare, a group fare, an excursion, APEX, or other discount ticket — your travel agent or airline tour desk will be able to tell you which one applies to the package you choose, depending on when you travel, how far in advance you book, and other factors. (An individual tour-basing fare is a fare computed as part of a package that includes land arrangements, thereby entitling a carrier to reduce the air portion almost to the absolute minimum. Though it always represents a saving over full-fare coach or economy, lately the individual tour-basing fare has not been as inexpensive as the excursion and other discount fares that also are available to individuals. The group fare usually is the least expensive fare, and it is the tour operator, not you, who makes up the group.) When the brochure does include round-trip transportation in the package price, don't forget to add the cost of round-trip transportation from your home to the departure city to come up with the total cost of the package.

Finally, read the general information regarding terms and conditions and the responsibility clause (usually in fine print at the end of the descriptive literature) to determine the precise elements for which the tour operator is — and is not — liable. Here the tour operator frequently expresses the right to change services or schedules as long as equivalent arrangements are offered. This clause also absolves the operator of responsibility for circumstances beyond human control, such as avalanches, earthquakes, or floods, or injury to you or your property. While reading, ask the following questions:

1. Does the tour include airfare or other transportation, sightseeing, meals, transfers, taxes, baggage handling, tips, or any other services? Do you want all these services?
2. If the brochure indicates that "some meals" are included, does this mean a welcoming and farewell dinner, two breakfasts, or every evening meal?
3. What classes of hotels are offered? If you will be traveling alone, what is the single supplement?
4. Does the tour itinerary or price vary according to the season?
5. Are the prices guaranteed; that is, if costs increase between the time you book and the time you depart, can surcharges unilaterally be added?
6. Do you get a full refund if you cancel? If not, be sure to obtain cancellation insurance.
7. Can the operator cancel if too few people join? At what point?

One of the consumer's biggest problems is finding enough information to judge the reliability of a tour packager, since individual travelers seldom have direct contact with the firm putting the package together. Usually, a retail travel agent is interposed between customer and tour operator, and much depends on his or her candor and cooperation. So ask a number of questions about the tour you are considering. For example:

- Has the travel agent ever used a package provided by this tour operator?
- How long has the tour operator been in business? Check the Better Business Bureau in the area where the tour operator is based to see if any complaints have been filed against it.
- Is the tour operator a member of the *United States Tour Operators Association*

(*USTOA;* 211 E. 51st St., Suite 12B, New York, NY 10022; phone: 212-944-5727)? *USTOA* will provide a list of its members on request; it also offers a useful brochure called *How to Select a Package Tour.*
- How many and which companies are involved in the package?

■ **A word of advice:** Purchasers of vacation packages who feel they're not getting their money's worth are more likely to get a refund if they complain in writing to the operator — and bail out of the whole package immediately. Alert the tour operator to the fact that you are dissatisfied, that you will be leaving for home as soon as transportation can be arranged, and that you expect a refund. They may have forms to fill out detailing your complaint; otherwise, state your case in a letter. Even if difficulty in arranging immediate transportation home detains you, your dated, written complaint should help in procuring a refund from the operator.

SAMPLE PACKAGES: Following is a list of some of the major tour operators that offer Las Vegas packages. Most companies offer several departure dates, depending on the length of the tour and subject matter. Some operators offer flexible city stays that start with 1 hotel night, with a choice of locations and prices available, to which may be added more nights and a wide variety of options, such as sightseeing, transfers, car rental and, in some cases, dine-around plans. As indicated, some operators are wholesalers only, and will deal only with a travel agent.

Adventure Tours (9818 Liberty Rd., Randallstown, MD 21133; phone: 301-922-7000 in Baltimore; 800-638-9040 elsewhere in the US). Offers flexible city stays. This company is a wholesaler; consult a travel agent.

American Express Travel Related Services (offices throughout the US; phone: 800-241-1700 for information and local branch offices). Markets flexible city stays in Las Vegas as well as independent and escorted tours throughout the US. The tour operator is a wholesaler, so use a travel agent.

Apple Vacations West (25 NW Point Blvd., Elk Grove Village, IL 60007; phone: 800-365-2775). Operators Las Vegas charters out of Chicago with city packages starting at 2 nights. This agency is a wholesaler, so use a travel agent.

Dixieland Tours & Cruises (8352 W. El Cajon, Baton Rouge, LA 70815; phone: 800-256-8747). Features hotel packages to Las Vegas.

Domenico Tours (751 Broadway, PO Box 144, Bayonne, NJ 07002; phone: 201-823-8687, 212-757-8687, or 800-554-8687). Operates a 15-day Las Vegas and Colorado Rockies motorcoach tour.

Funway Holidays/Funjet (8907 N. Port Washington Rd., PO Box 1460, Milwaukee, WI 53201-1460; phone: 800-558-3050). Charter operator, offering packages for a minimum of 2 nights with car rentals. This is a wholesaler only, so use a travel agent.

GoGo Tours (69 Spring St., Ramsey, NJ 07446-0507; phone: 201-934-3500 or call any of the 75 local *GoGo* offices.). Features land-only and air-inclusive city packages with sightseeing and car-rental options.

Kerrville Tours (3776 Youree Dr., Shreveport, LA 71105; phone: 800-442-8705). Operates a 9-day Las Vegas–Laughlin tour.

Las Vegas Connection (11010 Spring Hill Dr., Spring Hill, FL 34608; phone: 800-628-3427). Offers hotel packages in conjunction with Las Vegas charters from Florida.

Las Vegas Travel Center (1100 Jorie Blvd., Suite 151, Oak Brook, IL 60521; phone: 800-922-4252). Markets 2- to 7-day land or air/land packages with variety of options.

Mayflower Tours (1225 Warren Ave., PO Box 490, Downers Grove, IL 60515; phone: 800-323-7604 outside of Illinois, or 708-960-3430). Combines Arizona and Las Vegas in an 8-day holiday and offers a package combining Las Vegas with Laughlin and Mesquite.

MLT Vacations (5130 Hwy. 101, Minnetonka, MN 55345; phone: 800-328-0025). Charter operator offers packages including accommodations and transportation, as well as air seats only. This company is a wholesaler, so use a travel agent.

MTI Vacations (1220 Kensington Ct., Oak Brook, IL 60521; phone: 800-323-7285). This charter operators also offers city packages including air transportation and use of a car for a minimum of 2 nights. It is a wholesaler, so consult a travel agent.

PTI Tours (6340 Glennwood, Bldg. 7, Overland Park, KS 66202; phone: 800-666-7766). Offers land-only and air/land city packages.

SuperCities (Radisson Reservations Center, 11340 Blondo St., Omaha, NE 68164; phone: 800-333-1234). Offers highly flexible mix-and-match city packages. This tour operator is a wholesaler, so use a travel agent.

For runners, *Marathon Tours* (108 Main St., Charlestown, MA 02129; phone: 800-783-0024 or 617-242-7845) will make the arrangements for them to run in marathons throughout the country. The *Las Vegas International Marathon* will be held February 6 this year.

Many of the major air carriers maintain their own tour departments or subsidiaries to stimulate vacation travel to the cities they serve. In all cases, the arrangements may be booked through a travel agent or directly with the company. Air/hotel Las Vegas packages are offered by the following tour operations of airlines serving the city:

American Airlines FlyAAway Vacations (Southern Reservation Center, Mail Drop 1000, Box 619619, Dallas/Ft. Worth Airport, TX 75261-9619; phone: 800-321-2121).

America West Vacations (1150 E. University, Suite 201, Tempe, AZ 85281; phone: 800-356-6611).

Continental's Grand Destinations (PO Box 1460, Milwaukee, WI 53201-1460; phone: 800-634-5555).

Delta's Dream Vacations (PO Box 1525, Ft. Lauderdale, FL 33302; phone: 800-872-7786).

Northwest Vacations Center (5101 Northwest Dr., St. Paul, MN 55111-3034; phone: 800-692-8687).

TWA Getaway (10 E. Stow Rd., Marlton, NJ 08053; phone: 800-GETAWAY).

Whether visiting Las Vegas independently or on one of the above city packages, if you would like to include some organized touring, *Ray & Ross Transport* (300 W. Owens, Las Vegas, NV 89106; phone: 800-338-8111 or 702-646-4661) and *Gray Line of Las Vegas* (1550 S. Industrial Rd., Las Vegas, NV 89102; phone: 800-634-6579 or 702-384-1234) offer 1-day or shorter guided tours of the city as well as excursions to nearby attractions such as Lake Mead, Boulder City, and Red Rock Canyon. In both cases, reservations are either desirable or necessary.

A very popular excursion from Las Vegas is a flightseeing ride over Lake Mead and up to the Grand Canyon. Four companies specializing in that trip are *Scenic Airlines* (241 E. Reno Ave., Las Vegas, NV 89115; phone: 800-634-6801 or 702-739-1900), *Air Nevada Airlines* (5700 S. Haven, Las Vegas, NV 89119; phone: 800-634-6377 or 702-736-8900), *Las Vegas Airlines* (PO Box 15105, Las Vegas, NV 89114; phone: 800-634-6851 or 702-647-3056), and *Helicop-Tours* (135 E. Reno Ave., Las Vegas, NV 89119; phone: 702-736-0606). Some of these companies offer a variety of tours — the air trip only or in combination with ground sightseeing at Grand Canyon.

Another popular excursion outside the city is provided by *Lake Mead Cruises* (PO

Box 62465, Boulder City, NV 89006; phone: 702-293-6180), which operates lunch and dinner or cocktail cruises on Lake Mead, as well as breakfast sailings on Saturdays and Sundays.

- **Note:** Frequently, the best city packages are offered by the hotels, which are trying to attract guests during the weekends, when business travel drops off, and during other slow periods. These packages are sometimes advertised in local newspapers and in the Sunday travel sections of major metropolitan papers, such as *The Los Angeles Times* and *The New York Times,* which has a national edition available in most parts of the US. It's worth asking about packages, especially family and special-occasion offerings, when you call to make a hotel reservation. Calling several hotels can garner you a variety of options from which to choose.

Preparing

Calculating Costs

DETERMINING A BUDGET: A realistic appraisal of travel expenses is the most crucial bit of planning before any trip. It also is, unfortunately, one for which it is most difficult to give precise practical advice.

Estimating travel expenses for Las Vegas depends on the mode of transportation you choose and how long you will stay, as well as the kind of trip you are planning.

When calculating costs, start with the basics, the major expenses being transportation, accommodations, and food. For Las Vegas that will mean $95 or more a night for a double at an expensive hotel, $40 to $60 for a moderate property, and somewhat under $40 for an inexpensive one. Dinner for two runs to over $55 at an expensive restaurant, $30 to $45 at a moderate one, and under $25 at an inexpensive one. Then there are breakfast and lunch to consider.

Don't forget such extras as local transportation, shopping, and such miscellaneous items as laundry and tips. The reasonable cost of these items often is a positive surprise to your budget. And ask about discount passes on local transportation.

Other expenses, such as the cost of local sightseeing tours and other excursions, should be included. Tourist information offices and most of the better hotels will have someone at the front desk to provide a rundown on the cost of local tours and full-day excursions in and out of Las Vegas. Travel agents also can provide this information.

In planning any travel budget, it also is wise to allow a realistic amount for both entertainment and recreation. Are you planning to spend time sightseeing and visiting local tourist attractions? Is tennis or golf a part of your plan? Are you traveling with children who want to visit every site? Finally, allow for the extra cost of nightlife, if such is your pleasure. This one item alone can add a great deal to your daily expenditures.

If at any point in the planning process it appears impossible to estimate expenses, consider this suggestion: The easiest way to put a ceiling on the price of all these elements is to buy a package tour with transportation, rooms, meals, sightseeing, local travel, tips, and a dinner show or two included and prepaid. This provides a pretty exact total of what the trip will cost beforehand, and the only surprise will be the one you spring on yourself by succumbing to some irresistible souvenir.

Planning a Trip

Travelers fall into two categories: those who make lists and those who do not. Some people prefer to plot the course of their trip to the finest detail, with contingency plans and alternatives at the ready. For others, the joy of a voyage is its spontaneity; exhaustive planning only lessens the thrill of anticipation and the sense of freedom.

For most travelers, however, a week-plus trip can be too expensive for an "I'll take my chances" attitude. Even perennial gypsies and anarchistic wanderers have to take into account the time-consuming logistics of getting around and, even with minimal baggage, they need to think about packing. Hence, at least some planning is crucial.

This is not to suggest that you work out your itinerary in minute detail before you go, but it's still wise to decide certain basics at the very start: where to go, what to do, and how much to spend. These decisions require a certain amount of consideration. So before rigorously planning specific details, you might want to establish your general travel objectives:

1. How much time will you have for the entire trip, and how much of it are you willing to spend getting where you're going?
2. What interests and/or activities do you want to pursue while on vacation?
3. At what time of year do you want to go?
4. Do you want peace and privacy or lots of activity and company?
5. How much money can you afford to spend for the entire vacation?

You now can make almost all of your own travel arrangements if you have time to follow through with hotels, airlines, tour operators, and so on. But you'll probably save considerable time and energy if you have a travel agent make arrangements for you. The agent also should be able to advise you of alternative arrangements of which you may not be aware. Only rarely will a travel agent's services cost a traveler any money, and they may even save you some (see *How to Use a Travel Agent,* below).

Pay particular attention to the dates when off-season rates go into effect. In major resort areas, accommodations may cost less during the off-season (and the weather often is perfectly acceptable at this time). Off-season rates frequently are lower for other facilities, too, although don't expect to save much on car rental costs during any season. In general, it is a good idea to beware of holiday weeks, as rates at hotels generally are higher during these periods and rooms normally are heavily booked.

Make plans early. During the summer months and holidays, make hotel reservations at least a month in advance. If you are flying at these times and want to benefit from savings offered through discount fares, purchase tickets as far ahead as possible. The less flexible your schedule requirements, the earlier you should book. Many hotels require deposits before they will guarantee reservations, and this most often is the case during peak travel periods. (Be sure to get a receipt for any deposit or, better yet, charge the deposit to a credit card.)

When packing, make a list of any valuable items you are carrying with you, including credit card numbers and the serial numbers of your traveler's checks. Put copies in your purse or pocket, and leave other copies at home. Put a label with your name and home address on the inside of your luggage for identification in case of loss. Put your name and business address — *never your home address* — on a label on the outside of your luggage. (Those who run businesses from home should use the office address of a friend or relative.)

Review your travel documents. If you are traveling by air, check that your ticket has been filled in correctly. The left side of the ticket should have a list of each stop you will make (even if you are stopping only to change planes), beginning with your departure point. Be sure that the list is correct, and count the number of copies to see that you have one for each plane you will take. If you have confirmed reservations, be sure that the column marked "status" says "OK" beside each flight. Have in hand vouchers or proof of payment for any reservation for which you've paid in advance; this includes hotels, transfers to and from the airport, sightseeing tours, car rentals, and tickets to special events.

Although policies vary from carrier to carrier, it's still smart to reconfirm your flight 48 to 72 hours before departure, both going and returning. If you are traveling by car, bring your driver's license, car registration, and proof of insurance, as well as gasoline credit cards and auto service card (if you have them).

Finally, you always should bear in mind that despite the most careful plans, things do not always occur on schedule. If you maintain a flexible attitude and try to accept minor disruptions as less than cataclysmic, you will enjoy yourself a lot more.

How to Use a Travel Agent

A reliable travel agent remains the best source of service and information for planning a trip, whether you have a specific itinerary and require an agent only to make reservations or you need extensive help in sorting through the maze of airfares, tour offerings, hotel packages, and the scores of other arrangements that may be involved in your trip.

Know what you want from a travel agent so that you can evaluate what you are getting. It is perfectly reasonable to expect your travel agent to be a thoroughly knowledgeable travel specialist, with information about your destination and, even more crucial, a command of current airfares, ground arrangements, and other wrinkles in the travel scene.

Most travel agents work through computer reservations systems (CRS). These are used to assess the availability and cost of flights, hotels, and car rentals, and through them they can book reservations. Despite reports of "computer bias," in which a computer may favor one airline over another, the CRS should provide agents with the entire spectrum of flights available to a given destination and the complete range of fares, in considerably less time than it takes to telephone the airlines individually — and at no extra cost to the client.

Make the most intelligent use of a travel agent's time and expertise; understand the economics of the industry. As a client, traditionally you pay nothing for the agent's services; with few exceptions it's all free, from hotel bookings to advice on package tours. Any money the travel agent makes on the time spent arranging your itinerary — booking hotels, resorts, or flights, or suggesting activities — comes from commissions paid by the suppliers of these services — the airlines, hotels, and so on. These commissions generally run from 10% to 15% of the total cost of the service, although suppliers often reward agencies that sell their services in volume with an increased commission called an override.

A travel agent sometimes may charge a fee for special services. These chargeable items may include long-distance telephone costs incurred in making a booking, for reserving a room in a place that does not pay a commission (such as a small, out-of-the way hotel), or for a special attention such as planning a highly personalized itinerary. A fee also may be assessed in instances of deeply discounted airfares.

Choose a travel agent with the same care with which you would choose a doctor or lawyer. You will be spending a good deal of money on the basis of the agent's judgment, so you have a right to expect that judgment to be mature, informed, and interested. At the moment, unfortunately, there aren't many standards within the travel agent industry to help you gauge competence, and the quality of individual agents varies enormously.

At present, only nine states have registration, licensing, or other forms of travel agent–related legislation on their books. Rhode Island licenses travel agents; Florida, Hawaii, Iowa, and Ohio register them; and California, Illinois, Oregon, and Washington have laws governing the sale of transportation or related services. While state licensing of agents cannot absolutely guarantee competence, it can at least ensure that an agent has met some minimum requirements.

38 GETTING READY / Insurance

Perhaps the best-prepared agents are those who have completed the CTC Travel Management program offered by the *Institute of Certified Travel Agents (ICTA)* and carry the initials CTC (Certified Travel Counselor) after their names. This indicates a relatively high level of expertise. For a free listing of CTCs in your area, send a self-addressed, stamped, #10 envelope to *ICTA,* 148 Linden St., PO Box 56, Wellesley, MA 02181 (phone: 617-237-0280 in Massachusetts; 800-542-4282 elsewhere in the US).

An agent's membership in the *American Society of Travel Agents (ASTA)* can be a useful guideline in making a selection. But keep in mind that *ASTA* is an industry organization, requiring only that its members be licensed in those states where required; be accredited to represent the suppliers whose products they sell, including airline and cruise tickets; and adhere to its Principles of Professional Conduct and Ethics code. *ASTA* does not guarantee the competence, ethics, or financial soundness of its members, but it does offer some recourse if you feel you have been dealt with unfairly. Complaints may be registered with *ASTA* (Consumer Affairs Dept., 1101 King St., Alexandria, VA 22314; phone: 703-739-2782). First try to resolve the complaint directly with the supplier. For a list of *ASTA* members in your area, send a self-addressed, stamped, #10 envelope to *ASTA* (Public Relations Dept.) at the address above.

There also is the *Association of Retail Travel Agents (ARTA),* a smaller but highly respected trade organization similar to *ASTA.* Its member agencies and agents similarly agree to abide by a code of ethics, and complaints about a member can be made to *ARTA*'s Grievance Committee, 1745 Jefferson Davis Hwy., Suite 300, Arlington, VA 22202-3402 (phone: 800-969-6069 or 703-553-7777).

Perhaps the best way to find a travel agent is by word of mouth. If the agent (or agency) has done a good job for your friends over a period of time, it probably indicates a certain level of commitment and competence. Always ask for the name of the company *and* for the name of the specific agent with whom your friends dealt, for it is that individual who will serve you, and quality can vary widely within a single agency.

Insurance

It is unfortunate that most decisions to buy travel insurance are impulsive and usually are made without any real consideration of the traveler's existing policies. Therefore, the first person with whom you should discuss travel insurance is your own insurance broker, not a travel agent or the clerk behind the airport insurance counter. You may discover that the insurance you already carry — homeowner's policies and/or accident, health, and life insurance — protects you adequately while you travel and that your real needs are in the more mundane areas of excess value insurance for baggage or trip cancellation insurance.

TYPES OF INSURANCE: To make insurance decisions intelligently, however, you first should understand the basic categories of travel insurance and what they cover. Then you can decide what you should have in the broader context of your personal insurance needs, and you can choose the most economical way of getting the desired protection: through riders on existing policies; with onetime, short-term policies; through a special program put together for the frequent traveler; through coverage that's part of a travel club's benefits; or with a combination policy sold by insurance companies through brokers, automobile clubs, tour operators, and travel agents.

There are seven basic categories of travel insurance:

1. Baggage and personal effects insurance
2. Personal accident and sickness insurance
3. Trip cancellation and interruption insurance

4. Default and/or bankruptcy insurance
5. Flight insurance (to cover injury or death)
6. Automobile insurance (for driving your own or a rented car)
7. Combination policies

Baggage and Personal Effects Insurance – Ask your insurance agent if baggage and personal effects are included in your current homeowner's policy, or if you will need a special floater to cover you for the duration of a trip. The object is to protect your bags and their contents in case of damage or theft anytime during your travels, not just while you're in flight, where only limited protection is provided by the airline. Baggage liability varies from carrier to carrier, but generally speaking, on domestic flights, luggage usually is insured to $1,250 — that's per passenger, not per bag. This limit should be specified on your airline ticket, but to be awarded any amount, you'll have to provide an itemized list of lost property, and if you're including new and/or expensive items, be prepared for a request that you back up your claim with sales receipts or other proof of purchase.

If you are carrying goods worth more than the maximum protection offered by the airlines, consider excess value insurance. Additional coverage is available from airlines at an average, currently, of $1 to $2 per $100 worth of coverage, up to a maximum of $5,000. This insurance can be purchased at the airline counter when you check in, though you should arrive early to fill out the necessary forms and to avoid holding up other passengers.

Major credit card companies provide coverage for lost or delayed baggage — and this coverage often is over and above what the airline will pay. The basic coverage usually is automatic for all cardholders who use the credit card to purchase tickets, but to qualify for additional coverage, cardholders generally must enroll.

American Express: Provides $500 coverage for checked baggage; $1,250 for carry-on baggage; and $250 for valuables, such as cameras and jewelry.

Carte Blanche and Diners Club: Provide $1,250 free insurance for checked or carry-on baggage that's lost or damaged.

Discover Card: Offers $500 insurance for checked baggage and $1,250 for carry-on baggage — but to qualify for this coverage cardholders first must purchase additional flight insurance (see "Flight Insurance," below).

MasterCard and Visa: Baggage insurance coverage set by the issuing institution.

Additional baggage and personal effects insurance also is included in certain of the combination travel insurance policies discussed below.

■**A note of warning:** Be sure to read the fine print of any excess value insurance policy; there often are specific exclusions, such as cash, tickets, furs, gold and silver objects, art, and antiques. Insurance companies ordinarily will pay only the depreciated value of the goods rather than their replacement value. The best way to protect your property is to take photos of your valuables, and keep a record of the serial numbers of such items as cameras, typewriters, laptop computers, radios, and so on. This will establish that you do, indeed, own the objects. If your luggage disappears en route or is damaged, deal with the situation immediately. If an airline loses your luggage, you will be asked to fill out a Property Irregularity Report before you leave the airport. Also report the loss to the police (since the insurance company will check with the police when processing the claim).

Personal Accident and Sickness Insurance – This covers you in case of illness during your trip or death in an accident. Most policies insure you for hospital and doctors' expenses, lost income, and so on. In most cases, it is a standard part of existing health insurance policies (especially where domestic travel is concerned), though you should check with your insurance broker to be sure of the conditions for which your policy will pay. If your coverage is insufficient, take out a separate vacation accident policy or an entire vacation insurance policy that includes health and life coverage.

One example of such comprehensive health and life insurance coverage is the travel insurance package offered by *Wallach & Co.* This insurance package, which can be purchased for periods of 10 to 180 days, is offered for two age groups: Men and women up to age 75 receive $25,000 medical insurance and a $50,000 death benefit; those from age 75 to 84 are eligible for $12,500 medical insurance and a $25,000 death benefit. For either policy, the cost for a 10-day period is $25, with decreasing rates up to 75 days, after which the rate is $1.50 per day. This basic program also may be bought in combination with trip cancellation and baggage insurance at extra cost. For further information, write to *Wallach & Co.,* 107 W. Federal St., Box 480, Middleburg, VA 22117-0480 (phone: 703-687-3166 in Virginia; 800-237-6615 elsewhere in the US).

Trip Cancellation and Interruption Insurance – Most package tour passengers pay for their travel well before departure. The disappointment of having to miss a vacation because of illness or any other reason pales before the awful prospect that not all (and sometimes none) of the money paid in advance might be returned. So cancellation insurance for any package tour is a must.

Although cancellation penalties vary (they are listed in the fine print of every tour brochure, and before you purchase a package tour you should know exactly what they are), rarely will a passenger get more than 50% of this money back if forced to cancel within a few weeks of scheduled departure. Therefore, if you book a package tour, you should have trip cancellation insurance to guarantee full reimbursement or refund should you, a traveling companion, or a member of your immediate family get sick, forcing you to cancel your trip or *return home early.*

The key here is *not* to buy just enough insurance to guarantee full reimbursement for the cost of the package in case of cancellation. The proper amount of coverage should include reimbursement for the cost of having to catch up with a tour after its departure or having to travel home at the full economy airfare if you have to forgo the return flight tied to the package. There usually is quite a discrepancy between an excursion or other special airfare and the amount charged to travel the same distance on a regularly scheduled flight at full economy fare.

Trip cancellation insurance is available from travel agents and tour operators in two forms: as part of a short-term, all-purpose travel insurance package (sold by the travel agent); or as specific cancellation insurance designed by the operator for a specific tour. Generally, tour operators' policies are less expensive, but also less inclusive. Cancellation insurance also is available directly from insurance companies or their agents as part of a short-term, all-inclusive travel insurance policy.

Before you decide on a policy, read each one carefully. (Either type can be purchased from a travel agent when you book the package tour.) Be sure to check the fine print for stipulations concerning "family members" and "pre-existing medical conditions," as well as allowances for living expenses if you must delay your return due to injury or illness.

Default and/or Bankruptcy Insurance – Although trip cancellation insurance usually protects you if *you* are unable to complete — or begin — your trip, a fairly recent innovation is coverage in the event of default and/or bankruptcy on the part of the tour operator, airline, or other travel supplier. In some travel insurance packages, this contingency is included in the trip cancellation portion of the coverage; in others, it is a separate feature. Either way, it is becoming increasingly important. Whereas sophisticated travelers have long known to beware of the possibility of default or bankruptcy when buying a tour package, in recent years more than a few respected airlines have unexpectedly revealed their shaky financial condition, sometimes leaving

GETTING READY / Insurance   41

hordes of stranded ticket holders in their wake. While default/bankruptcy insurance will not ordinarily result in reimbursement in time to pay for new arrangements, it can ensure that you will get your money back, and even independent travelers buying no more than an airplane ticket may want to consider it.

Flight Insurance – US airlines' liability for injury or death to passengers on domestic flights currently is determined on a case-by-case basis in court — this means potentially unlimited liability. But remember, this liability is not the same thing as an insurance policy; every penny that an airline eventually pays in the case of death or injury likely will be subject to a legal battle.

But before you buy last-minute flight insurance from an airport vending machine, consider the purchase in light of your total existing insurance coverage. A careful review of your current policies may reveal that you already are amply covered for accidental death. Be aware that airport insurance, the kind typically bought at a counter or from a vending machine, is among the most expensive forms of life insurance coverage, and that even within a single airport, rates for approximately the same coverage vary widely.

If you buy your plane ticket with a major credit card, you generally receive automatic insurance coverage at no extra cost. Additional coverage usually can be obtained at extremely reasonable prices, but a cardholder must sign up for it in advance.

Automobile Insurance – If you have an accident in a state that has "no fault" insurance, each party's insurance company pays his or her expenses up to certain specified limits. When you rent a car, the rental company is required to provide you with collision protection.

In your car rental contract, you'll see that for about $5 to $13 a day, you may buy optional collision damage waiver (CDW) protection. Some companies, such as *Hertz* and *Avis*, now call the option a loss damage waiver (LDW). (If partial coverage with a deductible is included in the rental contract, the CDW will cover the deductible in the event of an accident, and can cost as much as $25 per day.)

If you do not accept the CDW coverage, you may be liable for as much as the full retail value of the rental car if it is damaged or stolen; by paying for the CDW, you are relieved of all responsibility for any damage to the car. Before agreeing to this coverage, however, check with your own broker about your own existing personal automobile insurance policy. It very well may cover your entire liability exposure without any additional cost, or you automatically may be covered by the credit card company to which you are charging the cost of your rental. To find out the amount of rental car insurance provided by major credit cards, contact the issuing institutions.

You also should know that an increasing number of the major US car rental companies automatically are including the cost of the CDW in their basic rates. Car rental prices have increased to include this coverage, although rental company ad campaigns may promote this as a new, improved rental package feature. The disadvantage of this inclusion is that you may not have the option to turn down the CDW — even if you already are adequately covered by your own insurance policy or through a credit card company.

Combination Policies – Short-term insurance policies, which may include a combination or all of the types of insurance discussed above, are available through retail insurance agencies, automobile clubs, and many travel agents. These combination policies are designed to cover you for the duration of a single trip.

The following companies provide such coverage for the insurance needs discussed above:

> *Access America International:* A subsidiary of the Blue Cross/Blue Shield plans of New York and Washington, DC, now available nationwide. Contact *Access*

America, PO Box 90310, Richmond, VA 23230 (phone: 800-284-8300 or 804-285-3300).

Carefree: Underwritten by The Hartford. Contact *Carefree Travel Insurance,* Arm Coverage, PO Box 310, Mineola, NY 11501 (phone: 800-645-2424 or 516-294-0220).

NEAR Services: In addition to a full range of travel services, this organization offers a comprehensive travel insurance package. An added feature is coverage for lost or stolen airline tickets. Contact *NEAR Services,* 450 Prairie Ave., Suite 101, Calumet City, IL 60409 (phone: 708-868-6700 in the Chicago area; 800-654-6700 elsewhere in the US and Canada).

Tele-Trip: Underwritten by the Mutual of Omaha Companies. Contact *Tele-Trip Co.,* 3201 Farnam St., Omaha, NE 68131 (phone: 402-345-2400 in Nebraska; 800-228-9792 elsewhere in the US).

Travel Assistance International: Provided by Europ Assistance Worldwide Services, and underwritten by Transamerica Occidental Life Insurance Company. Contact *Travel Assistance International,* 1133 15th St. NW, Suite 400, Washington, DC 20005 (phone: 202-331-1609 in Washington, DC; 800-821-2828 elsewhere in the US).

Travel Guard International: Underwritten by the Insurance Company of North America, it is available through authorized travel agents; or contact *Travel Guard International,* 1145 Clark St., Stevens Point, WI 54481 (phone: 715-345-0505 in Wisconsin; 800-826-1300 elsewhere in the US).

Travel Insurance PAK: Underwritten by The Travelers. Contact *The Travelers Companies,* Ticket and Travel Plans, One Tower Sq., Hartford, CT 06183-5040 (phone: 203-277-2319 in Connecticut; 800-243-3174 elsewhere in the US).

Hints for Handicapped Travelers

From 40 to 50 million people in the US alone have some sort of disability, and over half this number are physically handicapped. Like everyone else today, they — and the uncounted disabled millions around the world — are on the move. More than ever before, they are demanding facilities they can use comfortably, and they are being heard. With the 1990 passage of the Americans with Disabilities Act, the physically handicapped increasingly will be finding better access to places and services throughout the US. The provisions of the act relating to public accommodations and transportation, which took effect in January 1992, mandate that means of access be provided except where the cost would be prohibitive, and creative alternatives are being encouraged. As the impact of the law spreads across the country, previous barriers to travel in the US should be somewhat ameliorated.

PLANNING: Make your travel arrangements well in advance and specify to services involved the exact nature of your condition or restricted mobility, as your trip will be much more comfortable if you know that there are accommodations and facilities to suit your needs. The best way to find out if your intended destination can accommodate a handicapped traveler is to write or call the local tourist authority or hotel and ask specific questions. It is also advisable to call the hotel you are considering and ask specific questions. If you require a corridor of a certain width to maneuver a wheelchair or if you need handles on the bathroom walls for support, ask the manager (many large hotels have rooms specially designed for the handicapped). A travel agent or the local chapter or national office of the organization that deals with your particular disability — for example, the *American Foundation for the Blind* or the *American Heart Association* — will supply the most up-to-date information on the subject.

GETTING READY / Hints for Handicapped Travelers 43

Many Las Vegas hotels offer information packets for disabled guests (separate ones for the visually handicapped, hearing-impaired, or physically limited) detailing the property's services and giving useful advice on such things as shortcuts. Most of the hotel showrooms are wheelchair accessible and provide listening devices for the hearing-impaired.

The following organizations also offer general information on access:

ACCENT on Living (PO Box 700, Bloomington, IL 61702; phone: 309-378-2961). This information service for persons with disabilities provides a free list of travel agencies specializing in arranging trips for the disabled; for a copy send a self-addressed, stamped envelope. It also offers a wide range of publications, including a quarterly magazine ($10 per year; $17.50 for 2 years) for persons with disabilities.

Direct Link (PO Box 1036, Solvang, CA 93463; phone: 805-688-1603). This company provides an on-line computer service and links the disabled and their families with a wide range of information, including accessibility, attendant care, transportation, and travel necessities.

Disabled Individuals Assistance Line (*DIAL;* 100 W. Randolph St., Suite 8-100, Chicago, IL 60601; 800-233-DIAL both voice and TDD — telecommunications device for the deaf). This toll-free hotline provides information about public and private resources available to people with disabilities.

Information Center for Individuals with Disabilities (Fort Point Pl., 1st Floor, 27-43 Wormwood St., Boston, MA 02210; phone: 800-462-5015 in Massachusetts; 617-727-5540/1 elsewhere in the US; all numbers provide voice and TDD). The center offers information and referral services on disability-related issues, publishes fact sheets on travel agents, tour operators, and other travel resources, and can help you research your trip.

Mobility International USA (*MIUSA;* PO Box 3551, Eugene, OR 97403; phone: 503-343-1284 both voice and TDD). This US branch of *Mobility International* (the main office is at 228 Borough High St., London SE1 1JX, England; phone: 44-71-403-5688), a nonprofit British organization with affiliates worldwide, offers members advice and assistance — including information on accommodations and other travel services, and publications applicable to the traveler's disability. *Mobility International* also offers a quarterly newsletter and a comprehensive sourcebook, *A World of Options for the 90s: A Guide to International Education Exchange, Community Service and Travel for Persons with Disabilities* ($14 for members; $16 for non-members). Membership includes the newsletter and is $20 a year; subscription to the newsletter alone is $10 annually.

National Rehabilitation Information Center (8455 Colesville Rd., Suite 935, Silver Spring, MD 20910; phone: 301-588-9284). A general information, resource, research, and referral service.

Paralyzed Veterans of America (*PVA;* PVA/ATTS Program, 801 18th St. NW, Washington, DC 20006; phone: 202-416-7708 in Washington, DC; 800-424-8200 elsewhere in the US). The members of this national service organization all are veterans who have suffered spinal cord injuries, but it offers advocacy services and information to all persons with a disability. *PVA* also sponsors *Access to the Skies (ATTS),* a program that coordinates the efforts of the national and international air travel industry in providing airport and airplane access for the disabled. Members receive several helpful publications, as well as regular notification of conferences on subjects of interest to the disabled traveler.

Society for the Advancement of Travel for the Handicapped (*SATH;* 347 5th Ave., Suite 610, New York, NY 10016; phone: 212-447-7284). To keep abreast of developments in travel for the handicapped as they occur, you may want to join

44 GETTING READY / Hints for Handicapped Travelers

SATH, a nonprofit organization whose members include consumers, as well as travel service professionals who have experience (or an interest) in travel for the handicapped. For an annual fee of $45 ($25 for students and travelers who are 65 and older), members receive a quarterly newsletter and have access to extensive information and referral services. *SATH* also offers two useful publications: *Travel Tips for the Handicapped* (a series of informative fact sheets) and *The United States Welcomes Handicapped Visitors* (a 48-page guide covering domestic transportation and accommodations, as well as useful hints for travelers with disabilities); to order, send a self-addressed, #10 envelope and $1 per title for postage.

Travel Information Service (Moss Rehabilitation Hospital, 1200 W. Tabor Rd., Philadelphia, PA 19141-3099; phone: 215-456-9600 for voice; 215-456-9602 for TDD). This service assists physically handicapped people in planning trips and supplies detailed information on accessibility, for a nominal fee.

Blind travelers should contact the *American Foundation for the Blind* (15 W. 16th St., New York, NY 10011; phone: 800-829-0500 or 212-620-2147) and *The Seeing Eye* (Box 375, Morristown, NJ 07963-0375; phone: 201-539-4425); both provide useful information on resources for the visually impaired. The *American Society for the Prevention of Cruelty to Animals* (*ASPCA,* Education Dept., 441 E. 92nd St., New York, NY 10128; phone: 213-876-7700) offers a useful booklet, *Traveling With Your Pet,* which lists inoculation and other requirements by state. It is available for $5 (including postage and handling).

In addition, there are a number of publications — from travel guides to magazines — of interest to handicapped travelers. Among these are the following:

Access to the World, by Louise Weiss, offers sound tips for the disabled traveler. Published by Facts on File (460 Park Ave. S., New York, NY 10016; phone: 212-683-2244 in New York State; 800-322-8755 elsewhere in the US; 800-443-8323 in Canada), it costs $16.95 and is available only in paperback. Check with your local bookstore; it also can be ordered from the publisher by phone with a credit card.

The Diabetic Traveler (PO Box 8223 RW, Stamford, CT 06905; phone: 203-327-5832) is a useful quarterly newsletter for travelers with diabetes. Each issue highlights a single destination or type of travel and includes information on general resources and hints for diabetics. A 1-year subscription costs $18.95. When subscribing, ask for the free fact sheet including an index of special articles; back issues are available for $4 each.

Guide to Traveling with Arthritis, a free brochure available by writing to the Upjohn Company (PO Box 307-B, Coventry, CT 06238), provides lots of good, commonsense tips on planning your trip and how to be as comfortable as possible when traveling by car, bus, train, cruise ship, or plane.

The Handicapped Driver's Mobility Guide, compiled by the *AAA,* lists over 1,100 sources of equipment and services for the handicapped, including manufacturers and retailers of special adaptive devices for automobiles. This guide also provides listings of car rental companies that can fit cars with hand controls, as well as information on accessibility of hotels and public transportation to the handicapped. Available for $5.95, plus shipping and handling, from the *AAA* chapter in your area or from the national office, 1000 AAA Dr., Heathrow, FL 32746 (phone: 407-444-7000).

Handicapped Travel Newsletter is regarded as one of the best sources of information for the disabled traveler. It is edited by wheelchair-bound Vietnam veteran Michael Quigley, who has traveled to 93 countries around the world. Issued

GETTING READY / Hints for Handicapped Travelers 45

every 2 months (plus special issues), a subscription is $10 per year. Write to *Handicapped Travel Newsletter,* PO Box 269, Athens, TX 75751 (phone: 903-677-1260).

Handi-Travel: A Resource Book for Disabled and Elderly Travellers, by Cinnie Noble, is a comprehensive travel guide full of practical tips for those with disabilities affecting mobility, hearing, or sight. To order this book, send $12.95, plus shipping and handling, to the *Canadian Rehabilitation Council for the Disabled,* 45 Sheppard Ave. E., Suite 801, Toronto, Ontario M2N 5W9, Canada (phone: 416-250-7490 both voice and TDD).

The Itinerary (PO Box 2012, Bayonne, NJ 07002-2012; phone: 201-858-3400). This quarterly travel magazine for people with disabilities includes information on accessibility, listings of tours, news of adaptive devices, travel aids, and special services, as well as numerous general travel hints. A subscription costs $10 a year.

The Physically Disabled Traveler's Guide, by Rod W. Durgin and Norene Lindsay, rates accessibility of a number of travel services and includes a list of organizations specializing in travel for the disabled. It is available for $9.95, plus shipping and handling, from Resource Directories, 3361 Executive Pkwy., Suite 302, Toledo, OH 43606 (phone: 419-536-5353 in the Toledo area; 800-274-8515 elsewhere in the US).

Ticket to Safe Travel offers useful information for travelers with diabetes. A reprint of this article is available free from local chapters of the *American Diabetes Association.* For the nearest branch, contact the central office at 1660 Duke St., Alexandria, VA 22314 (phone: 703-549-1500 in Virginia; 800-232-3472 elsewhere in the US).

Travel for the Patient with Chronic Obstructive Pulmonary Disease, a publication of the George Washington University Medical Center, provides some sound practical suggestions for those with emphysema, chronic bronchitis, asthma, or other lung ailments. To order, send $2 to Dr. Harold Silver, 1601 18th St. NW, Washington, DC 20009 (phone: 202-667-0134).

Traveling Like Everybody Else: A Practical Guide for Disabled Travelers, by Jacqueline Freedman and Susan Gersten, offers the disabled tips on traveling by car, cruise ship, and plane, as well as lists of accessible accommodations, tour operators specializing in tours for disabled travelers, and other resources. It is available for $11.95, plus postage and handling, from Modan Publishing, PO Box 1202, Bellmore, NY 11710 (phone: 516-679-1380).

Travel Tips for Hearing-Impaired People, a free pamphlet for deaf and hearing-impaired travelers, is available from the *American Academy of Otolaryngology* (One Prince St., Alexandria, VA 22314; phone: 703-836-4444). For a copy, send a self-addressed, stamped, business-size envelope to the academy.

Travel Tips for People with Arthritis, a 31-page booklet published by the *Arthritis Foundation,* provides helpful information regarding travel by car, bus, train, cruise ship, or plane, planning your trip, medical considerations, and ways to conserve your energy while traveling. It also includes listings of helpful resources, such as associations and travel agencies that operate tours for disabled travelers. For a copy, contact your local *Arthritis Foundation* chapter, send $1 to the national office, PO Box 19000, Atlanta, GA 30326 (phone: 404-872-7100).

The Wheelchair Traveler, by Douglass R. Annand, lists accessible hotels, motels, restaurants, and other sites by state throughout the US. This valuable resource is available directly from the author. For the price of the most recent edition, contact Douglass R. Annand, 123 Ball Hill Rd., Milford, NH 03055 (phone: 603-673-4539).

A few more basic resources to look for are *Travel for the Disabled,* by Helen Hecker ($19.95), and by the same author, *Directory of Travel Agencies for the Disabled* ($19.95). *Wheelchair Vagabond,* by John G. Nelson, is another useful guide for travelers confined to a wheelchair (hardcover, $14.95; paperback, $9.95). All three titles are published by Twin Peaks Press, PO Box 129, Vancouver, WA 98666 (phone: 800-637-CALM or 206-694-2462). The publisher also offers a catalogue of 26 other books on travel for the disabled for $2.

PLANE: The US Department of Transportation (DOT) has ruled that US airlines must accept all passengers with disabilities. As a matter of course, US airlines were pretty good about accommodating handicapped passengers even before the ruling, although each airline has somewhat different procedures. Most carriers can accommodate passengers in wheelchairs, although advance notice usually is required. Ask for specifics when you book your flight.

Disabled passengers should always make reservations well in advance and should provide the airline with all relevant details of their conditions. These details include information on mobility and equipment that you will need the airline to supply — such as a wheelchair for boarding or portable oxygen for in-flight use. Be sure that the person to whom you speak fully understands the degree of your disability — the more details provided, the more effective help the airline can give you.

On the day before the flight, call back to make sure that all arrangements have been prepared, and arrive early on the day of the flight so that you can board before the rest of the passengers. It's a good idea to bring a medical certificate with you, stating your specific disability or the need to carry particular medicine.

Because most airports have jetways (corridors connecting the terminal with the door of the plane), a disabled passenger usually can be taken as far as the plane, and sometimes right onto it, in a wheelchair. If not, a narrow boarding chair may be used to take you to your seat. Your own wheelchair, which will be folded and put in the baggage compartment, should be tagged as escort luggage to assure that it's available at planeside upon landing rather than in the baggage claim area. Travel is not quite as simple if your wheelchair is battery-operated: Unless it has non-spillable batteries, it might not be accepted on board, and you will have to check with the airline ahead of time to find out how the batteries and the chair should be packaged for the flight. Usually people in wheelchairs are asked to wait until other passengers have disembarked. If you are making a tight connection, be sure to tell the attendant.

Passengers who use oxygen may not use their personal supply in the cabin, though it may be carried on the plane as cargo when properly packed (the tank must be empty) and labeled. If you will need oxygen during the flight, the airline will supply it to you (there is a charge), provided you have given advance notice — 24 hours to a few days, depending on the carrier.

The free booklet *Air Transportation of Handicapped Persons* explains the general guidelines that govern air carrier policies. For a copy, write to the US Department of Transportation (Distribution Unit, Publications Section, M-443-2, Washington, DC 20590) and ask for "Free Advisory Circular #AC-120-32." *Access Travel: A Guide to the Accessibility of Airport Terminals,* a free publication of the *Airport Operators Council International,* provides information on more than 500 airports worldwide and offers ratings of 70 features, such as accessibility to bathrooms, corridor width, and parking spaces. For a copy, contact the Consumer Information Center, Dept. 563W, Pueblo, CO 81009 (phone: 719-948-3334).

The following airlines have TDD toll-free lines in the US for the hearing-impaired:

American: 800-582-1573 in Ohio; 800-543-1586 elsewhere in the US.
America West: 800-526-8077.

GETTING READY / Hints for Handicapped Travelers   47

Continental: 800-343-9195.
Delta: 800-831-4488.
Northwest: 800-328-2298.
TWA: 800-252-0622 in California; 800-421-8480 elsewhere in the US.
United: 800-942-8819 in Illinois: 800-323-0170 elsewhere in the US.
USAir: 800-242-1713 in Pennsylvania; 800-245-2966 elsewhere in the US.

McCarran International Airport offers a booklet, *Handicapped Services, A Special Guide to McCarran Airport,* that includes access and other information. It is available from the Clark County Dept. of Aviation, McCarran Airport, PO Box 11005, Las Vegas, NV 89111 (phone: 702-739-7511).

GROUND TRANSPORTATION: Perhaps the simplest solution to getting around is to travel with an able-bodied companion who can drive. If you are accustomed to driving your own hand-controlled car and want to rent one, you are in luck. Some rental companies will fit cars with hand controls. *Avis* (phone: 800-331-1212) can convert a car to hand controls with as little as 24 hours' notice, though it's a good idea to arrange further in advance. *Hertz* (phone: 800-654-3131) requires a minimum of 4 days to install the controls, and makes the additional stipulation that the car be returned to the office from which it was rented. Most companies do not charge extra for hand controls, but *Budget* (phone: 800-527-0700) requires an additional $50 deposit (refunded when the care is returned). *Alamo* (phone: 800-327-9633) and *Avis* will fit hand controls only on full-size cars — which tend to be among the most expensive models to rent. In addition, companies may request that you bring your handicapped-driver's permit with you. Hand controls often are installed only at some locations of a given company, and there usually are a limited number of these devices available, so make arrangements as early as possible.

In Las Vegas three cab companies have cars equipped to carry wheelchairs, which they do at no extra cost. The companies are *ABC Union Cab* (phone: 702-736-8444), *Ace Cab Co.* (phone: 702-736-8383), and *Vegas Western Cab* (phone: 702-736-6121). In addition, the Strip and downtown buses and trolleys of the *Las Vegas Transit System* (1550 Industrial Rd.; phone: 702-384-3540) are equipped with wheelchair lifts; and some are kneeling buses.

A relatively new company, *Wheelchair Getaways,* rents vans accommodating 1 or 2 wheelchairs and up to 5 other passengers. Each vehicle has tie-downs for wheelchairs, air conditioning, and stereo. The Pennsylvania-based company (PO Box 819, Newtown, PA 18940; phone: 800-642-2042 or 215-579-9120) has franchises in a number of US cities, although at press time nothing in the Las Vegas area. It would be worthwhile, however, to call the headquarters when making travel plans to find out if the company has extended service to Las Vegas.

TOURS: Programs designed for the physically impaired are run by specialists who have researched hotels, restaurants, and sites to be sure they present no insurmountable obstacles. The following travel agencies and tour operators specialize in making group and individual arrangements for travelers to Las Vegas with physical or other disabilities:

> *Access: The Foundation for Accessibility by the Disabled* (PO Box 356, Malverne, NY 11565; phone: 516-887-5798). A travelers' referral service that acts as an intermediary with tour operators and agents worldwide, and provides information on accessibility at various locations.
>
> *Accessible Journeys* (412 S. 45th St., Philadelphia, PA 19104; phone: 215-747-0171). Arranges for medical-professional traveling companions — registered or licensed practical nurses, therapists, or doctors (all are experienced travelers). Several prospective companions' profiles and photos are sent to the client for

perusal, and if one is acceptable, the "match" is made. The client usually pays all travel expenses for the companion, plus a certain amount in "earnings" to replace wages the companion would be making at his or her usual job.

Accessible Tours/Directions Unlimited (720 N. Bedford Rd., Bedford Hills, NY 10507; phone: 914-241-1700 in New York State; 800-533-5343 elsewhere in the continental US). Arranges group or individual tours for disabled persons traveling in the company of able-bodied friends or family members. Accepts the unaccompanied traveler if completely self-sufficient.

Dahl Good Neighbor Travel Service (124 S. Main St., Viroqua, WI 54665; phone: 608-637-2128; and 535 N. St. Mary's Rd., Libertyville, IL 60048; phone: 708-362-0129). This agency can supply an array of services and provide necessities to travelers with any special needs, mental or physical.

Evergreen Travel Service (4114 198th St. SW, Suite 13, Lynnwood, WA 98036-6742; phone: 800-435-2288 or 206-776-1184 throughout the continental US and Canada). Offers worldwide tours and cruises for the disabled (Wings on Wheels Tours), sight-impaired/blind (White Cane Tours), and hearing-impaired/deaf (Flying Fingers Tours). Most programs are first class or deluxe, and include a trained escort. It also offers programs for people who are not disabled but who want a slower pace (Lazybones Tours), and arranges special programs for people who need dialysis.

Flying Wheels Travel (143 W. Bridge St., Box 382, Owatonna, MN 55060; phone: 507-451-5005 or 800-535-6790). Handles both tours and individual arrangements for the disabled.

The Guided Tour (613 W. Cheltenham Ave., Suite 200, Melrose Park, PA 19126-2414; phone: 215-782-1370). Arranges tours, including to Las Vegas, for people with developmental and learning disabilities and sponsors separate tours for members of the same population who also are physically disabled or who simply need a slower pace.

Hinsdale Travel (201 E. Ogden Ave., Hinsdale, IL 60521; phone: 708-325-1335 or 708-469-7349). The tour leader, Janice Perkins, leads an active groups of handicapped travelers on the road, making arrangements to meet their special needs.

USTS Travel Horizons (11 E. 44th St., New York, NY 10017; phone: 800-487-8787 or 212-687-5121). Travel agent and registered nurse Mary Ann Hamm designs trips for individual travelers requiring all types of kidney dialysis and handles arrangements for the dialysis.

Weston Travel Agency (134 N. Cass Ave., PO Box 1050, Westmont, IL 60559; phone: 800-633-3725 outside of Illinois, or 708-968-2513). It specializes in travel services for people with cerebral palsy and those who are wheelchair-bound.

Travelers who would benefit from being accompanied by a nurse or physical therapist also can hire a companion through *Traveling Nurses' Network,* a service provided by Twin Peaks Press (PO Box 129, Vancouver, WA 98666; phone: 800-637-CALM or 206-694-2462). For a $10 fee, clients receive the names of three nurses, whom they can then contact directly; for a $125 fee, the agency will make all the hiring arrangements for the client. Travel arrangements also may be made in some cases — the fee for this further service is determined on an individual basis.

A similar service is offered by *MedEscort International* (ABE International Airport, PO Box 8766, Allentown, PA 18105; phone: 800-255-7182 in the continental US; elsewhere, call 215-791-3111). Clients can arrange to be accompanied by a nurse, paramedic, respiratory therapist, or physician through *MedEscort.* The fees are based on the disabled traveler's needs. This service also can assist in making travel arrangements.

Hints for Single Travelers

Just about the last trip in human history on which the participants were neatly paired was the voyage of Noah's Ark. Ever since, passenger lists and tour groups have reflected the same kind of asymmetry that occurs in real life, as countless individuals set forth to see the world unaccompanied (or unencumbered, depending on your outlook) by spouse, lover, friend, companion, or relative. Unfortunately, traveling alone can turn a traveler into a second class citizen.

The truth is that the travel industry is not very fair to people who vacation by themselves. People traveling alone almost invariably end up paying more than individuals traveling in pairs. Most travel bargains, including package tours, accommodations, resort packages, and cruises, are based on *double occupancy* rates. This means that the per-person price is offered on the basis of two people traveling together and sharing a double room (which means they each will spend a good deal more on meals and extras). The single traveler will have to pay a surcharge, called a single supplement, for exactly the same package. In extreme cases, this can add as much as 35% — and sometimes more — to the basic per-person rate.

Don't despair, however. Throughout the US, there are scores of smaller hotels and other hostelries where, in addition to a cozier atmosphere, prices still are quite reasonable for the single traveler.

The obvious, most effective alternative is to find a traveling companion. Even special "singles' tours" that promise no supplements usually are based on people sharing double rooms. Perhaps the most recent innovation along these lines is the creation of organizations that "introduce" the single traveler to other single travelers. Some charge fees, while others are free, but the basic service offered is the same: to match an unattached person with a compatible travel mate, often as part of the company's own package tours. Among such organizations are the following:

Jane's International (2603 Bath Ave., Brooklyn, NY 11214; phone: 718-266-2045). This service puts potential traveling companions in touch with one another. It has started a new organization, *Sophisticated Women Travelers,* to create groups for single women to travel together. No age limit, no fee for either.

Odyssey Network (118 Cedar St., Wellesley, MA 02181; phone: 800-487-6059 or 617-237-2400). Originally founded to match single female travelers, this company now includes men in its enrollment. *Odyssey* offers a quarterly newsletter for members who are seeking a travel companion and makes independent arrangements for them. A $50 membership fee includes the newsletter.

Partners-in-Travel (PO Box 491145, Los Angeles, CA 90049; phone: 213-476-4869). Members receive a list of singles seeking traveling companions; prospective companions make contact through the agency. The membership fee is $40 per year and includes a chatty newsletter (6 issues per year).

Travel Companion Exchange (PO Box 833, Amityville, NY 11701; phone: 516-454-0880). This group publishes a newsletter for singles and a directory of individuals looking for travel companions. On joining, members fill out a lengthy questionnaire and write a small listing (much like an ad in a personal column). Based on these listings, members can request copies of profiles and contact prospective traveling companions. It is wise to join well in advance of your planned vacation so that there's enough time to determine compatibility and plan a joint trip. Membership fees, including the newsletter, are $30 for 6 months or $60 a year for a single-sex listing; $66 and $120, respectively, for a complete listing. Subscription to the newsletter alone costs $24 for 6 months or $36 per year.

In addition, a number of tour packagers cater to single travelers. These companies offer packages designed for individuals interested in vacationing with a group of single travelers or in being matched with a traveling companion. Among the better established of these agencies are the following:

Gallivanting (515 E. 79th St., Suite 20F, New York, NY 10021; phone: 800-933-9699 or 212-988-0617). Offers matching service for singles ages 25 through 55 willing to share accommodations in order to avoid paying single supplement charges, with the agency guaranteeing this arrangement if bookings are paid for at least 75 days in advance.

Marion Smith Singles (611 Prescott Pl., N. Woodmere, NY 11581; phone: 516-791-4852, 516-791-4865, or 212-944-2112). Specializes in tours for singles ages 20 to 50, who can choose to share accommodations to avoid paying single supplement charges.

Saga International Holidays (222 Berkeley St., Boston MA 02116; phone: 800-343-0273 or 617-451-6808). A subsidiary of a British company specializing in older travelers, many of them single, *Saga* offers a broad selection of packages for people age 60 and over or those 50 to 59 traveling with someone 60 or older. Although anyone can book a *Saga* trip, a club membership (no fee) includes a subscription to their newsletter, as well as other publications and travel services — such as a matching service for single travelers.

Singles in Motion (545 W. 236th St., Suite 1D, Riverdale, NY 10463; phone: 718-884-4464). Has a scheduled program.

Travel in Two's (239 N. Broadway, Suite 3N. Tarrytown, NY 10591; phone: 914-631-8409). For city programs, this company matches up solo travelers and then customizes programs for them. The firm also puts out a quarterly *Singles Vacation Newsletter,* which costs $7.50 per issue or $20 per year.

A good book for single travelers is *Traveling On Your Own,* by Eleanor Berman, which offers tips on traveling solo and includes information on trips for singles. Available in bookstores, it also can be ordered by sending $12.95, plus postage and handling, to Random House, Order Dept., 400 Hahn Rd., Westminster, MD 21157 (phone: 800-733-3000).

Single travelers also may want to subscribe to *Going Solo,* a newsletter that offers helpful information on going on your own. Issued eight times a year, a subscription costs $36. Contact Doerfer Communications, PO Box 1035, Cambridge, MA 02238 (phone: 617-876-2764).

Those interested in a particularly cozy type of accommodation should consider going the bed and breakfast route. Though a single person will likely pay more than half of the rate quoted for a couple even at a bed and breakfast establishment, the prices still are quite reasonable, and the homey atmosphere will make you feel less conspicuously alone.

Hints for Older Travelers

Special discounts and more free time are just two factors that have given Americans over age 65 a chance to see the world at affordable prices. Senior citizens make up an ever-growing segment of the travel population, and the trend among them is to travel more frequently and for longer periods of time.

PLANNING: When planning a vacation, prepare your itinerary with one eye on your own physical condition and the other on your interests. One important factor to keep in mind is not to overdo anything and to be aware of the effects that the weather may have on your capabilities.

Older travelers may find the following publications of interest:

GETTING READY / Hints for Older Travelers 51

Discount Guide for Travelers Over 55, by Caroline and Walter Weintz, is an excellent book for budget-conscious older travelers. Published by Penguin USA, it is currently out of print; check your local library.

International Health Guide for Senior Citizen Travelers, by Dr. W. Robert Lange, covers such topics as trip preparations, food and water precautions, adjusting to weather and climate conditions, finding a doctor, motion sickness, jet lag, and so on. Also includes a list of resource organizations that provide medical assistance for travelers. It is available for $4.95 postpaid from Pilot Books, 103 Cooper St., Babylon, NY 11702 (phone: 516-422-2225).

Mature Traveler is a monthly newsletter that provides information on travel discounts, places of interest, useful tips, and other topics of interest for travelers 49 and up. To subscribe, send $24.95 to GEM Publishing Group, PO Box 50820, Reno, NV 89513 (phone: 702-786-7419).

Senior Citizen's Guide to Budget Travel in the US and Canada, by Paige Palmer, provides specific information on economical travel options for senior citizens. To order, send $4.95, plus $1 for postage and handling, to Pilot Books (address above).

Take a Camel to Lunch and Other Adventures for Mature Travelers, by Nancy O'Connell, offers offbeat and unusual adventures for travelers over 50. Available at bookstores or directly from Bristol Publishing Enterprises (PO Box 1737, San Leandro, CA 94577; phone: 800-346-4889 or 510-895-4461) for $8.95, plus shipping and handling.

Travel Easy: The Practical Guide for People Over 50, by Rosalind Massow, discusses a wide range of subjects — from trip planning, transportation options, and preparing for departure to avoiding and handling medical problems en route. The book is out of print, so check your local library.

Unbelievably Good Deals & Great Adventures That You Absolutely Can't Get Unless You're Over 50, by Joan Rattner Heilman, offers travel tips for older travelers, including discounts on accommodations and transportation, as well as a list of organizations for seniors. It is available for $7.95, plus shipping and handling, from Contemporary Books, 180 N. Michigan Ave., Chicago, IL 60601 (phone: 312-782-9181).

HEALTH: Pre-trip medical and dental checkups are strongly recommended. In addition, be sure to take along any prescription medication you need, enough to last *without a new prescription* for the duration of your trip; pack all medications with a note from your doctor for the benefit of airport authorities. If you have specific medical problems, bring prescriptions and a "medical file" composed of the following:

1. A summary of your medical history and current diagnosis.
2. A list of drugs to which you are allergic.
3. Your most recent electrocardiogram, if you have heart problems.
4. Your doctor's name, address, and telephone number.

DISCOUNTS AND PACKAGES: Since guidelines change from place to place, it is a good idea to inquire in advance about discounts on transportation, hotels, concerts, movies, museums, and other activities. For instance, the National Park Service has a Golden Age Passport, which entitles people over 62 (and those in the car with them) to free entrance to all national parks and monuments (available by showing a Medicare card or driver's license as proof of age at any national park).

Many hotel chains, airlines, cruise lines, bus companies, car rental companies, and other travel suppliers offer discounts to older travelers. For instance, *United* offers senior citizen coupon books — with either four or eight coupons each — that can be exchanged for tickets on domestic flights of up to 2,000 miles. These coupons are good 7 days a week for travel in all 50 states, although some peak travel periods are omitted. Other airlines also offer discounts for passengers age 60 (or 62) and over, which may be applicable to one traveling companion per senior. Among the airlines that often offer such discounted airfares are *America West, Continental,* and *TWA.* Given the continuing changes in the airline industry, however, these discounted fares may not be available when you purchase your tickets. For information on current prices and applicable restrictions, contact the individual carriers.

Some discounts, however, are extended only to bona fide members of certain senior citizens organizations. Because the same organizations frequently offer package tours to both domestic and international destinations, the benefits of membership are twofold: Those who join can take advantage of discounts as individual travelers and also reap the savings that group travel affords. In addition, because the age requirements for some of these organizations are quite low (or nonexistent), the benefits can begin to accrue early. In order to take advantage of these discounts, you should carry proof of your age (or eligibility). A driver's license, membership card in a recognized senior citizens organization, or a Medicare card should be adequate. Among the organizations dedicated to helping older travelers see the world are the following:

American Association of Retired Persons (*AARP;* 601 E St. NW, Washington, DC 20049; phone: 202-434-2277). The largest and best known of these organizations. Membership is open to anyone 50 or over, whether retired or not; dues are $8 a year, $20 for 3 years, or $45 for 10 years, and include spouse. The *AARP* Travel Experience Worldwide program, available through *American Express Travel Related Services,* offers members tours and other travel programs designed exclusively for older travelers. For example, it offers an independent Las Vegas city program. Members can book these services by calling *American Express* at 800-927-0111 for land and air travel.

Golden Companions (PO Box 754, Pullman, WA 99163-0754; phone: 509-334-9351). This club assists members in finding suitable traveling companions. Its Travel Companion Network includes a mail exchange service and bimonthly newsletter for those age 45 and over. Other services include vacation home exchanges, discounts on hotels and package tours, and group trips and cruises, some of which are sponsored by the club.

Mature Outlook (Customer Service Center, 6001 N. Clark St., Chicago, IL 60660; phone: 800-336-6330). Through its *Travel Alert* program, tours, cruises, and other vacation packages are available to members at special savings. Hotel and car rental discounts and travel accident insurance also are available. Membership is open to anyone 50 years of age or older, costs $9.95 a year, and includes a bimonthly newsletter and magazine, as well as information on package tours.

National Council of Senior Citizens (1331 F St. NW, Washington, DC 20005; phone: 202-347-8800). Here, too, the emphasis is on keeping costs low. This nonprofit organization offers members a different roster of package tours each year, as well as individual arrangements through its affiliated travel agency *(Vantage Travel Service).* Although most members are over 50, membership is open to anyone (regardless of age) for an annual fee of $12 per person or couple. Lifetime membership costs $150.

Certain travel agencies and tour operators offer special trips geared to older travelers. Among them are the following:

Evergreen Travel Service (4114 198th St. SW, Suite 13, Lynnwood, WA 98036-6742; phone: 800-435-2288 or 206-776-1184 throughout the continental US and Canada). This specialist in trips for persons with disabilities recently introduced Lazybones Tours, a program offering leisurely tours for older travelers, including to Las Vegas. Most programs are first class or deluxe, and include an escort.

Saga International Holidays (222 Berkeley St., Boston MA 02116; phone: 800-343-0273 or 617-451-6808). A subsidiary of a British company catering to older travelers, *Saga* offers a broad selection of packages for people age 60 and over or those 50 to 59 traveling with someone 60 or older. Although anyone can book a *Saga* trip, a club membership (no fee) includes a subscription to their newsletter, as well as other publications and travel services.

Many travel agencies, particularly the larger ones, are delighted to make presentations to help a group of senior citizens select destinations. A local chamber of commerce should be able to provide the names of such agencies. Once a time and place are determined, an organization member or travel agent can obtain group quotations for transportation, accommodations, meal plans, and sightseeing. Larger groups usually get the best breaks.

Another choice open to older travelers is a trip that includes an educational element. *Elderhostel,* a nonprofit organization, offers programs at educational institutions in the US, including Las Vegas, and worldwide. The domestic programs generally last 1 week and include double-occupancy accommodations in hotels or student residence halls and all meals. Travel to the programs usually is by designated scheduled flights, and participants can arrange to extend their stay at the end of the program. Elderhostelers must be at least 60 years old (younger if a spouse or companion qualifies), in good health, and not in need of special diets. For a free catalogue describing the program and current offerings, write to *Elderhostel* (75 Federal St., Boston, MA 02110; phone: 617-426-7788). Those interested in the program also can borrow slides at no charge or purchase an informational videotape for $5.

Hints for Traveling with Children

What better way to encounter some of the different byways of Las Vegas than in the company of the young, wide-eyed members of your family? Their presence does not have to be a burden or an excessive expense. The current generation of discounts for children and family package deals can make a trip together quite reasonable.

PLANNING: Here are several hints for making a trip with children easy and fun:

1. Children, like everyone else, will derive more pleasure from a trip if they know something about their destination before they arrive. Begin their education about a month before you leave. Using maps, travel magazines, and books, give children a clear idea of where you are going and how far away it is.
2. Children should help to plan the itinerary, and where you go and what you do should reflect some of their ideas. If they already know something about the city and the sites they will visit, they will have the excitement of recognition when they arrive.
3. Give children specific responsibilities: The job of carrying their own flight bags and looking after their personal things, along with some other light chores, will give them a stake in the journey.
4. Give each child a travel diary or scrapbook to take along.

Children's books about Las Vegas provide an excellent introduction and can be found at children's bookstores (see *Books, Magazines, and Newsletters*), many general bookstores, and in libraries.

And for parents, *Travel With Your Children* (*TWYCH;* 45 W. 18th St., New York, NY 10011; phone: 212-206-0688) publishes a newsletter, *Family Travel Times,* that focuses on families with young travelers and offers helpful hints. An annual subscription (10 issues) is $35 and includes a copy of the "Airline Guide" issue (updated every

54 GETTING READY / Hints for Traveling with Children

other year), which focuses on the subject of flying with children. This special issue is available separately for $10.

Another newsletter devoted to family travel is *Getaways*. This quarterly publication provides reviews of family-oriented literature, activities, and useful travel tips. To subscribe, send $25 to *Getaways*, Att. Ms. Brooke Kane, PO Box 8282, McLean, VA 22107 (phone: 703-534-8747).

Also of interest to parents traveling with their children is *How to Take Great Trips With Your Kids*, by psychologist Sanford Portnoy and his wife, Joan Flynn Portnoy. The book includes helpful tips from fellow family travelers, tips on economical accommodations and touring by car, as well as over 50 games to play with your children en route. It is available for $8.95, plus shipping and handling, from Harvard Common Press, 535 Albany St., Boston, MA 02118 (phone: 617-423-5803). Another title worth looking for is *Great Vacations with Your Kids*, by Dorothy Jordan (Dutton, $12.95).

Another book on family travel, *Travel with Children*, by Maureen Wheeler, offers a wide range of practical tips on traveling with children. It is available for $10.95, plus shipping and handling, from Lonely Planet Publications, Embarcadero W., 112 Linden St., Oakland, CA 94607 (phone: 510-893-8555).

Finally, parents arranging a trip with their children may want to deal with an agency specializing in family travel such as *Let's Take the Kids* (1268 Devon Ave., Los Angeles, CA 90024; phone: 800-726-4349 or 213-274-7088). In addition to arranging and booking trips for individual families, this group occasionally organizes trips for single-parent families traveling together. They also offer a parent travel network, whereby parents who have been to a particular destination can evaluate it for others.

PLANE: Begin early to investigate all available discount flights, as well as any package deals and special rates offered by the major airlines. Booking is sometimes required up to 2 months in advance. You may well find that charter companies offer no reduction for children, or not enough to offset the risk of last-minute delays or other inconveniences to which charters are subject. Some of the major scheduled airlines, on the other hand, do provide hefty discounts for children. When using local transportation such as a bus, or train, ask about lower fares for children or family rates.

When you make your reservation, tell the airline that you are traveling with a child. Where discounts are offered, children ages 2 through 11 generally travel at about 80% of the adult fare on domestic flights. As a general rule, children under 2 fly free if they sit on an adult's lap. A second infant without a second adult would pay the fare applicable to children ages 2 through 11.

Although some airlines will, on request, supply bassinets for infants, most carriers encourage parents to bring their own safety seat on board, which then is strapped into the airline seat with a regular seat belt. This is much safer — and certainly more comfortable — than holding the child in your lap. If you do not purchase a seat for your baby, you have the option of bringing the infant restraint along on the off chance that there might be an empty seat next to yours — in which case some airlines will let you use that seat at no charge for your baby and infant seat. However, if there is no empty seat available, the infant seat no doubt will have to be checked as baggage (and you may have to pay an additional charge), since it generally does not fit under the airplane seats or in the overhead racks. The safest bet is to pay for a seat.

Be forewarned: Some safety seats designed primarily for use in cars do not fit into plane seats properly. Although nearly all seats manufactured since 1985 carry labels indicating whether they meet federal standards for use aboard planes, actual seat sizes may vary from carrier to carrier. At the time of this writing, the FAA was in the process of reviewing and revising the federal regulations regarding infant travel and safety devices — it was still to be determined if children should be *required* to sit in safety seats and whether the airlines will have to provide them.

GETTING READY / Hints for Traveling with Children

If using one of these infant restraints, you should try to get bulkhead seats, which will provide extra room to care for your child during the flight. You also should request a bulkhead seat when using a bassinet — again, this is not as safe as strapping the child in. On some planes the bassinet hooks into a bulkhead wall; on others they are placed on the floor in front of you. (Note that bulkhead seats often are reserved for families traveling with small children.) As a general rule, babies should be held during takeoff and landing.

Request seats on the aisle if you have a toddler or if you think you will need to use the bathroom frequently. Carry onto the plane all you will need to care for and occupy your children during the flight — formula, diapers, a sweater, books, favorite stuffed animals, and so on. Dress your baby simply, with a minimum of buttons and snaps, because the only place you may have to change a diaper is at your seat or in a small lavatory.

On most US carriers, you can ask for a hot dog or hamburger instead of the airline's regular lunch or dinner if you give at least 24 hours' notice. Some, but not all, airlines have baby food aboard, and the flight attendant can warm a bottle for you. While you should bring along toys from home, also ask about children's diversions. Some carriers have terrific free packages of games, coloring books, and puzzles.

When the plane takes off and lands, make sure your baby is nursing or has a bottle, pacifier, or thumb in its mouth. This sucking will make the child swallow and help to clear stopped ears. A piece of hard candy will do the same for an older child.

Parents traveling by plane with toddlers, children, or teenagers may want to consult *When Kids Fly,* a free booklet published by Massport (Public Affairs Dept., 10 Park Plaza, Boston, MA 02116-3971; phone: 617-973-5600), which includes helpful information on airfares for children, infant seats, what to do in the event of overbooked or canceled flights, and so on.

■ **Note:** Newborn babies, whose lungs may not be able to adjust to the altitude, should not be taken aboard an airplane. And some airlines may refuse to allow a pregnant woman in her 8th or 9th month to fly. Check with the airline ahead of time, and carry a letter from your doctor stating that you are fit to travel — and indicating the estimated date of birth.

ACCOMMODATIONS: Often a cot for a child will be placed in a hotel room at little or no extra charge. If you wish to sleep in separate rooms, special rates sometimes are available for families; some places do not charge for children under a certain age. In many of the larger chain hotels, the staffs are more used to children. These hotels also are likely to have swimming pools or gamerooms — both popular with most youngsters. Many large resorts also have recreation centers for children. Cabins, bungalows, condominiums, and other rental options offer families privacy, flexibility, some kitchen facilities, and often lower costs.

At mealtime, don't deny yourself or your children the delights of a new style of cooking. Encourage them to try new foods. Children like to know what kind of food to expect, so it will be interesting to look up regional specialties. And don't forget about picnics.

Things to Remember
1. If you are visiting many sites, pace the days with children in mind. Break the trip into half-day segments, with running around or "doing" time built in.
2. Don't forget that a child's attention span is far shorter than an adult's. Children don't have to see every sight or all of any sight to learn something from their trip; watching, playing with, and talking to other children can be equally enlightening.
3. Let your children lead the way sometimes; their perspective is different from yours, and they may lead you to things you would never have noticed on your own.

4. Remember the places that children love to visit: aquariums, zoos, amusement parks, beaches, nature trails, and so on. Among the activities that may pique their interest are bicycling, horseback riding, boat trips, visiting planetariums and children's museums, and viewing natural habitat exhibits. The perennial attractions for children are the *Wet 'n' Wild* theme park, the non-gambling action at the *Circus Circus Hotel/Casino,* the *Guinness World of Records Museum,* the *Lied Discovery Children's Museum, Ripley's Believe It or Not Odditorium,* and the *Dolphin Habitat* in the *Mirage* hotel).

On the Road

Credit Cards and Traveler's Checks

It may seem hard to believe, but one of the greatest (and least understood) costs of travel is money itself. Your one single objective in relation to the care and retention of your travel funds is to make them stretch as far as possible. When you do spend money, it should be on things that expand and enhance your travel experience, with no buying power lost due to carelessness or lack of knowledge. This requires more than merely ferreting out the best airfare or the most charming budget hotel. It means being canny about the management of money itself. Herewith, a primer on making money go as far as possible while traveling.

TRAVELER'S CHECKS: It's wise to carry traveler's checks while on the road instead of (or in addition to) cash, since it's possible to replace them if they are stolen or lost; in the US, you usually can receive partial or full replacement funds the same day if you have your purchase receipt and proper identification. Issued in various denominations, with adequate proof of identification (credit cards, driver's license, passport), traveler's checks are as good as cash in most hotels, restaurants, stores, and banks. Don't assume, however, that restaurants, small shops, and other establishments are going to be able to change checks of large denominations. More and more establishments are beginning to restrict the face amount of traveler's checks they will accept or cash, so it is wise to purchase at least some of your checks in small denominations — say, $10 and $20.

Every type of traveler's check is legal tender in banks around the world, and each company guarantees full replacement if checks are lost or stolen. After that the similarity ends. Some charge a fee for purchase, while others are free; you can buy traveler's checks at almost any bank, and some are available by mail. Most important, each traveler's check issuer differs slightly in its refund policy — the amount refunded immediately, the accessibility of refund locations, the availability of a 24-hour refund service, and the time it will take you to receive replacement checks. For instance, *American Express* offers a 3-hour replacement of lost traveler's checks at any *American Express* office — other companies may not be as prompt. (Note that *American Express*'s 3-hour policy is based on the traveler's being able to provide the serial numbers of the lost checks. Without these numbers, refunds can take much longer.) *American Express*'s offices in Las Vegas are located in *Caesars Palace* (3570 Las Vegas Blvd. S.; phone: 702-731-7705) and in the *Gold Coast Hotel* (4000 W. Flamingo; phone: 702-876-1410).

We cannot overemphasize the importance of knowing how to replace lost or stolen checks. All of the traveler's check companies have agents throughout the US, both in their own name and at associated agencies (usually, but not necessarily, banks), where refunds can be obtained during business hours. Most of them also have 24-hour toll-free telephone lines, and some even will provide emergency funds to tide you over on a Sunday.

Be sure to make a photocopy of the refund instructions that will be given to you by the issuing institution at the time of purchase. To avoid complications should you need to redeem lost checks (and to speed up the replacement process), keep the purchase receipt and an accurate list, by serial number, of the checks that have been spent or cashed. You may want to incorporate this information in an "emergency packet," also including the numbers of the credit cards you are carrying, and any other bits of information you shouldn't be without. Always keep these records separate from the checks and the original records themselves (you may want to give them to a traveling companion to hold).

Several of the major traveler's check companies charge 1% for the acquisition of their checks; others don't. To receive fee-free traveler's checks you may have to meet certain qualifications — for instance, *Thomas Cook*'s checks issued in US currency are free if you make your travel arrangements through its travel agency. *American Express* traveler's checks are available without charge to members of the *American Automobile Association (AAA)*. Holders of some credit cards (such as the *American Express Platinum* card) also may be entitled to free traveler's checks. The issuing institution (e.g., the particular bank at which you purchase them) may itself charge a fee. If you purchase traveler's checks at a bank in which you or your company maintains significant accounts (especially commercial accounts of some size), the bank may absorb the 1% fee as a courtesy.

American Express, Bank of America, Citicorp, MasterCard, Thomas Cook, and *Visa* all offer traveler's checks. Here is a list of the major companies issuing traveler's checks and the numbers to call to report lost or stolen checks throughout the US:

American Express: 800-221-7282.
Bank of America: 800-227-3460.
Citicorp: 800-645-6556.
MasterCard: Note that *Thomas Cook MasterCard* (below) is now handling all *MasterCard* traveler's check inquiries and refunds (see below).
Thomas Cook MasterCard: 800-223-7373.
Visa: 800-227-6811.

CREDIT CARDS: Some establishments you may encounter during the course of your travels may not honor any credit cards and some may not honor all cards, so there is a practical reason to carry more than one. The following is a list of credit cards that enjoy wide domestic and international acceptance:

American Express: Cardholders can cash personal checks for traveler's checks and cash at *American Express* or its representatives' offices in the US up to the following limits (within any single 21-day period): $1,000 for *Green* and *Optima* cardholders; $5,000 for *Gold* cardholders; and $10,000 for *Platinum* cardholders. Check cashing also is available to cardholders who are guests at participating hotels (up to $250), and for holders of airline tickets at participating airlines (up to $50). Free travel accident, baggage, and car rental insurance is provided if the ticket or rental is charged to the card; additional insurance also is available for additional cost. For further information or to report a lost or stolen *American Express* card, call 800-528-4800 throughout the continental US.

Carte Blanche: Free travel accident, baggage, and car rental insurance if ticket or rental is charged to card; additional insurance also is available at additional cost. For medical, legal, and travel assistance, call 800-356-3448 throughout the US. For further information or to report a lost or stolen *Carte Blanche* card, call 800-525-9135 throughout the US.

Diners Club: Emergency personal check cashing for cardholders staying at participating hotels and motels (up to $250 per stay). Free travel accident, baggage, and car rental insurance if ticket or rental is charged to card; additional insurance also is available for an additional fee. For medical, legal, and travel assist-

GETTING READY / Credit Cards and Traveler's Checks 59

ance worldwide, call 800-356-3448 throughout the US. For further information or to report a lost or stolen *Diners Club* card, call 800-525-9135 throughout the US.

Discover Card: Offered by a subsidiary of Sears, Roebuck & Co., it provides cardholders with cash advances at numerous automatic teller machines and *Sears* stores throughout the US. For further information or to report a lost or stolen *Discover* card, call 800-DISCOVER throughout the US.

MasterCard: Cash advances are available at participating banks worldwide. Check with your issuing bank for information. *MasterCard* also offers a 24-hour emergency lost card service; call 800-826-2181 throughout the US.

Visa: Cash advances are available at participating banks worldwide. Check with your issuing bank for information. *Visa* also offers a 24-hour emergency lost card service; call 800-336-8472 throughout the US.

SENDING MONEY: If you have used up your traveler's checks, cashed as many emergency personal checks as your credit card allows, drawn on your cash advance line to the fullest extent, and still need money, have it sent to you via one of the following services:

American Express (phone: 800-543-4080). Offers a service called "Moneygram," completing money transfers in as little as 15 minutes. The sender can go to any *American Express* office in the US and transfer money by presenting cash, a personal check, money order, or credit card — *Discover, MasterCard, Visa,* or *American Express Optima* (no other *American Express* or other credit cards are accepted). *American Express Optima* cardholders also can arrange for this transfer over the phone. The minimum transfer charge is $12, which rises with the amount of the transaction; the sender can forward funds of up to $10,000 per transaction (credit card users are limited to the amount of their pre-established credit line). To collect at the other end, the receiver must show identification (driver's license or other picture ID) at an *American Express* branch office. The company's offices in Las Vegas are listed above in the *Traveler's Checks* section.

Western Union Telegraph Company (phone: 800-325-4176 throughout the US). A friend or relative can go, cash in hand, to any *Western Union* office in the US, where, for a *minimum* charge of $13 (it rises with the amount of the transaction), the funds will be transferred to a centralized *Western Union* account. When the transaction is fully processed — generally within 30 minutes — you can go to any *Western Union* branch office to pick up the transferred funds (2 convenient locations in the Strip area — at the *Landmark Pharmacy* at 252 Convention Center Dr.; phone: 702-731-0041; and *Mail Boxes Etc.* at 3049 Las Vegas Blvd. S.; phone: 702-731-6245; downtown, another *Mail Boxes Etc.* location is at 316 Bridger Ave.; phone: 702-737-4110). For an additional fee of $2.95 you will be notified by phone when the money is available. For a higher fee, the sender may call *Western Union* with a *MasterCard* or *Visa* number to send up to $2,000, although larger transfers will be sent to a predesignated location.

CASH MACHINES: Automatic teller machines (ATMs) are increasingly common throughout the US. If your bank participates in one of the international ATM networks (most do), the bank will issue you a "cash card" along with a personal identification code or number (also called a PIC or PIN). You can use this card at any ATM in the same electronic network to check your account balances, transfer monies between checking and savings accounts, and — most important for a traveler — withdraw cash instantly. Network ATMs generally are located in banks, commercial and transportation centers, and near major tourist attractions.

Some financial institutions offer exclusive automatic teller machines for their own customers only at bank branches. At the time of this writing, ATMs that *are* connected generally belong to one of the following two international networks:

CIRRUS: Has over 70,000 ATMs in more than 45 countries, including over 65,000 locations in the US — about 200 in Las Vegas. *MasterCard* holders also may use their cards to draw cash against their credit lines. For further information on the *CIRRUS* network, call 800-4-CIRRUS.

PLUS: Has over 70,000 automatic teller machines worldwide, including over 50,000 locations in the US — about 245 of them in Las Vegas. *MasterCard* and *Visa* cardholders also may use their cards to draw cash against their credit lines. For further information on the *PLUS* network, call 800-THE-PLUS.

Information about the *CIRRUS* and *PLUS* systems also is available at member bank branches, where you can obtain free booklets listing the locations worldwide. Note that a recent change in banking regulations permits financial institutions to subscribe to *both* the *CIRRUS* and *PLUS* systems, allowing users of either network to withdraw funds from ATMs at participating banks.

Time Zone and Business Hours

TIME ZONE: Las Vegas is in the Pacific time zone and observes daylight saving time beginning on the first Sunday in April and continuing until the last Sunday in October.

BUSINESS HOURS: Las Vegas maintains business hours that are fairly standard throughout the country: 9 AM to 5 PM, Mondays through Fridays.

Banks generally are open weekdays from 9 AM to 3 PM, and 24-hour "automatic tellers" or "cash machines" are increasingly common (for information on national networks, see *Credit Cards and Traveler's Checks,* in this section).

Retail stores usually are open from 9:30 or 10 AM to 5:30 or 6 PM, 7 days a week. Shops in the malls generally are open until 9 PM.

Mail, Telephone, and Electricity

MAIL: The main post office at 1001 E. Sunset Rd. (phone: 702-361-9212) is open from 8:30 AM to 8 PM weekdays. It has a 24-hour self-service section in the lobby for weighing packages and buying stamps.

Stamps also are available at most hotel desks. There are vending machines for stamps in drugstores, transportation terminals, and other public places. Stamps cost more from these machines than they do at the post office. Convenient post office branches for visitors are the Circus Circus Station (1001 Circus Circus Dr.; phone: 702-735-2525), which is open 8:30 AM to 5 PM weekdays; the Downtown Station (301 E. Stewart Ave.; phone: 702-385-8944), open 9 AM to 5 PM weekdays; and the Airport Station (phone: 702-361-9356), open the same hours weekdays and 9 AM to 1:30 PM on Saturdays.

There are several places that will receive and hold mail for travelers. Mail sent to you at a hotel and clearly marked "Guest Mail, Hold for Arrival" is one safe approach. Post offices will extend this service to you if the mail is sent to you in care of General Delivery in the city or town you will visit. This will direct it to the main post office in any large city. Ask the sender to put "Hold for 30 Days" (the maximum period of

GETTING READY / Mail, Telephone, and Electricity 61

time that the US Postal Service will hold correspondence), as well as a return address on the envelope so that the post office can return it if you are unable to pick it up. To claim this mail, go to the main post office in Las Vegas (see above for address), ask for General Delivery, and present identification (driver's license, credit cards, birth certificate, or passport). Mail must be collected in person.

If you are an *American Express* customer (a cardholder, a carrier of *American Express* traveler's checks, or traveling on an *American Express Travel Related Services* tour) you can have mail sent to its Las Vegas office. Letters are held free of charge — registered mail and packages are not accepted. You must be able to show an *American Express* card, traveler's checks, or a voucher proving you are on one of the company's tours to qualify. Those who aren't clients cannot use the service. Mail should be addressed to you, care of *American Express,* and should be marked "Client Mail Service." Additional information on its mail service and the addresses of *American Express* offices throughout the US are listed in the pamphlet *American Express Travelers' Companion,* available from any American Express branch office.

Members of the *American Automobile Association (AAA)* also can have mail held free of charge at any *AAA* office in the US. Instruct the sender to mark the envelope "Hold for Arrival." For more information regarding *AAA*'s mail service and branch locations, contact your local chapter or the national office, 1000 AAA Dr., Heathrow, FL 32745-5063 (phone: 407-444-8544).

For rapid, overnight delivery to other cities, *Federal Express* can be useful. The phone number to call for pick-up in Las Vegas is 800-238-5355, while convenient drop-off addresses include 5870 S. Eastern Ave. and 316 E. Bridger. Another useful overnight service is *DHL Worldwide Courier Express;* call 702-798-4090.

TELEPHONE: Public pay telephones are available just about everywhere — including transportation terminals, hotel lobbies, restaurants, drugstores, libraries, post offices, and other municipal buildings, as well as major tourist centers.

The statewide area code is 702.

Although you can use a telephone company credit card number on any phone, pay phones that take major credit cards (*American Express, MasterCard, Visa,* and so on) are increasingly common, particularly in transportation and tourism centers. Also now available is the "affinity card," a combined telephone calling card/bank credit card that can be used for domestic and international calls. Cards of this type include the following:

AT&T/Universal (phone: 800-662-7759)
Executive Telecard International (phone: 800-950-3800)

Similarly, *MCI VisaPhone* (phone: 800-866-0099) can add phone card privileges to the services available through your existing *Visa* card. This service allows you to use your *Visa* account number, plus an additional code, to charge calls on any touch-tone phone.

You must first dial 1 to indicate that you are making a long-distance call. The nationwide number for information is 555-1212. If you need a number in another area code, dial 1 + the area code + 555-1212. (If you don't know the area code, simply dial 0 for an operator who will tell you.)

Long-distance rates are charged according to when the call is placed: weekday daytime; weekday evenings; and nights, weekends, and holidays. Least expensive are the calls you dial yourself from a private phone at night and on weekends and major holidays. It generally is more expensive to call from a pay phone than it is to call from a private phone, and you must pay for a minimum 3-minute call. If the operator assists you, calls are more expensive. This includes credit card, bill-to-a-third-number, collect, and time-and-charge calls, as well as person-to-person calls, which are the most expensive. Rates are fully explained in the front of the white pages of every telephone directory.

Hotel Surcharges – Before calling from any hotel room, inquire about any surcharges the hotel may impose. These can be excessive, but are avoidable by calling collect, using a telephone credit card (see above), or calling from a public pay phone. (Note that when calling from your hotel room, even if the call is made collect or charged to a credit card number, some establishments still may add on a nominal line usage charge — so ask before you call.)

Emergency Number – As in most US cities, 911 is the number to dial in the event of an emergency in Las Vegas. Operators at this number will get you the help you need from the police, fire department, or ambulance service. It is, however, a number that should be used for real emergencies only.

Other Resources – Particularly useful for planning a trip is *AT&T's Toll-Free 800 Directory*, which lists thousands of companies with 800 numbers, both alphabetically (white pages) and by category (yellow pages), including a wide range of travel services — from travel agents to transportation and accommodations. Issued in a consumer edition for $9.95 and a business edition for $14.95, both are available from *AT&T Phone Centers* or by calling 800-426-8686. Other useful directories for use before you leave and on the road include the *Toll-Free Travel & Vacation Information Directory* ($4.95 postpaid from Pilot Books, 103 Cooper St., Babylon, NY 11702; phone: 516-422-2225) and *The Phone Booklet*, which lists the nationwide, toll-free (800) numbers of travel information sources and suppliers — such as major airlines, hotel and motel chains, car rental companies, and tourist information offices (send $2 to *Scott American Corporation*, Box 88, W. Redding, CT 06896).

ELECTRICITY: All 50 US states have the same electrical current system: 110 volts, 60 cycles, alternating current (AC). Appliances running on standard current can be used throughout the US without adapters or converters.

Staying Healthy

The surest way to return home in good health is to be prepared for medical problems that might occur on vacation. As is always the case with both diseases and accidents, prevention is the best cure. Below, we've outlined some things you need to think about before your trip.

BEFORE YOU GO: Older travelers or anyone suffering from a chronic medical condition, such as diabetes, high blood pressure, cardiopulmonary disease, asthma, or ear, eye, or sinus trouble, should consult a physician before leaving home. Those with conditions requiring special consideration when traveling should consider seeing, in addition to their regular physician, a specialist in travel medicine. For a referral in a particular community, contact the nearest medical school or ask a local doctor to recommend such a specialist. Dr. Leonard Marcus, a member of the *American Committee on Clinical Tropical Medicine and Travelers' Health*, provides a directory of more than 100 travel doctors across the country. For a copy, send a 9-by-12-inch self-addressed, stamped envelope to Dr. Marcus at 148 Highland Ave., Newton, MA 02165 (phone: 617-527-4003).

Also be sure to check with your insurance company ahead of time about the applicability of your hospitalization and major medical policies while you're away. If your medical policy does not protect you while you're traveling, there are comprehensive

GETTING READY / Staying Healthy 63

combination policies specifically designed to fill the gap. (For a discussion of medical insurance and a list of inclusive combination policies, see *Insurance,* in this section.)

First Aid – Put together a compact, personal medical kit including Band-Aids, first-aid cream, antiseptic, nose drops, insect repellent, aspirin or non-aspirin pain reliever, an extra pair of prescription glasses or contact lenses (and a copy of your prescription for glasses or contact lenses), sunglasses, over-the-counter remedies for diarrhea, indigestion, and motion sickness, a thermometer, and a supply of those prescription medicines you take regularly.

In a corner of your kit, keep a list of all the drugs you have brought and their purpose, as well as duplicate copies of your doctor's prescriptions (or a note from your doctor). As brand names may vary in different parts of the US, it's a good idea to ask your doctor for the generic name of any drugs you use so that you can ask for their equivalent should you need a refill.

It also is a good idea to ask your doctor to prepare a medical identification card that includes such information as your blood type, your social security number, any allergies or chronic health problems you have, and your medical insurance information. Considering the essential contents of your medical kit, keep it with you, rather than in your checked luggage.

MINIMIZING THE RISKS: In the US, travelers do not face many of the health risks encountered in visits to many destinations around the world (such as Mexico or South America). Certainly travel always entails *some* possibility of injury or illness, but neither is inevitable and, with some basic precautions, your trip should proceed untroubled by ill health.

Food and Water – The tap water in the US is thoroughly purified, so feel free to drink it; fruit, vegetables, and dairy products are likewise safe. However, you should avoid swimming in or drinking water from freshwater streams, rivers, or pools, as they may be contaminated with *Leptospira,* a bacterium that causes a disease call leptospirosis (its symptoms resemble influenza).

Sunburn – The burning power of the sun can quickly cause severe sunburn or sunstroke. To protect yourself against these ills, wear sunglasses, take along a broad-brimmed hat and cover-up, and, most important, use a sunscreen lotion.

Following these precautions will not guarantee an illness-free trip, but should minimize the risk. For more information regarding preventive health care for travelers, contact the *International Association for Medical Assistance to Travelers (IAMAT;* 417 Center St., Lewiston, NY 14092; phone: 716-754-4883). This organization also assists travelers in obtaining emergency medical assistance around the world.

MEDICAL ASSISTANCE IN LAS VEGAS: Nothing ruins a vacation or business trip more effectively than sudden injury or illness. Fortunately, should you need medical attention, competent health professionals perfectly equipped to handle any medical problem can be found throughout the country. Most towns and cities of any size have a hospital in the area, and generally, even the smallest of towns has at least a medical clinic or private physician nearby. All hospitals are prepared for emergency cases — although the sophistication of facilities may vary — and many hospitals also have walk-in clinics to serve people who do not really need emergency service, but who have no place to go for immediate medical attention. The level of medical care in the US, especially in the larger cities, generally is excellent, providing all the basic specialties and services.

Emergency Treatment – You will find, in the event of an emergency, that most tourist facilities — transportation companies, hotels, theme parks, and resorts — are equipped to handle the situation quickly and efficiently. If a bona fide emergency occurs, dial 911, the emergency number, and immediately state the nature of your problem and your location. If you are able to, another alternative is to go directly to the emergency room of the nearest hospital. In Las Vegas, major medical institutions with top emergency facilities include *Humana Hospital–Sunrise* (3186 Maryland Pkwy.; phone: 702-731-8000), which also operates a physician referral service (phone: 702-731-8211), and *University Medical Center* (1800 W. Charleston; phone: 702-383-2074.)

Non-Emergency Care – If a doctor is needed for something less than an emergency, there are several ways to find one. If you are staying in a hotel or at a resort, ask for help in reaching a doctor or other emergency service, or for the house physician, who may visit you in your room or ask you to visit an office. When you register at a hotel, it's not a bad idea to include your home address and telephone number; this will facilitate the process of notifying friends, relatives, or your own doctor in case of emergency.

Pharmacies and Prescriptions – There should be no problem finding a 24-hour drugstore in most cities and large towns throughout the country. In some areas, pharmacies may take turns staying open for 24 hours. *White Cross Drugs* (1700 Las Vegas Blvd. S.; phone: 702-382-1733) stays open 24 hours, 7 days a week. The *Village East* (5025 S. Eastern Ave.; phone: 702-736-7081) is open daily 8 AM to midnight.

If you need to refill a prescription from your own doctor, you should be aware that in some states pharmacists only will fill prescriptions made out by a doctor licensed to practice in that state, so you may have to have a local doctor rewrite a prescription. Even in an emergency — such as a diabetic needing insulin — a traveler more than likely will be given only enough of a drug to last until a local prescription can be obtained. Generally, a hospital emergency room or walk-in clinic can provide a refill from its pharmaceutical department or a prescription that can be filled at a nearby pharmacy.

ADDITIONAL RESOURCES: Information and medical assistance also is available from various organizations, some of which offer programs designed to assist travelers who have chronic ailments or whose illness requires them to return home. Among these are the following:

International Association for Medical Assistance to Travelers (IAMAT; 417 Center St., Lewiston, NY 14092; phone: 716-754-4883). Entitles members to the services of participating doctors around the world, as well as clinics and hospitals in various locations. Participating physicians agree to adhere to a basic charge of around $50 to see a patient referred by *IAMAT.* To join, simply write to *IAMAT;* in about 3 weeks you will receive a membership card, the booklet of members, and an inoculation chart. A nonprofit organization, *IAMAT* appreciates donations; with a donation of $25 or more, you will receive a set of worldwide climate charts detailing weather and sanitary conditions. (Delivery can take up to 5 weeks, so plan ahead.)

International Health Care Service (New York Hospital–Cornell Medical Center, 525 E. 68th St., Box 210, New York, NY 10021; phone: 212-746-1601). This provides a variety of travel-related health services, including a complete range of immunizations at moderate per-shot rates. A pre-travel counseling and immunization package costs $255 for the first family member and $195 for each additional member; a post-travel consultation is $175 to $275, plus lab work. Consultations are by appointment only, from 4 to 8 PM Mondays through Thursdays, although 24-hour coverage is available for urgent travel-related problems. In addition, sending $4.50 (with a self-addressed envelope) to the address above will procure the service's publication, *International Health Care Travelers Guide,* a compendium of facts and advice on health care and diseases around the world.

International SOS Assistance (PO Box 11568, Philadelphia, PA 19116; phone: 800-523-8930 or 215-244-1500). Subscribers are provided with telephone ac-

GETTING READY / Staying Healthy 65

cess — 24 hours a day, 365 days a year — to a worldwide, monitored, multilingual network of medical centers. A phone call brings assistance ranging from a telephone consultation to transportation home by ambulance or aircraft, or, in some cases, transportation of a family member to wherever you are hospitalized. Individual rates are $35 for 2 weeks of coverage ($3.50 for each additional day), $70 for 1 month, or $240 for 1 year; couple and family rates also are available.

Medic Alert Foundation (2323 N. Colorado, Turlock, CA 95380; phone: 800-ID-ALERT or 209-668-3333). If you have a health condition that may not be readily perceptible to the casual observer — one that might result in a tragic error in an emergency situation — this organization offers identification emblems specifying such conditions. The foundation also maintains a computerized central file from which your complete medical history is available 24 hours a day by phone (the telephone number is clearly inscribed on the emblem). The onetime membership fee (between $35 and $50) is based on the type of metal from which the emblem is made — the choices range from stainless steel to 10K gold-filled.

TravMed (PO Box 10623, Baltimore, MD 21204; phone: 800-732-5309 or 410-296-5225). For $3 per day, subscribers receive comprehensive medical assistance while abroad. Major medical expenses are covered up to $100,000, and special transportation home or of a family member to wherever you are hospitalized is provided at no additional cost.

Helpful Publications – Practically every phase of health care — before, during, and after a trip — is covered in *The New Traveler's Health Guide,* by Drs. Patrick J. Doyle and James E. Banta. It is available for $4.95, plus postage and handling, from Acropolis Books Ltd., 13950 Park Center Rd., Herndon, VA 22071 (phone: 800-451-7771 or 703-709-0006).

The *Traveling Healthy Newsletter,* which is published six times a year, also is brimming with health-related travel tips. For a year's subscription, which costs $24, contact Dr. Karl Neumann (108-48 70th Rd., Forest Hills, NY 11375; phone: 718-268-7290). A sample issue is available for $4. Dr. Neumann also is the editor of the useful free booklet *Traveling Healthy,* which is available by writing to the *Travel Healthy Program* (Clark O'Neill, 1 Broad Ave., Fairview, NJ 07022; phone: 201-947-3400).

For more information regarding preventive health care for travelers, contact the Centers for Disease Control, which publishes an interesting booklet called *Health Information for International Travel.* To order send a check or money order for $5 to the Superintendent of Documents (US Government Printing Office, Washington, DC 20402), or charge it to your credit card by calling 202-783-3238. For information on vaccination requirements, disease outbreaks, and other health information pertaining to traveling abroad, you also can call the Centers for Disease Control's 24-hour International Health Requirements and Recommendations Information Hotline: 404-332-4559.

■ **Note:** Those who are unable to take a reserved flight due to personal illness or who must fly home unexpectedly due to a family emergency should be aware that airlines may offer a discounted airfare (or arrange a partial refund) if the traveler can demonstrate that his or her situation is indeed a legitimate emergency. Your inability to fly or the illness or death of an immediate family member usually must be substantiated by a doctor's note or the name, relationship, and funeral home from which the deceased will be buried. In such cases, airlines often will waive certain advance purchase restrictions or you may receive a refund check or voucher for future travel at a later date. Be aware, however, that this bereavement fare may not necessarily be the least expensive fare available and, if possible, it is best to have a travel agent check all possible flights through a computer reservations system (CRS).

Legal Aid

The best way to begin looking for legal aid in an unfamiliar area is to call your own lawyer. If you don't have, or cannot reach, your own attorney, most cities offer legal referral services (sometimes called attorney referral services) maintained by county bar associations. In Las Vegas, the *State Bar of Nevada* offers a *Lawyer Referral Service* (201 Las Vegas Blvd. S.; phone: 702-382-0504). Such referral services see that anyone in need of legal representation gets it. (Attorneys also are listed in the yellow pages.) The referral service is almost always free. If your case goes to court, you are entitled to court-appointed representation if you can't get a lawyer or can't afford one.

In the case of minor traffic accidents (such as a fender bender), it often is most expedient to settle the matter before the police get involved. If you get a traffic or parking ticket, pay it. For most violations, you will receive a citation at most, and be required to appear in court on a specified date.

Drinking and Drugs

DRINKING: As in all 50 states, the legal drinking age in Nevada is 21. There are basically few other laws governing the sale or purchase of liquor. Alcoholic drinks may be served in restaurants, bars, and lounges 24 hours a day, 7 days a week. The same laissez-faire approach applies to retail purchases of liquor, wine, and beer, which are sold at package stores, supermarkets, and convenience stores.

DRUGS: Despite the US government's intensified and concerted effort to stamp out drugs, illegal narcotics still are prevalent in the US, as elsewhere. Enforcement of drug laws is becoming increasingly strict throughout the nation, however, and local narcotics officers are renowned for their absence of understanding and lack of a sense of humor.

Opiates, barbiturates, and other increasingly popular drugs — "white powder" substances like heroin, cocaine, and "crack" (the cocaine derivative) and ICE (a crystallized amphetamine) — continue to be of major concern to narcotics officials. **Warning:** Authorities warn those traveling with children that ICE is virtually indistinguishable from rock salt and rock candy, so it is particularly important to stress to children not to accept anything from strangers.

Possession of marijuana in Nevada brings a felony charge, no matter what amount, as does possession of cocaine or heroin. Conviction will result in 1 to 20 years in prison, depending on the circumstances and whether sale is involved. It is important to bear in mind that the quantity of drugs involved is of minor importance. The best advice we can offer is this: Don't carry, use, buy, or sell illegal drugs.

To avoid difficulties during spot luggage inspections at the airport, those who carry medicines that contain a controlled drug such as codeine should be sure to have current doctor's prescription.

■ **Be Forewarned:** US narcotics agents warn travelers of the increasingly common ploy of drug dealers asking travelers to transport a "gift" or other package for them. In other words, do not, under any circumstances, agree to take anything with you for a stranger.

Tipping

While tipping is at the discretion of the person receiving the service, 50¢ is the rock-bottom tip for anything, and $1 is the current customary minimum for small services. In restaurants, tip between 10% and 20% of the bill. For average service in an average restaurant, a 15% tip to the waiter is reasonable, although one should never hesitate to penalize poor service or reward excellent and efficient attention by leaving less or more.

Although it's not necessary to tip the maître d' of most restaurants — unless he has been especially helpful in arranging a special party or providing a table (slipping the maître d' something *may*, however, get you seated sooner or procure a preferred table) — when tipping is desirable or appropriate, the least amount should be $5. In the finest restaurants, where a multiplicity of servers are present, plan to tip 5% to the captain in addition to the gratuity left for the waiter. The sommelier (wine waiter) is tipped approximately 10% of the price of the bottle of wine.

In allocating gratuities at a restaurant, pay particular attention to what has become the standard credit card charge form, which now includes separate places for gratuities for waiters and/or captains. If these separate boxes are not on the charge slip, simply ask the waiter or captain how these separate tips should be indicated. In some establishments, tips indicated on credit card receipts may not be given to the help, so you may want to leave tips in cash.

In a large hotel, where it is difficult to determine just who out of a horde of attendants actually performed particular services, it is perfectly proper for guests to ask to have an extra 10% to 15% added to their bill. For those who prefer to distribute tips themselves, a chambermaid generally is tipped at the rate of around $1 a day. Tip the concierge or hall porter for specific services only, with the amount of such gratuities dependent on the level of service provided. For any special service you receive in a hotel, a tip is expected — $1 being the minimum for a small service.

Bellhops, doormen, and porters at hotels and transportation centers generally are tipped at the rate of $1 per piece of luggage, along with a small additional amount if a doorman helps with a cab or car. Taxi drivers should get about 15% of the total fare.

Miscellaneous tips: Sightseeing tour guides should be tipped. If you are traveling in a group, decide together what you want to give the guide and present it from the group at the end of the tour ($1 per person is a reasonable tip). If you have been individually escorted, the amount paid should depend on the degree of your satisfaction, but it should not be less than 10% of the tour price. Museum and monument guides also are usually tipped a few dollars.

In barbershops and beauty salons, tip as you would at home, keeping in mind that the percentages vary according to the type of establishment — 10% in the most expensive salons; 15% to 20% in less expensive establishments. (As a general rule, the person who washes your hair should get a small additional tip.) Washroom attendants should get a small tip — they usually set out a little plate with a coin (or coins) already on it indicating the suggested denomination. Coat checks are worth about 50¢ to $1 a coat. And don't forget service station attendants, for whom a tip of around 50¢ for cleaning the windshield or other attention is not unusual.

Tipping always is a matter of personal preference. In the situations covered above, as well as in any others that arise where you feel a tip is expected or due, feel free to express your pleasure or displeasure. Again, never hesitate to reward excellent and efficient attention or to penalize poor service. Give an extra gratuity and a word of thanks when someone has gone out of his or her way for you. Either way, the more personal the act of tipping, the more appropriate it seems. And if you didn't like the service — or the attitude — don't tip.

Religion on the Road

The surest source of information on religious services in an unfamiliar community is the desk clerk of the hotel or resort in which you are staying; the local tourist information office or a church of another religious affiliation also may be able to provide this information. For a full range of options, joint religious councils often provide circulars with the addresses and times of services of other houses of worship in the area. These often are printed as part of general tourist guides provided by the local tourist and convention center, or as part of a "what's going on" guide to the city. Many newspapers also provide a listing of religious services in their area in weekend editions.

You may want to use your vacation to broaden your religious experience by joining an unfamiliar faith in its service. This can be a moving experience, especially if the service is held in a church, synagogue, or temple that is historically significant or architecturally notable. You almost always will find yourself made welcome and comfortable.

Sources and Resources

Tourist Information

The Nevada Commission on Tourism's address is 5151 S. Carson St., Carson City, NV 89710 (phone: 800-NEVADA-8 or 702-687-4322). The Las Vegas Chamber of Commerce is at 2301 E. Sahara Ave., Las Vegas, NV 89104 (phone: 702-457-4664). For other local tourist information, see *Sources and Resources* in THE CITY.

Books, Magazines, and Newsletters

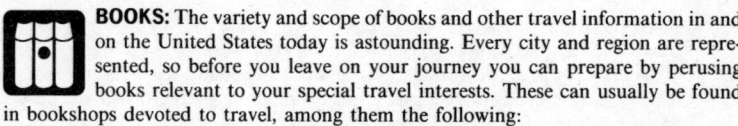

BOOKS: The variety and scope of books and other travel information in and on the United States today is astounding. Every city and region are represented, so before you leave on your journey you can prepare by perusing books relevant to your special travel interests. These can usually be found in bookshops devoted to travel, among them the following:

Book Passage (51 Tamal Vista Blvd., Corte Madera, CA 94925; phone: 415-927-0960 in California; 800-321-9785 elsewhere in the US). Travel guides and maps to all areas of the world. A free catalogue is available.

The Complete Traveller (199 Madison Ave., New York, NY 10016; phone: 212-685-9007). Travel guides and maps. A catalogue is available for $2.

Forsyth Travel Library (PO Box 2975, Shawnee Mission, KS 66201-1375; phone: 800-367-7984 or 913-384-3440). Travel guides and maps, old and new, to all parts of the world. Ask for the "Worldwide Travel Books and Maps" catalogue.

Globe Corner (1 School St., Boston, MA 02180; phone: 617-523-6658). Travel guides, maps, and histories.

Phileas Fogg's Books and Maps (87 *Stanford Shopping Center,* Palo Alto, CA 94304; phone: 800-533-FOGG or 415-327-1754). Travel guides and maps.

Powell's Travel Store (Pioneer Courthouse Sq., 701 SW 6th Ave., Portland, OR 97204; phone: 503-228-1108). A wealth of travel-related books (over 15,000 titles) and reference materials (globes, an extensive selection of maps and so on), as well as luggage and travel accessories (travel irons and the like). There is even a travel agency on the premises.

Tattered Cover (2955 E. First Ave., Denver, CO 80206; phone: 800-833-9327 or 303-322-7727). The travel department alone of this enormous bookstore carries over 7,000 books, as well as maps and atlases. No catalogue is offered (the list is too extensive), but a newsletter, issued three times a year, is available on request.

Thomas Brothers Maps & Travel Books (603 W. Seventh St., Los Angeles, CA 90017; phone: 213-627-4018). Maps (including road atlases, street guides, and wall maps), guidebooks, and travel accessories.

Traveldays Book Shop (317 Columbus City Center, Columbus, OH 43215; phone: 614-221-0506). Maps, guidebooks, and travel videos.

Traveller's Bookstore (22 W. 52nd St., New York, NY 10019; phone: 212-664-0995). Travel guides, maps, literature, and accessories. A catalogue is available for $2.

MAGAZINES: As sampling the regional fare is likely to be one of the highlights of any visit, you will find reading about local edibles worthwhile before you go or after you return. *Gourmet,* a magazine specializing in food, frequently features mouth-watering articles on food and restaurants in the US, although its scope is much broader than domestic fare alone. It is available at newsstands nationwide for $2.50 an issue or for $18 a year from *Gourmet,* PO Box 53780, Boulder, CO 80322 (phone: 800-365-2454).

There are numerous additional magazines for every special interest available; check at your library information desk for a directory of such publications, or look over the selection offered at a well-stocked newsstand.

NEWSLETTERS: One of the very best sources of detailed travel information is *Consumer Reports Travel Letter.* Published monthly by Consumers Union (PO Box 53629, Boulder, CO 80322-3629; phone: 800-999-7959), it offers comprehensive coverage of the travel scene on a wide variety of fronts. A year's subscription costs $37; 2 years, $57.

In addition, the following travel newsletters provide useful up-to-date information on travel services and bargains:

Entree (PO Box 5148, Santa Barbara, CA 93150; phone: 805-969-5848). Monthly; a year's subscription costs $59. Subscribers also have access to a 24-hour hotline providing information on restaurants and accommodations around the world. This newsletter caters to a sophisticated, discriminating traveler with the means to explore the places mentioned.

The Hideaway Report (Harper Associates, Subscription Office: PO Box 300, Whitefish, MO 59937; phone: 406-862-3480). This monthly source highlights retreats — including domestic idylls — for sophisticated travelers. A year's subscription costs $90.

Romantic Hideaways (217 E. 86th St., Suite 258, New York, NY 10028; phone: 212-969-8682). This newsletter leans toward those special places made for those traveling in twos. A year's subscription to this monthly publication costs $65.

Travel Smart (Communications House, 40 Beechdale Rd., Dobbs Ferry, NY 10522; phone: 914-693-8300 in New York; 800-327-3633 elsewhere in the US). This monthly newsletter covers a wide variety of trips and travel discounts. A year's subscription costs $44.

COMPUTER SERVICES: Anyone who owns a personal computer and a modem can subscribe to a database service providing everything from airline schedules and fares to restaurant listings. Two such services to try:

CompuServe (5000 Arlington Center Blvd., Columbus, OH 43220; phone: 800-848-8199 or 614-457-8600). It costs $39.95 to join, plus hourly usage fees of $6 to $12.50.

Prodigy Services (445 Hamilton Ave., White Plains, NY 10601; phone: 800-822-6922 or 914-993-8000). A month's subscription costs $12.95, plus variable phone charges.

■ **Note:** Before using any computer bulletin-board services, be sure to take precautions to prevent downloading of a computer "virus." First install one of the programs designed to screen out such nuisances.

Cameras and Equipment

Vacations (and even some business trips) are everybody's favorite time for taking pictures and home movies. After all, most of us want to remember the places we visit — and to show them off to others. Here are a few suggestions to help you get the best results from your travel photography or videography.

BEFORE THE TRIP

If you're taking your camera or camcorder out after a long period in mothballs, or have just bought a new one, check it thoroughly before you leave to prevent unexpected breakdowns or disappointing pictures.

1. Still cameras should be cleaned carefully and thoroughly, inside and out. If using a camcorder, run a head cleaner through it. You also may want to have your camcorder professionally serviced (opening the casing yourself will violate the manufacturer's warranty). Always use filters to protect your lens while traveling.
2. Check the batteries for your camera's light meter and flash, and take along extras just in case yours wear out during the trip. For camcorders, bring along extra Nickel-Cadmium (Ni-Cad) batteries; if you use rechargeable batteries, a recharger will cut down on the extras.
3. Using all the settings and features, shoot at least one test roll of film or one videocassette, using the type you plan to take along with you.

EQUIPMENT TO TAKE ALONG

Keep your gear light and compact. Items that are too heavy or bulky to be carried comfortably on a full-day excursion will likely remain in your hotel room.

1. Invest in a broad camera or camcorder strap if you now have a thin one. It will make carrying the camera much more comfortable.
2. A sturdy canvas, vinyl, or leather camera or camcorder bag, preferably with padded pockets (not an airline bag), will keep your equipment organized and easy to find. If you will be doing much shooting around the water, a waterproof case is best.
3. For cleaning, bring along a camel's hair brush that retracts into a rubber squeeze bulb. Also take plenty of lens tissue, soft cloths, and plastic bags to protect equipment from dust and moisture.

FILM AND TAPES: If you are concerned about airport security X-rays damaging rolls of undeveloped still film (X-rays do not affect processed film) or tapes, store them in one of the lead-lined bags sold in camera shops. This possibility is not as much of a threat as it used to be, however. In the US, incidents of X-ray damage to unprocessed film (exposed or unexposed) are few because low-dosage X-ray equipment is used virtually everywhere. If you're traveling without a protective bag, you may want to ask to have your photo equipment inspected by hand. One type of film that should never be subjected to X-rays is the very high speed ASA 1000 film; there are lead-lined bags made especially for it — and, in the event that you are refused a hand inspection, this is the only way to save your film. The walk-through metal detector devices at airports do not affect film, though the film cartridges may set them off.

You should have no problem finding film or tapes in Las Vegas. When buying film, tapes, or photo accessories the best rule of thumb is to stick to name brands with which you are familiar. The availability of film processing labs and equipment repair shops will vary.

For tips on some of Las Vegas's most photogenic spots, see *A Shutterbug's Las Vegas* in DIVERSIONS.

THE CITY

LAS VEGAS

There may be no other place on earth so forbidding and yet so alluring as Las Vegas, that glittering oasis in the midst of mountainous Nevada desert. It has an aura of unreality, a lack of connection to the humdrum of everyday life. To some it's a 24-hour city of fantasy, to others an unending nightmare. Your opinion just may depend on your tolerance for the phantasmagorical and your affinity for the type of place where one of the major hotel-casinos has a volcano in its front yard that emits piña colada–scented smoke. But whether it's loved as a vacation paradise or damned as "Sin City," the maze of contradictions that are bred here makes the place fascinating.

The unabashed glitz of this city is striking when seen from a descending plane at night. Las Vegas emerges from nearly total darkness as a stream of bright lights, scattered like brilliant jewels on black velvet. The city promises visitors the ultimate in excess — and that's just what it delivers.

Despite its current standing as "Entertainment Capital of the World," Las Vegas had rather humble beginnings. In 1905, it was incorporated as a town without much fanfare, and people paid little attention to it. Even the legalization of gambling by the Nevada Legislature in 1931 created only a minor dust storm. Las Vegas languished, a tiny gambling town stuck in the middle of the desert, until the arrival of one Benjamin "Bugsy" Siegel.

Today, you won't see memorials or tributes to Siegel anywhere in the city, but he had more to do with the development of Las Vegas as a sparkling Shangri-la than any other individual — as anyone who has seen the Warren Beatty film *Bugsy* knows. Siegel was enamored of the make-believe world of Hollywood and decided that transforming Las Vegas into an equally make-believe, luxurious gambling showplace would attract big-name stars and big-time dollars. In 1945, he began to turn his dream into reality, building a lavish hotel-casino at the south end of what would eventually become the Strip. Even though building materials were scarce (after all, World War II had just ended) and his cronies were dismissing his scheme as a crazy waste of money, he persevered. The *Flamingo* — named for his flamboyant girlfriend, Virginia Hill — opened on *Christmas Day,* 1946. A financial bust, the hotel closed almost immediately. Siegel himself barely outlived his creation; he died in typical gangland style a year later, his Las Vegas dream not yet realized (the *Flamingo* was taken over by one of his original partners shortly afterward). But he had planted the seed of an idea, and little by little, it began to grow.

About 20 years after Siegel's death, another fan of Hollywood and the movie industry gave Las Vegas a boost. In 1966, reclusive billionaire Howard Hughes stayed in the penthouse of the *Desert Inn* during a visit here. He and his entourage did not gamble, and the management, disturbed by this strange aberration, requested that he move out to make room for high-rolling guests. Hughes politely declined — and bought the hotel. Where Hughes led, other corporations followed, including the Hilton group, which began building hotels along the Strip. Although inevitably linked with gambling (and the sometimes seedy characters it attracts), Las Vegas began to take on an air of respectability, which it has attempted — with some measure of success — to enhance ever since.

With the legalization of gambling in Atlantic City and other communities across the country, a new age has dawned. Since the 1950s, Las Vegas has reigned as the unchallenged gambling resort of the world, and it is not about to surrender its throne without a fight. A sense of competition has swept the city, and several of the older hotels have received dramatic face-lifts while the new structures that continue to spring up place special emphasis on extras and freebies. Some of this effort seems to have paid off. In 1991, the US census reported that Las Vegas was the fastest-growing city in the country, with 6,000 people a month moving to this desert demi-dreamscape (perhaps because of the pleasantly dry climate and favorable real estate values compared to other similarly sized cities), and over 21 million visitors (an increase of about 83% over the past 10 years).

By and large, these visitors see one face of Las Vegas: the façade of the "Entertainment Capital of the World." But this doesn't begin to describe it. The cavernous air conditioned vastness of countless Strip casinos aims at total sensory bombardment with a maelstrom of sights and sounds: the ringing bells and flashing lights of the slot machines, the rolling wheels of fortune, the dice dancing on the green tables, the smoke-filled air mixed with a heavy undercurrent of free-flowing alcohol. Throngs of people crowd the casinos at every hour of the day and night. In Las Vegas, time doesn't matter — indeed, it barely exists. There are no clocks in the casinos, and many places serve breakfast and dinner 24 hours a day at such bargain prices that it might make sense to eat both at one sitting. Cocktail waitresses keep the thirst quenched by bringing drinks on the house for those gambling steadily. The casinos offer these extras so that Vegas visitors can spend their time indulging in the town's one overwhelming obsession — the desire to gamble. If gratification is not found instantly, there is a choice of a few hundred other places whose neon signs blare bigger and better attractions. By the way, it is considered the height of gauche insensitivity to forget to tip a dealer working for you on your big win. Local protocol dictates that you toss a few largish chips his or her way. Never openly hand over money. This could be considered even worse than doing nothing, and the dealer will not be able to accept the gratuity.

Just venture outside on the Strip (in Las Vegas, going outside is a big step) and you will see one huge hotel-casino after another: *Caesars Palace, Riviera,* the *Sahara,* the *Mirage,* the *Sands, Aladdin, Excalibur, Bally's.* The names promise magic, but it's mostly an optical illusion. Underneath those opulent exteriors and plush decors is a foundation of sand. Certainly, some of the biggest names in entertainment perform here and everyone flocks to see them, but the real business is gambling; anything else is done simply to draw people to the casinos. That's the real trick and that's what keeps Las Vegas going. Money is the god here, and it created poker chips in its own image. It also created some vast resort complexes — castles built on the desert that promise paradise at the next throw of the dice. The newest kid on the block will be the *MGM Grand;* scheduled to open later this year, it's billed as the biggest hotel in the world — 5,000 rooms of luxury and glamour under one roof. Once the *Grand* is up and running, Las Vegas will have the world's ten largest hotels, no small feat for what was once a desert hamlet.

But if you do manage to break the spell of the casinos and get outside — beyond the Strip and town — you will discover that the world out there is worth a good deal more than the few rounds of golf or tennis between poker games. Contrary to preconceived notions of the desert as a lifeless, joyless, uniformly bland stretch of rock and sand, you will value the treeless expanse for its incredible beauty — a magnificent variety of colors — and the utter freedom of its open spaces. Within miles of Las Vegas, but on the other side of the barrier of unreality, lie the dramatic red and gold sandstone formations of the Red Rock Canyon Conservation Area and the subtle desert colors of the Valley of Fire. These, with the nearby cool green mountains of Mt. Charleston and the manmade Lake Mead, make the desert as attractive a proposition as the Strip.

LAS VEGAS AT-A-GLANCE

SEEING THE CITY: The *Skye Room* restaurant in *Binion's Horseshoe* hotel (128 Fremont St.; phone: 382-1600) offers a panoramic view of Las Vegas. As you ascend in the glass elevator, all of downtown Las Vegas glitters around you. As you reach the top, the expanse of surrounding desert appears, and your eye is drawn to the neon of the Strip, a long stream of hotels and casinos, and, to the west, the green heights of Mt. Charleston. Riding in the glass-enclosed elevator on the north side of the *Las Vegas Hilton* (3000 Paradise Rd.; phone: 732-5111), closer to the Strip, offers another fine vantage point.

SPECIAL PLACES: Gambling is the name of the game in Las Vegas. The cultural aspects of the city are limited, but expanding, and its history has been all but obliterated by its rapid growth. But the surrounding area is rich in outdoor diversions that can fill your days with a wide variety of non-casino pleasures, leaving the nights for the air conditioned paradise of green felt, dazzling neon, and flashy production numbers.

THE STRIP

If gambling is the game, the Strip is the place. Shining brightly in the desert sun, this 3½-mile stretch of highway about 2 miles south of downtown glows more intensely at night, ablaze with the glittering opulence of a seemingly never-ending stream of hotels. The *MGM Grand* and *Treasure Island* hotels are under construction, and the Egyptian-theme *Luxor* (a *Circus Circus* property) is scheduled to open in October. The sky's the limit here, and one after another of the big hotels offer it — the *Sahara, Circus Circus, Flamingo Hilton, Harrah's, Riviera, Sands, Caesars Palace, Tropicana, Mirage,* and *Excalibur.* From slot machines, poker, and blackjack to the esoteric keno and baccarat of the casinos, to the production spectaculars with a cavalcade of stars in the main showrooms, to 24-hour breakfasts or dinners, it's all here and rolling around the clock. Las Vegas Blvd., just south of the city. Here are a few highlights:

Mirage – The brainchild of Steve Wynn, owner of the *Golden Nugget,* this 3,000-

room property cost $725 million to build — so far, the most expensive price tag in Las Vegas. Its opulent design features a gold-and-white Y-shaped edifice, cascading waterfalls, and a 60-foot volcano that erupts a piña colada–scented spray into the air every 15 minutes in the evenings. The volcano is rapidly becoming the city's trademark, like the Eiffel Tower — albeit on a smaller and far less tasteful scale. 3400 Las Vegas Blvd. S. (phone: 791-7111).

Excalibur – With 4,032 rooms, it's the newest and largest hotel in the world (until later this year, when the 5,007-room *MGM Grand* is scheduled to open). The façade looks like a castle out of a Hans Christian Andersen tale, complete with white turrets. 3850 Las Vegas Blvd. S. (phone: 597-7777).

Caesars Palace – Las Vegas's stab at ancient Rome, *Caesars Palace* outdoes its namesake in gaming. The only other similarities are the Romanesque names of casino areas and the fact that cocktail waitresses and keno runners dress in distinctive mini-togas. Otherwise, it's still one of the plushest in town. It also boasts one of the city's most lavish shopping centers, the recently opened *Forum Shops*. Superstars perform often; be sure to make reservations. 3570 Las Vegas Blvd. S. (phone: 731-7110).

Circus Circus – The first Vegas hotel to cater to families with children, with gambling on the ground and gamboling in the air. In this tent-shaped casino, trapeze and high-wire artists, clowns, acrobats, and dancers perform to the music of a brass band. The observation gallery at circus level is lined with food and carnival stands. Children are permitted in the gallery but not on the casino floor, so bring them along and everybody can have his or her own circus. Circus open 11 AM to midnight. No admission charge. 2880 Las Vegas Blvd. S. (phone: 734-0410).

Wet 'n' Wild – A 26-acre family-oriented water playground with a surf lagoon, water chutes, rapids, flumes, a 70-foot water drop called Der Stuka, and even pearl diving. Family rates and discount tickets are available at the Strip hotels. Open daily, early April to early October. 2600 Las Vegas Blvd. S., next to the *Sahara* hotel (phone: 737-3819).

Convention Center – One of the world's major convention destinations, this is Las Vegas's center. This modern steel structure is a million-square-foot complex. On Paradise Rd., next to the *Las Vegas Hilton,* off the Strip (phone: 733-2323).

DOWNTOWN

Golden Nugget – The most spectacular hotel downtown and one of the most glamorous in Las Vegas. Attractions include a marble-and-brass lobby, the biggest gold nugget in the world (weighing in at about 63 pounds), the $50-million Town House Tower with just 27 duplex suites, *Elaine's* and *Stefano's* restaurants for fine dining, and a 500-seat theater-ballroom. This is the only downtown property that does not use neon to decorate its exterior; instead, the outside of the building is encased in Italian marble. A must-see during any visit. 129 E. Fremont St. (phone: 385-7111).

THE OUTDOORS

Hoover Dam and Lake Mead – Completed in 1936, Hoover Dam is an awesome monument to man's engineering capabilities, a 726-foot-high concrete wall that tamed the mighty Colorado River and supplies electricity to Nevada, Arizona, and California. Daily tours. Modest admission charge; no admission charge for children under 15. Lake Mead, produced when the Colorado backed up behind the dam, is, at 115 miles long, one of the largest manmade lakes in the world. Fishing (bass, crappie, and catfish), swimming, and boating are available year-round. The visitors' center for Hoover Dam (phone: 293-1081) and the headquarters of Lake Mead National Recreation Area (phone: 293-8907) are 30 minutes south of the city on Boulder Highway (US 95). For information on guided tours, call 293-8321.

Mt. Charleston – Just 35 minutes west of the city, the 12,000-foot Mt. Charleston dramatically exhibits the effects of increased elevation with a wide variety of trees and wildlife. With plenty of cool, fresh mountain air, it's an excellent place for camping or hiking. During the winter months, snow covers the ground and temperatures often hover below freezing at the Lee Canyon ski slopes while vacationers swim in Las Vegas hotel pools just half an hour away. Take US 95 north to the Mt. Charleston exit, then follow the signs.

Red Rock Canyon Conservation Area – A beautiful desert locale featuring red and gold hues of sandstone formations, and spectacular views of steep canyons, Red Rock is becoming a popular rock climbing area. Just a few miles farther west, the Spring Mountain State Park has Old West buildings on a ranch that has belonged to such well-known capitalists as Howard Hughes and the German Krupp family (the armament folks). State rangers lead tours through the old buildings. W. Charleston Blvd., 15 miles west of the city (phone: 363-1921).

■ **EXTRA SPECIAL:** Just 2 hours northwest of Las Vegas lies Death Valley, the hottest, driest, and lowest area in the US. It also is starkly beautiful. The high mountains surrounding the 120-mile-long valley have isolated it, and of the 600 species of plants that have been identified there, 21 grow nowhere else on earth. The variety of the colors and textures of nature in the raw is remarkable, from the jagged bluish rock salt formations of Devil's Golf Course, to the smoothly sculpted golden dunes of Mesquite Flat, to the rich reds and purples of Telescope Peak at sunrise. Scotty's Castle, an eccentric and intricate mansion built in the middle of this expanse by a Chicago millionaire, is the area's most incongruous wonder. Because of extremely high temperatures in the summer, the best time to visit the valley is from November through April. The *Furnace Creek Inn* (phone: 619-786-2345) offers excellent accommodations. Take US 95 north to Lathrop Wells, then south on Route 373 to Death Valley Junction, then north on Route 190; follow the signs to the park (phone: 619-786-2331). See also *Tour 6: Death Valley National Monument, Rhyolite* in DIRECTIONS.

SOURCES AND RESOURCES

TOURIST INFORMATION: The Las Vegas Chamber of Commerce (2301 E. Sahara Ave., Las Vegas, NV 89104; phone: 457-4664) and the Las Vegas Convention and Visitors Authority (3150 Paradise Rd., Las Vegas, NV 89109; phone: 892-0711) are the best sources for brochures, maps, suggestions, and general tourist information. Contact the Nevada state hotline (phone: 800-NEVADA-8) for maps, calendars of events, health updates, and travel advisories.

Local Coverage – *Review Journal,* morning daily. Several weekly entertainment guides are available at newsstands.

Television Stations – KVBC Channel 3–NBC; KVVU Channel 5–Fox; KLAS Channel 8–CBS; KLVX Channel 10–PBS; KTNV Channel 13–ABC.

Radio Stations – AM: KDWN 720 (talk); KORK 920 (big band); KNUU 970 (news); KFM 1410 (country); KENO 1460 (oldies). FM: KNPR 89.5 (National Public Radio); KILA 90.5 (Christian music); KUNV 91.5 (jazz); KOMP 92.3 (rock 'n' roll); KEYV 93.1 (new age music); KXTZ 95.5 (easy listening); KLUC 98.5 (top 40); KKLZ 103.5 (classic rock).

Food – *Dining Out in Las Vegas,* by Elliot S. Krane (Elliot S. Krane & Associates, Publishers; $14), offers a knowledgeable opinion on area restaurants. To order a copy, contact the publishers at 2822 Bridgepointe Dr., Las Vegas, NV 89121-4147.

Entertainment – *What's On,* a weekly entertainment guide to the city, covers everything from theater to music to nightlife. A sample copy costs $3.50 (send check or money order to *What's On,* 610 S. Third St., Las Vegas, NV 89101).

TELEPHONE: The area code for Las Vegas is 702.

SALES TAX: A tax of 7% is levied on all purchases except groceries; there also is an 8% hotel tax.

GETTING AROUND: Although Las Vegas is not really a large city, the summer heat makes walking difficult. If you are going any farther than a hundred yards or so, you'll probably do better on wheels.

Bus – The *Las Vegas Transit System* covers the downtown area and the Strip. The discount commuter ticket offers a real savings if you expect to use the buses frequently. Route information is available at 1550 Industrial Rd. (phone: 384-3540). All fares are $1.25.

Car Rental – For information on renting a car, see *On Arrival,* GETTING READY TO GO.

Taxi – Cabs can be hailed in the street, ordered on the phone, or picked up at taxi stands in front of hotels. Major companies are *Whittlesea Cab* (phone: 384-6111); *Yellow and Checker Cab* (phone: 873-2000); and *Desert Cab* (phone: 386-4828).

LOCAL SERVICES: Audiovisual Equipment – *Las Vegas Video Sound Rentals* (phone: 362-4660); *Nevada Audio Visual Services* (phone: 876-6272).

Baby-sitting – *Sandy's Sitter Service,* 24-hour service, 953 E. Sahara (phone: 731-2086).

Business Services – *Manpower Temporary Services,* 314 Las Vegas Blvd. N. (phone: 386-2626).

Check Cashing – *A-Able Check Cashing,* 3049 Las Vegas Blvd. S., across from the *Stardust* hotel (phone: 732-2541).

Computer Rental – *Business Computer Rentals,* 3560 Polaris Ave. (phone: 871-8009).

Dry Cleaner/Tailor – *Al Phillips, the Cleaner,* open 24 hours, 3659 S. Maryland Pkwy., in the *Maryland Square Shopping Center* (phone: 735-2805).

Limousine – *Bell Trans* (phone: 739-7990); *Lucky 7* (phone: 739-6277).

Mechanic – *Stiver's,* 2300 Western (phone: 385-2407).

Medical Emergency – *Humana Hospital–Sunrise* (3186 Maryland Pkwy.; phone: 731-8000); *University Medical Center* (1800 W. Charleston; phone: 383-2074).

Messenger Services – *Armored Transport* (phone: 457-3934).

National/International Courier – *Federal Express* (phone: 800-238-5355); *DHL Worldwide Courier Express* (phone: 798-4090).

Pharmacy – *White Cross Drugs,* open 24 hours (1700 Las Vegas Blvd. S.; phone: 382-1733); *Village East,* open 8 AM to midnight (5025 S. Eastern Ave.; phone: 736-7081).

Photocopies – *Kinko's* (4440 S. Maryland Pkwy.; phone: 735-4402); *PDQ,* (3820 S. Valley View; phone: 876-3235).

Post Office – Main office is near the airport (1001 E. Sunset Rd.; phone: 361-9212);

there is a downtown office (301 E. Stewart Ave.; phone: 385-8944); and there's another along the Strip (1001 Circus Circus Dr.; phone: 735-2525).

Professional Photographer – *Photo Finish* (phone: 732-1878); *Positive Images* (phone: 791-3287).

Secretary/Stenographer – *Best Business Support Services* (phone: 737-3900).

Teleconference Facilities – *Caesars Palace* (3570 Las Vegas Blvd. S.; phone: 731-7110) and *Las Vegas Hilton* (3000 Paradise Rd.; phone: 732-5111) offer facilities.

Translator – *Arriaga's Bilingual Services* (phone: 382-5497).

Typewriter Rental – *TAC*, 1-day minimum (phone: 736-2657).

Western Union/Telex – Many offices are located around the city (phone: 800-325-6000).

Other – The *Home Office* provides office space, photocopying, and typing services (phone: 873-5700).

■ **Wedding Bells Are Always Ringing in Las Vegas:** If you are at least 18 (16 with parental consent), and you feel a sudden urge to legally merge, it's easy to tie the knot on the spot. Just apply at the Las Vegas Marriage License Bureau at the Clark County Courthouse (3rd and Carson Sts.; phone: 455-3156; after hours, 455-4415); there's not even a blood test or waiting period, just a $35 fee for the license. Open round the clock on Fridays, Saturdays and holidays; till midnight Mondays through Thursdays. Then head to the altar, say "I do," and the deed is done. Many of the hotels in town have wedding chapels and offer honeymoon packages; other well-known places to get hitched are the *Candlelight Wedding Chapel* (2855 Las Vegas Blvd. S.; phone: 735-4179) and *Little Church of the West* (3960 Las Vegas Blvd. S.; phone: 739-7971), where Dudley Moore and Clark Gable got married (not to each other). They don't call this place the "Wedding Capital of the World" for nothing.

SPECIAL EVENTS: Las Vegas rings in the start of a new year with a huge *New Year's Eve* bash. The big hotels feature lavish entertainment — with name performers such as Frank Sinatra, Liza Minnelli, and Shirley MacLaine — and there are fancy-dress balls with dinner and dancing. Even if you didn't have enough forethought (or capital) to secure tickets to these events, you can still have a good time at the downtown block party, where 4 blocks of Fremont Street are closed off for *New Year's* revelers. At midnight, fireworks go off at the *Plaza* hotel.

The *Las Vegas International Marathon* will be held February 6 this year. In March or April, the *Desert Inn* (3145 Las Vegas Blvd. S.; phone: 733-4444) hosts the *LPGA International Golf Tournament;* the *World Series of Poker* is played at *Binion's Horseshoe* (128 Fremont St.; phone: 382-1600) in April or May. The *Senior Classic Golf Tournament* is held in April or May at the *Desert Inn.* During the *Helldorado Festival,* held from May 21 through May 30 this year, the city celebrates its western heritage with rodeos, parades, and beauty contests. The *Jaycees State Fair* takes place in October at the *Convention Center* and has carnival acts, magic shows, rides, livestock, and craft exhibits. The 5-day *Las Vegas Invitational Golf Tournament* is held in October at the *Desert Inn.* The 10-day *National Finals Rodeo* opens in early December at the *Thomas and Mack Center* (on the campus of the University of Nevada at Las Vegas; phone: 731-3900).

MUSEUMS: Though it's not noted for its cultural draw, Las Vegas and its environs do contain a few museums and places of interest. Many of the hotels have commercial art exhibitions with works of well-known artists. *Herigstad's Gallery* (2290 E. Flamingo Rd.; phone: 733-7366) has art shows as well as works for sale. Open from 10 AM to 6 PM; closed Sundays. Also worth a visit is *Minotaur Fine Arts Ltd.* (in the *Fashion Show Mall;* phone: 737-1400). Open weekdays 9:30 AM to 9 PM, Saturdays 9:30 AM to 7 PM, Sundays 11 AM to 6 PM. Some other museums of note are listed below.

Boulder City, Hoover Dam Museum – This place was established to preserve the historical artifacts relating to the construction of Hoover Dam (also known as Boulder Dam) in the 1930s. There are exhibits chronicling the workers' lifestyle during the time the dam was being built. A movie detailing the process of building the dam is shown several times daily. Open daily from 9 AM to 5 PM. Admission charge. 444 Hotel Plaza, Boulder City (phone: 294-1988).

Clark County Heritage Museum – Exhibits displayed in several buildings depict the early pioneer and mining history of southern Nevada. On the grounds — located between Las Vegas and Boulder City — is "Heritage Street," a row of houses from the 1920s, 1930s, and 1940s, complete with period furnishings, as well as a 1905 *Union Pacific* steam engine. Open 9 AM to 4:30 PM daily. Admission charge. 1830 S. Boulder Hwy., Henderson (phone: 455-7955).

Guinness World of Records Museum – A collection detailing many of the world records and feats found in the *Guinness Book of Records*. The museum is divided into six sections: Sports World; Amazing Humans; Nature's Wonders; Music, Arts, and Entertainment; Amazing Animals; and Buildings and Structures. Exhibits include a model of the world's tallest man (8 feet, 11 inches), displays on Death Valley, which holds the record for the highest temperature sustained over a long period of time (120F or more for 43 consecutive days), and the Grand Canyon (the world's largest land gorge), and videos of some of the records being set. There's also a special display focusing on Las Vegas. Open daily. Admission charge. 2780 Las Vegas Blvd. S., next to the *Circus Circus* hotel (phone: 792-3766).

Imperial Palace Auto Collection – More than 200 antique and classic vehicles are on display here, including a 1939 armored parade car that once belonged to Adolf Hitler, and one of Al Capone's cars. Open from 9 AM to 11:30 PM daily. Admission charge. 3535 Las Vegas Blvd. S., in the *Imperial Palace* hotel (phone: 731-3311).

Las Vegas Art Museum – Located in Lorenzi Park, this museum features a permanent collection of 20th-century Occidental art, as well as several galleries with temporary exhibits. Open Tuesdays through Saturdays from 10 AM to 3 PM; Sundays, from noon to 3 PM; closed Mondays. No admission charge. 3333 W. Washington Ave. (phone: 647-4300).

Las Vegas Natural History Museum – Exhibits feature animal life — from prehistoric to the present — including woodcarvings, wildlife paintings, artifacts, and more than 2,000 birds, fish, and mammals, preserved and mounted. Open from 9 AM to 4 PM daily. Admission charge. 900 Las Vegas Blvd. N. (phone: 384-3466).

Liberace Museum – Three buildings house the late, flamboyant entertainer's costumes, pianos, and automobiles, along with other memorabilia of his life and work. This is the third most popular attraction in the state, after the casinos and Hoover Dam. Open from 10 AM to 5 PM daily. Admission charge (the proceeds go toward music scholarships). 1775 E. Tropicana Ave. (phone: 798-5595).

Lied Discovery Children's Museum – Youngsters can learn about science and the humanities from the hands-on displays on pollution, weather, computers and electronics, and hot-air balloons. Open from 10 AM to 5 PM daily. Admission charge. 833 Las Vegas Blvd. N., across from the *Natural History Museum* (phone: 382-5437).

Mineral Collection – A display of 1,000 specimens of gems and minerals from the area and around the world. Open weekdays from 8 AM to 4:30 PM; closed weekends. No admission charge. At the University of Nevada at Las Vegas, Geoscience Hall, Room 103 (phone: 739-3262).

Museum of Natural History – Also at the University of Nevada at Las Vegas, this collection features Native American artifacts and live desert reptiles. Open weekdays from 9 AM to 4:45 PM; Saturdays, from 10 AM to 2 PM; closed Sundays. No admission charge. 4505 S. Maryland Pkwy. (phone: 739-3381).

Nevada State Museum and Historical Society – Four galleries contain dioramas depicting the history of southern Nevada, with emphasis on prehistoric humans. Native American culture and lifestyles over the past 13,000 years are shown, as are the area's characteristic plants, animals, and geographic features. Also included is an exhibit on the development and use of neon. Open from 8:30 AM to 4:30 PM daily. Admission charge. 700 Twin Lakes Dr., Lorenzi Park (phone: 486-5205).

Ripley's Believe It or Not Odditorium – Here are peculiar items from around the world, including shrunken heads, Rube Goldberg contraptions, and a photograph of a man with three eyes. Honest. Open daily from 9 AM to midnight. Admission charge. In the *Four Queens Hotel,* 202 Fremont St. (phone: 385-4011).

Other museums worth visiting are *Dolphin Habitat* (in the *Mirage Hotel;* 3400 Las Vegas Blvd. S.; phone: 791-7188) and the *Lost City Museum of Archaeology* (in the Valley of Fire area, 63 miles northeast of Las Vegas; phone: 397-2193).

MAJOR COLLEGES AND UNIVERSITIES: The University of Nevada at Las Vegas is the largest school in the area, with an enrollment of 24,000; 4505 S. Maryland Pkwy. (phone: 739-3011).

SHOPPING: It doesn't get top billing in Las Vegas; visitors come here to spend their money at the casinos, not to search for the best bargains. However, there are several shopping centers with high-fashion boutiques and chain department stores such as *Sears* and *JC Penney;* many of the top hotels contain posh arcades as well.

The Fashion Show Mall (3200 Las Vegas Blvd. S.; phone: 369-8382) is an upscale, 34-acre shopping center with 145 stores, including *Saks Fifth Avenue, Bullock's, Neiman Marcus,* and *May Company,* as well as *Chin's,* a first-rate Chinese restaurant (see *Eating Out*); the recently renovated *Boulevard Mall* (3528 S. Maryland Pkwy.; phone: 735-8268), located a few blocks from the Strip, has *Sears, JC Penney,* and *Dillard's* as its main stores. The *Meadows Mall,* 3 miles northwest of the Strip, has more than 140 stores, including *Sears, JC Penney, The Limited,* and *Frederick's of Hollywood* (4300 Meadows La.; phone: 878-4849). And the newest mall in town, the recently opened *Forum Shops* (located adjacent to *Caesars Palace;* 3570 Las Vegas Blvd. S.; phone: 731-7110), is a 240,000-square-foot luxury complex with such tony boutiques as *Victoria's Secret, Gucci, Louis Vuitton,* and *Porsche Design,* as well as a branch of *Spago,* the famous Los Angeles restaurant, and the *Palm,* the well-known New York and Los Angeles steakhouse.

There are also a couple of specialty shops focusing on — you guessed it — gambling. *Gambler's Book Club* deals primarily in both new and used books about aspects of gambling such as its history, rules of the games, and the influence of organized crime on its development (630 S. 11th St.; phone: 382-7555). Many types of gaming souvenirs and memorabilia, from dice and cards to slot machines, can be found at *Gambler's General Store* (800 S. Main St.; phone: 382-9903). For western-style clothing, try *Sam's Town Western Emporium;* you'll find a good selection of cowboy boots and hats, jewelry, belt buckles, and string ties (5111 Boulder Hwy.; phone: 454-8017).

SPORTS AND FITNESS: Las Vegas offers a wide variety of sporting events and fine facilities.

Baseball – The Las Vegas *Stars,* a farm club for the San Diego *Padres,* plays from April through September at *Cashman Field,* 850 Las Vegas Blvd. N. (phone: 386-7200).

Basketball – The University of Nevada at Las Vegas has fielded one of the finest collegiate basketball teams in the nation for several years — the *Runnin' Rebels* were the 1990 NCAA Champions. (Though they have fallen into some disfavor due to a recent recruiting scandal, their fans have remained loyal.) They play from February to April in the *Thomas and Mack Center,* an 18,000-seat arena. Tickets usually are available, but for really good seats your hotel bell captain or casino pit boss would be helpful (phone: 739-3267).

Betting – If you want to bet on almost any athletic event taking place outside of Nevada, numerous race and sports bookmakers dot the city. The most lavish facilities on the Strip are in *Caesars Palace* (3570 Las Vegas Blvd. S.; phone: 731-7110), the *Mirage* (3400 Las Vegas Blvd. S.; phone: 791-7111), the *Stardust* hotel (3000 Las Vegas Blvd.S.; phone: 732-6111), and the *Las Vegas Hilton* (3000 Paradise Rd.; phone: 732-5111). *Plaza's Book* tops the downtown locales for laying odds (1 Main St.; phone: 386-2110).

Boxing – If punching is your bag, the major hotels promote many boxing matches. Major bouts between professional heavyweight contenders are held from time to time at *Caesars Palace,* the *Las Vegas Hilton,* and the *Mirage.*

Fishing – You can wet a line all year round at Lake Mead, the manmade body of water created by Hoover Dam. Among the types of fish here are striped and largemouth bass, crappie, catfish, and bluegill. Licenses for 3 or 10 days can be purchased at any of the five marinas around the lake, and there are boats for rent, too. Lake Mead Marina (phone: 293-3484).

Fitness Centers – Most Las Vegas hotels have fitness centers. Among them: The health club at *Caesars Palace* has a whirlpool bath, steamroom, and exercise equipment, but no pool (3570 Las Vegas Blvd. S., 15th Floor; phone: 731-7110); the *Aristocrat Health Spa,* in the *Las Vegas Hilton,* has a sauna, whirlpool bath, and massage (3000 Paradise Rd., 3rd Floor on the pool deck; phone: 732-5111); a multimillion-dollar facility has been added to the *Desert Inn and Country Club* (3145 Las Vegas Blvd. S.; phone: 733-4444); the *Mirage* has men's and women's spa facilities, an exercise room and aerobics studios (3400 Las Vegas Blvd. S.; phone: 791-7111); and the *Golden Nugget* hotel sports a coed gym with sauna, whirlpool bath, and exercise equipment (129 E. Fremont St.; phone: 385-7111).

Football – From September to January, the University of Nevada at Las Vegas's *Rebels* football team plays at the *Sam Boyd Silver Bowl,* 7000 E. Russell Rd. (phone: 739-3900).

Golf – Dozens of courses dot the desert landscape. The *Sahara Country Club* (1911 E. Desert Inn Rd.; phone: 796-0013) and the *Desert Inn Country Club* (3145 Las Vegas Blvd. S.; phone: 733-4290) are the best. For lower greens fees, try the public courses. Best bet is the *Las Vegas Golf Club* (Washington Ave. and Decatur Blvd.; phone: 646-3003), which offers a reasonable challenge and good greens. The *Dunes* hotel (3650 Las Vegas Blvd. S.; phone: 737-4747) also has an 18-hole course that is open to non-guests. A few miles northwest of the city, *Angel Park Country Club* (100 S. Rampart Blvd.; phone: 254-4653) has an 18-hole Arnold Palmer–designed course, and a second course. Also just out of the city, in nearby Henderson, is the 18-hole, Arthur Hill–designed *Legacy Golf Club* (130 Par Excellence Dr., Henderson; phone: 897-2187). The city has more than 15 additional courses; for information, contact the Nevada Commission on Tourism (5151 S. Carson St., Carson City, NV 89710; phone: 687-4322).

Jogging – It's possible to run right along the Strip between Flamingo Road and Spring Mountain, where there are no cross streets to slow the pace (about one-half mile each way); stay on the *Caesars Palace* side. Another possibility is Squires Park, one-half mile from downtown; or drive to Sunset Park, 7 miles from downtown, or Bob Baskin Park, W. Oakey Blvd. at Rancho Dr. The University of Nevada at Las Vegas has a jogging track, as do most of the city's high schools. Note that at the height of the summer, the heat can make running a dangerous sport, even in the morning; however, determined joggers may run inside at the air conditioned *Fashion Show Mall* (3200 Las Vegas Blvd. S.) before its stores open at 10 AM.

Skiing – Believe it or not, Las Vegas is only an hour away from the slopes. *Lee Canyon,* a resort at Mt. Charleston, is about 45 miles northwest of the city. The 8,000-foot ski area, with natural and manmade snow, is good for downhill skiiing. The season runs from December through February (phone: 872-5462; for snow conditions, 593-9500).

Tennis – Many of the Strip hotels have good tennis facilities open to the public.

THEATER: For current performances, check the publications listed above. Outside of the entertainment at the Strip hotels, there are some old standbys, such as the *New West Stage Company* (phone: 876-6972), which presents its season at the *Charleston Heights Arts Center* (901 Brush St.; phone: 229-6383); and the *Actor's Repertory Theater,* which performs at the Clark County Library (1401 E. Flamingo Rd.; phone: 647-7469); plus a number of local theater groups that all keep the curtains raised. The best bet for shows is the *Repertory Theater* at *Judy Bayley Theatre* (University of Nevada at Las Vegas campus; phone: 739-3801). The Clark County Community College and other local companies are featured in *Theatre Under the Stars,* outdoors at the *Spring Mountain Ranch* in late June and early July. The creative sets make fine use of the environment, and the acting is first-rate. Tickets can be purchased at the ranch (Spring Mountain Rd., 18 miles west on Charleston Blvd.; phone: 875-4141). The *Nevada Dance Theatre* (phone: 739-3838) performs at the *Judy Bayley Theatre;* the *Nevada Opera Theatre* (phone: 737-6373), at *Artemus W. Ham Concert Hall.*

MUSIC: Symphony concerts, opera, and jazz are featured during the school year at *Artemus W. Ham Concert Hall* and the *Judy Bayley Theatre* on the UNLV campus. For tickets, call 739-3801. The *Las Vegas Chamber Orchestra,* under the baton of Rudolfo Fernandez, plays at the Clark County Library (1401 E. Flamingo Rd.; phone: 647-7469).

NIGHTCLUBS AND NIGHTLIFE: When it comes to nightlife, Las Vegas is king. The city never sleeps, and can keep visitors who want to keep the same hours entertained all night.

The Strip hotels offer a wide variety of entertainment, with musical and comedy headliners such as Liza Minnelli, Bill Cosby, Joan Rivers, Frank Sinatra, and Julio Iglesias. There are nightly production spectaculars, with dancing girls, lavish costumes and sets, and all kinds of specialty acts. *Jubilee* at *Bally's* (3645 Las Vegas Blvd. S.; phone: 739-4111), with a cast of more than 100 singers and dancers performing on one of the largest stages in the world, is the most extravagant. Other notables of this genre are Siegfried & Roy at the *Mirage* (3400 Las Vegas Blvd. S.; phone: 791-7111), featuring the famed illusionists performing magic on a grand and gaudy scale; *Splash* at the *Riviera* (2901 Las Vegas Blvd. S.; phone: 734-5110), with Esther Williams–style production numbers; the French cancan dancing of the *Folies Bergère* at the *Tropicana* (3801 Las Vegas Blvd. S.; phone: 739-2222); *City Lites* at the *Flamingo Hilton* (3555 Las Vegas Blvd. S.; phone: 733-3111), featuring both dance numbers and choreographed figure skating; and the newest, *Enter the Night* at the *Stardust* (3000 Las Vegas Blvd. S.; phone: 732-6111), with a gymnast/acrobat sharing the stage with some scantily clad showgirls. The *Imperial Palace* (3535 Las

Vegas Blvd. S.; phone: 731-3311) offers a show exclusively featuring dead performers — Elvis, Marilyn Monroe, Louis Armstrong, Buddy Holly, Judy Garland, Hank Williams — all portrayed by talented impersonators. *Boy-lesque,* at the *Plaza* hotel Downtown (1 Main St.; phone: 386-2110), is a Vegas institution (previously at the *Sahara* and then the *Stardust*) for specialized tastes — audiences who enjoy *La Cage aux Folles*-type shows in which boys will, if they put their minds to it, be girls. Smaller-scale productions can be seen at several hotels, including the *Sahara* (2535 Las Vegas Blvd. S.; phone: 737-2111) and the *Rio* (3700 W. Flamingo Rd.; phone: 252-7777).

In the main showrooms of all the other hotels on the Strip, a constant parade of stars performs to audiences of 800 to 1,200 people. The *Tropicana* and *Flamingo Hilton* serve dinner at the early show. There's no cover charge, but the minimum runs about $10 to $35 per person for dinner shows and $6 to $35 for late "drinks-only" shows. The *Excalibur* serves a Renaissance dinner, with two shows a night — depicting the Arthurian legend — for $24.95, including dinner, drink, taxes, tip, and show.

Note that the procedure for getting into these shows has changed. At many of the hotels, you can buy a ticket for a specific seat instead of making a general admission reservation and being seated by the maître d' at the door, as was done in the past. Keep a few things in mind when you are trying to get reservations or tickets to shows: Hotel guests get first priority for many shows, so consider staying at the hotel that has the show you most want to see. Always call in the morning, or better still, go in person to buy tickets or make reservations. Most hotels do *not* take show reservations or tickets more than 1 day in advance. The ticket booths open at 10 in the morning and stay open till show time, and the earlier you get there the better. If you've been gambling a good deal, ask the pit boss for assistance, and if you haven't you might try tipping the bell captain and hoping for the best. Bring along a sweater — or jacket — as powerful air conditioners are at work everywhere. And though dress is casual during the day, the showtime dress at night can be more formal and occasionally even elegant, but it's optional.

Often overlooked are the casino lounges, where lesser-known performers (many of whom — like Wayne Newton, Kenny Rogers, and Don Rickles — soon become better known) perform for just the cost of your drinks. Comedy clubs are gaining in popularity as well; the best ones are at *Bally's* (3645 Las Vegas Blvd. S.; phone: 739-4111), the *Aladdin* (3667 Las Vegas Blvd. S.; phone: 736-0111), the *Riviera* (2901 Las Vegas Blvd. S.; phone: 734-5110), and the *Tropicana* (3801 Las Vegas Blvd. S.; phone: 739-2222).

Favorite non-hotel clubs are the *Shark Club* (75 E. Harmon Ave.; phone: 795-7525), the *Hop* (1650 E. Tropicana Ave.; phone: 736-2020), *L.J.'s Sports Bar* (4405 W. Flamingo Rd.; phone: 871-1424), and the trendy *Metz* disco (3765 Las Vegas Blvd. S.; phone: 739-8855). Try the *Silver Dollar Saloon* (2501 E. Charleston Blvd.; phone: 382-6921), *Sam's Town Western Dance Hall* (5010 Boulder Hwy.; phone: 456-7777), or *Rockabilly's* (4660 Boulder Hwy.; phone: 458-0096) for live country-and-western music.

Las Vegas also presents the best-known burlesque/striptease artists in the world. Tops (or topless, more likely) is the *Palomino Club,* 1848 Las Vegas Blvd. N. (phone: 642-2984). Other choices are *Crazy Horse One and Two* (4034 Paradise Rd.; phone: 732-1116) and the *Can Can Room* (3155 Industrial Rd.; phone: 737-1161).

- **SEX TEASE CLUBS:** Watch out for brothels masquerading as legitimate nightclubs (some places even advertise in the local yellow pages). Once you enter the club, a "waitress" will offer to perform certain favors if you purchase a $300 bottle of champagne (and we're not talking Dom Perignon). If you find yourself in this situation, keep in mind that although prostitution is legal in some areas of Nevada, it is *not* legal in Las Vegas; your best bet is to steer clear of these clubs.

BEST IN TOWN

CHECKING IN: In Vegas, the hotel's the thing. The Strip (Las Vegas Boulevard South) is a 4-mile stream of hotel-casinos and motels, nearly matched in number — though usually not in quality — by the downtown "Glitter Gulch" area. Though most hotels feature gambling as one of their main attractions, there are some places that provide accommodations without the high-rolling betting atmosphere. Competition is fierce among the major hotels, and keeps room costs modest and on a par with one another; rates are lowest during the 2 weeks before *Christmas;* discounts can be as much as 60%, even at the most luxurious hotels. In general, expect to pay $95 and up for a double room per night in the expensive range; $40 to $60, moderate; around $20 to $35, inexpensive. All telephone numbers are in the 702 area code unless otherwise indicated.

Alexis Park – The first place in town not to offer an on-premises casino, this 500-suite hotel offers luxurious accommodations, fine dining, and the convenience of being close to the airport and the *Convention Center.* Every suite is tastefully decorated, and some boast Jacuzzis. There is a swimming pool nestled in 20 acres of gardens and waterfalls, and *Pegasus,* the restaurant, is first-rate (see *Eating Out*). Other amenities include 24-hour room service (though you can get hot food only between 6 AM and 11 PM), tennis courts, an exercise room, and 2 meeting rooms. 375 E. Harmon Ave. (phone: 796-3300 or 800-582-2228; fax: 796-0766). Expensive.

Bally's – More grandiose than ever: with 3,000 rooms, it also has 6 restaurants — among them *Caruso's* for Italian food and *Gigi* for elegant fish and seafood dishes (see *Eating Out* for both) — a 40-store shopping arcade, the *Ziegfeld Room* for lavish production numbers, and the *Celebrity Room* for top-name entertainment. The hotel also features two excellent buffets, the Sterling Brunch on Sundays and the Big Kitchen Buffet daily, served in a dining room on the second floor. Health spas, tennis courts, an Olympic-size swimming pool, 24-hour room service, 42 meeting rooms, A/V equipment, photocopiers, CNN, and express checkout are some of the amenities offered here. 3645 Las Vegas Blvd. S. (phone: 739-4111 or 800-634-3434; fax: 739-4405). Expensive.

Caesars Palace – One of the images that immediately comes to mind when the subject of Las Vegas hotels is mentioned — it celebrated its *Silver Anniversary* in 1991. Even the most basic of its 1,600 rooms are ornate, while the high-roller suites are tributes to excess, with large classical statues to make you feel right at home — if you've just flown in from ancient Rome. Ten of the suites are 2-level units with 4 bedrooms, mirrored ceilings, private dining rooms, in-room saunas, sunken Roman tubs, and a commanding view of the Strip. The service is excellent, and the location — midway on the Strip — puts guests right in the middle of the action. It has big-name entertainment, cafés, bars, restaurants (see *Eating Out*), an Olympic-size swimming pool, tennis, golf privileges, the *Forum Shops* (a posh new shopping arcade), and free parking. Reservations are a must during the summer, especially on holiday weekends. There are 40 meeting rooms for business needs, as well as A/V equipment and photocopiers. Express checkout, CNN, and 24-hour room service are other pluses. 3570 Las Vegas Blvd. S. (phone: 731-7110 or 800-634-6661; fax: 731-6636). Expensive.

Desert Inn – This place occupies a singular position in Las Vegas history: Its purchase by Howard Hughes in 1966 sparked the influx of investment that turned the fledgling gambling center into the resort complex it is today. More like a city than a hotel, the accommodations here are vast (though it is far from the largest hotel in the city). There are 5 locations on 2,000 acres with rooms and suites (820 separate units altogether), each offering something unique. There's the Wimbledon, for example, a 7-story pyramid structure which practically sits on the golf course. Or, if you'd like to look out over the Strip and the mountains of Nevada, Augusta Tower can satisfy both desires. The rooms include amenities such as wet bars, refrigerators, private patios and swimming pools, and phones in the bathroom. The dining facilities are numerous and just as varied, including the exquisite *Monte Carlo Room* (see *Eating Out*). There is a spectacular casino, several bars, a health spa, golf courses, a pool, tennis courts, and many shops, including separate golf and tennis pro shops. Plus 6 meeting rooms (with A/V equipment and photocopiers available), CNN, and a *Hertz* rental car counter, if you should feel the need (but why?) to leave. Room service is available around the clock; express checkout. 3145 Las Vegas Blvd. S. (phone: 733-4444 or 800-634-6906; fax: 733-4774). Expensive.

Marriott's Residence Inn – Offering the casual comfort of apartment living and the amenities of a hotel, its 192 suites have fully equipped kitchens and living rooms with fireplaces; there's also a swimming pool and exercise facilities, a complimentary continental breakfast, and a grocery shopping service. While there is no restaurant, several excellent dining spots are nearby, particularly in the *Las Vegas Hilton* across the street. A coin-operated laundry is on the premises. Note: There is no casino or gambling here. 3225 Paradise Rd. (phone: 796-9300 or 800-331-3131). Expensive.

Mirage – Among the newer Strip spots, this $725-million property has become the talk of the town. The theme is decidedly tropical: The lobby is decorated with lush plants, waterfalls, lagoons, and an aquarium stocked with exotic fish, and a volcano — complete with flames and piña colada–scented smoke — erupts outside every 15 minutes after dark. Set on 100 acres, the resort has 3,000 rooms with light-colored cane and rattan furnishings, bright, cheerful fabrics, and tropical flowers; guests may choose among double rooms of varying sizes, 1- and 2-bedroom suites, and deluxe penthouse suites. Other amenities include international dining in 8 restaurants, a spa and salon, shops, convention facilities, 15 meeting rooms, and a Polynesian-theme casino. Natural habitats in the lobby display a rain forest, sharks, and white tigers, and there is a dolphin pool near the swimming pool. Illusionists Siegfried and Roy perform here regularly and make everything from tigers to full-size elephants disappear. The hotel's photocopiers and A/V equipment are at guests' disposal, as are 24-hour room service and express checkout. 3400 Las Vegas Blvd. S. (phone: 791-7111 or 800-627-6667; fax: 791-7414). Expensive.

St. Tropez – Next door to the *Alexis Park*, this is another non-gaming, all-suite hotel. Its 150 attractively furnished suites include 2-line phones, work areas with computer hookups, and VCRs. Fitness facilities feature a swimming pool, exercise room, and a spa; there is a concierge and a ballroom that can accommodate up to 300 people. 455 E. Harmon Ave. (phone: 369-5400 or 800-666-5400; fax: 369-5845). Expensive.

Golden Nugget – One of the glitzier of the downtown spots, combining an overall turn-of-the-century look with mountains of marble, brass, and crystal in its casino, spa, and entertainment room. The 1,908 rooms are attractively decorated in light colors. *Stefano's* and *Elaine's,* named after owners Steve and Elaine Wynn, feature fine, elegant continental fare. Displayed in the lobby is the largest gold nugget in the world; discovered in Wetterburn, Australia, it weighs about 63 pounds. Amenities include 24-hour room service, a health spa with a fully equipped exercise room, Jacuzzis, steambaths, and saunas, a concierge desk, 12 meeting rooms,

A/V equipment, photocopiers, CNN, and express checkout. 129 E. Fremont St. (phone: 385-7111 or 800-634-3454; fax: 386-8362). Expensive to moderate.

Las Vegas Hilton – With 3,100 rooms, it claimed the title of "Biggest in Vegas" until the coming of the *Excalibur*. Off the Strip next to the *Convention Center*, it's not in the middle of the glitter, but neither is it in the center of traffic. With star entertainment, a café, bars, restaurants (see *Eating Out*), a 10-acre rooftop recreation center with a pool, tennis, a health club, putting greens and golf privileges, shops, and free parking. Business facilities include 41 meeting rooms, A/V equipment, CNN, and photocopiers. Twenty-four-hour room service can easily provide you with a quick bite, and express checkout expedites your departure. 3000 Paradise Rd. (phone: 732-5111 or 800-HILTONS; fax: 732-5249). Expensive to moderate.

Aladdin – The former owners ditched the Arabian theme and spent $30 million to give all its 1,100 rooms, 8 restaurants, and reception and public areas a more modern look. The *Florentine Room* features Italian fare, and *Fisherman's Port* has a Cajun/seafood menu. Other facilities include the Baghdad showroom, pools, meeting rooms, shops, and tennis courts. 3667 Las Vegas Blvd. S. (phone: 736-0111). Moderate.

Excalibur – At 4,032 rooms, this is the world's largest resort (though it will be relegated to second-largest when the *MGM Grand* opens later this year). The rooms have a castle-like decor, with red and blue fabrics and wallpaper that resembles stonework; baths have oversize showers and tubs. The medieval theme is continued by the staff, who dress in clothing reminiscent of the time of King Henry VIII, and the jugglers, magicians, and sword swallowers who perform on the second floor, near the restaurants. Two dinner shows nightly offer Arthurian performances and royal feasting in Renaissance style, and there are 6 other restaurants, as well. The *Magic Motion Theater* gives guests the feeling of being on a roller coaster ride without leaving their seats. Room service is available until 11 PM. Other conveniences are photocopiers and express checkout. 3850 Las Vegas Blvd. S. (phone: 597-7777 or 800-939-7777; fax: 798-3388). Moderate.

Flamingo Hilton – Benjamin "Bugsy" Siegel opened this hotel as the *Flamingo* in 1946; after its almost instant failure, it passed from owner to owner until the Hilton group took it over in 1971. Its 3,529 comfortable guestrooms, decorated in contemporary style in lavender, gray, and maroon, include the "Bugsy Siegel Suite," which has a secret passageway leading to the street — just in case. *City Lites,* one of the few remaining dinner shows in the city, is performed nightly. There are 8 restaurants, including the *Flamingo Room* (see *Eating Out*); other amenities include a fitness center with exercise equipment, Jacuzzis, and massage, 14 meeting rooms, A/V equipment, and express checkout. 3555 Las Vegas Blvd. S. (phone: 733-3111 or 800-732-2111; fax: 733-3499). Moderate.

Harrah's – Formerly the *Holiday Casino,* this property recently was acquired by Harrah's, which at press time was planning some renovations. In the heart of the Strip, the building looks like a riverboat lit up with neon — one of the most unusual façades in the city; it contains 725 comfortable but unprepossessing rooms. There are 5 restaurants, including *Claudine's* (see *Eating Out*), Amenities include a showroom, a swimming pool, and a spa and fitness center; the limited business services feature a fax machine and a photocopier and meeting space that can accommodate up to 1,200. 3475 Las Vegas Blvd. S. (phone: 369-5000 or 800-634-6765). Moderate.

Plaza – Recently acquired by Jackie Gaughan, who owns several smaller Las Vegas properties, this large (1,020-room) place, with the most complete facilities downtown, sits at the entranceway to the downtown "Glitter Gulch" action. Facilities include a pool, tennis courts, a café, a bar, a restaurant, shops, 11 meeting rooms, and a casino. Room service is available until 10:30 PM. 1 Main St. (phone: 386-2110 or 800-634-6575; fax: 382-8281). Moderate.

Rio – An all-suite hotel near the Strip, all of the 424 rooms have floor-to-ceiling windows, a separate dressing area, maple furniture, and king-size beds; refrigerators and coffee makers (with complimentary coffee) are also included. Some of the suites offer views overlooking *Caesars Palace* and the rest of the Strip. The hotel swimming pool has waterfalls and a "beach" made of real sand (purportedly from Rio de Janeiro), and there are volleyball courts. Other amenities include 7 restaurants, among them the first-rate *Antonio's* (see *Eating Out*), 24-hour room service, and express checkout. 3700 W. Flamingo Rd. (phone: 252-7777 or 800-888-1808; fax: 252-0080). Moderate.

Riviera – One of the oldest hotels in the city, now owned by wannabe star Pia Zadora and her entrepreneur husband, Meshulam Riklis, it claims to have the largest casino in the world (125,000 square feet). Its 2,032 rooms and 168 suites, distributed among 5 separate towers, are decorated in pastel colors and feature a variety of styles, from English Tudor to contemporary; some feature Oriental-inspired furnishings. There are 6 restaurants, a food court with 10 fast-food eateries, and 5 showrooms; its *Splash* production show is a popular nighttime attraction. Business amenities include 100,000 square feet of meeting space, a fully equipped business center, 24-hour room service, and express checkout. 2901 Las Vegas Blvd. S. (phone: 734-5110 or 800-634-6753; fax: 794-9230). Moderate.

Sahara – First stop on the Strip, and notable for its relatively tasteful decor and traditional style. This friendly sophistication characterized Las Vegas a long time ago but exists in fewer hotels each year. The service at this large (1,500-room) property is personalized and generally excellent. There also is nightly entertainment, the *House of Lords* restaurant, a bar, pools, health club, 25 meeting rooms (A/V equipment and photocopiers are available), CNN, and shops. Express checkout and 24-hour room service are other pluses. 2535 Las Vegas Blvd. S. (phone: 737-2111 or 800-634-6666; fax: 791-2027). Moderate.

Sands – This circular hotel made a name for itself in the 1960s as the hangout of "the Rat Pack" — Frank Sinatra, Dean Martin, Sammy Davis, Jr., Peter Lawford, and Joey Bishop. Ask for a room facing the Strip if you want a good view of the *Mirage*'s piña colada–scented volcano. The hotel has its own convention center, with 14 meeting rooms; there are also 4 restaurants including the elegant *Regency Room* (see *Eating Out*), 2 swimming pools, a 9-hole putting green, fitness facilities, beauty and barber shops, and gift shops. Express checkout. 3355 Las Vegas Blvd. S. (phone: 733-5000 or 800-634-6901; fax: 734-7324). Moderate.

Stardust – Once the largest resort hotel on the Strip, it underwent a $100-million expansion in 1991; there are now 2,500 rooms and villas. The accommodations in the high-rise East Tower are the newest, decorated with gray contemporary furniture highlighted with either red-and-black or blue-and-copper spreads and drapes; there are also Southwestern-style villas done up in peach and fuchsia. There's a landscaped pool, 6 restaurants, including *Ralph's Diner* (see *Eating Out*), and *Enter the Night,* a lavish new production-number show. Amenities include 24-hour room service, 12 meeting rooms, A/V equipment, photocopiers, and express checkout. 3000 Las Vegas Blvd. S. (phone: 732-6111 or 800-634-6757; fax: 732-6525). Moderate.

Tropicana – Self-billed as "The Island of Las Vegas," it has 2,000 well-appointed guestrooms decorated with bamboo furniture in bright, tropical colors, and it is conveniently located near the airport. Many of the suites have hot tubs and large-screen TV sets. *Folies Bergère,* the longest-running show in the city and modeled after the original French production, with high-stepping cancan dancers, is located here. There are 8 restaurants, a pool (with swim-up blackjack tables),

18 meeting rooms, and express checkout. 3801 Las Vegas Blvd. S. (phone: 739-2222 or 800-634-4000; fax: 739-2323). Moderate.

Circus Circus – Of all the hotels on the Strip, the only one really dedicated to family entertainment (at family prices). With a full-scale circus operating, complete with sideshows, there's something for everyone. Lots for the children — carousel, a clown-shape swimming pool; for the adults, the excellent *Steak House* (see *Eating Out*), cafés, bars, meeting rooms, health club, sauna. 2,500 rooms. Among the extras are room service until 11 PM, photocopiers, and express checkout. 2880 Las Vegas Blvd. S. (phone: 734-0410 or 800-634-3450; fax: 734-2268). Inexpensive.

Motel 6 – Good clean accommodations at the best prices in town. The bargain is worthwhile since hotel-motel rooms get little use in Las Vegas, and most of the time you're in them, you're asleep. Also, you get a pool for your money. 880 rooms. 196 E. Tropicana Ave. (phone: 798-0728). Inexpensive.

EATING OUT: Probably the only sure bet in Vegas is the food. Between hotels, restaurants, and casinos there's plenty to eat, and the food is much better than standard hotel or nightclub fare. From the continental cuisine of the hotels' main restaurants to "all-you-can-eat" buffets, Las Vegas features both quantity and quality. Though the offerings are basically American and Italian — steaks, seafood, and pasta — there are a number of good ethnic restaurants. So eat up, and take advantage of the bargains in the casinos that are subsidized by gambling revenues; you're probably paying for them anyway. Our restaurant selections range in price from $55 or more for a dinner for two in the expensive range; $30 to $45 in the moderate range; and $20 or less, inexpensive. Prices do not include drinks, wine, or tips. All telephone numbers are in the 702 area code unless otherwise indicated.

André's – A French restaurant in an old home, it is a favorite of the crowd in the downtown area. Open for lunch Mondays through Fridays; dinner nightly. Reservations necessary. Major credit cards accepted. 401 S. 6th St. (phone: 385-5016). Expensive.

Aristocrat – Charming 80-seat dining spot featuring continental cooking in the Rancho Circle area; one of the best dishes is sautéed pheasant in port wine. Open daily; lunch served weekdays, dinner nightly. Reservations advised. Major credit cards accepted. 850 S. Rancho Dr. (phone: 870-1977). Expensive.

Gigi – As close as you can get in Vegas to dining at Versailles. Elegance is the hallmark both in the atmosphere — pale green brocade, reproductions of Impressionist paintings, and fine crystal and china — and in the service. The menu features imaginative preparations of mostly fish and seafood, plus a few poultry, lamb, and beef selections and exotic desserts. Dinner only. Closed Mondays and Tuesdays. Reservations advised. Major credit cards accepted. *Bally's,* 3645 Las Vegas Blvd. S. (phone: 739-4651). Expensive.

Michael's – A gem of a restaurant in the Times Square section of the Strip. Among the offerings are shrimp served on frosted globes and double-dipped chocolate desserts. Outstanding service. Open for dinner nightly. Reservations essential. Major credit cards accepted. *Barbary Coast,* 3595 Las Vegas Blvd. S. (phone: 737-7111). Expensive.

Monte Carlo Room – Formerly *La Vie En Rose,* this second-floor dining room overlooks the lush poolside vegetation. Steak Diane with fresh mushrooms and quail in red wine are just two of the menu entrées. The pride of the *Desert Inn,* this room's service is expensive — but worth it. Dinner only. Closed Tuesdays and Wednesdays. Reservations advised. Major credit cards accepted. 3145 Las Vegas Blvd. S. (phone: 733-4524). Expensive.

Le Montrachet – The best of the *Las Vegas Hilton*'s dining dozen. Try the medallions of veal or venison. Desserts are imaginative, rich, and very tempting. Open for dinner nightly. Reservations essential. Major credit cards accepted. 3000 Paradise Rd. (phone: 732-5111). Expensive.

Palace Court – Considered the ultimate in dining grace in Las Vegas, at *Caesars Palace*. Candelabra, vermeil flatware, and hand-blown crystal are the accoutrements of an unforgettable experience. The sommelier pours wine from the hotel's distinguished wine cellar. Open for dinner nightly. Reservations essential. Major credit cards accepted. 3570 Las Vegas Blvd. S. (phone: 731-7110). Expensive.

Pamplemousse – This charming, romantic little spot (its name translates to "grapefruit") offers a taste of French countryside dining in the glitzy setting of Las Vegas. There is no printed menu; instead, the waiters recite the day's offerings. The items change based on what fresh ingredients the chef has at his disposal, but they are likely to include innovative presentations of duck, chicken, and veal. Dinner only. Closed Mondays. Reservations essential. Major credit cards accepted. 400 E. Sahara Ave. (phone: 733-2066). Expensive.

Pegasus – An elegant dining room in the *Alexis Park*, one of only two major hotels (the other being the *St. Tropez*) without gaming. Specialties of the house include sautéed veal with sauce Périgueux and pâté, beef Wellington, and fettuccine baked in a paper bag with shellfish; dinner is accompanied by attentive service and background harp music. Open for dinner nightly. Reservations essential. Major credit cards accepted. In the *Alexis Park Hotel*, 375 E. Harmon Ave. (phone: 796-3300). Expensive.

Chin's – An expanded version of the original, now nestled in the glittering *Fashion Show Mall* on the Strip. It serves crisp salads, *Chin's* beef, and pudding. A special elevator delivers diners from the parking garage. Open daily. Reservations advised. Major credit cards accepted. *Fashion Show Mall* (phone: 733-8899). Expensive to moderate.

Hugo's Cellar – Set in the *Four Queens* hotel, this is one of the most respected dining rooms in the city. The romantic atmosphere is enhanced by its remote, quiet location (well away from the casino) and the fresh red roses presented to the ladies. The menu items feature many excellent preparations of duck; also recommended are medallions of lobster. Open for dinner nightly. Reservations advised. Major credit cards accepted. In the *Four Queens Hotel*, 202 Fremont St. (phone: 385-4011). Expensive to moderate.

Regency Room – This elegant hotel dining room is one of the oldest in the city. The atmosphere and decor are reminiscent of a baronial mansion, and there are 2 separate menus: for lunch, there is a buffet of Italian specialties; the dinner menu features classic American dishes such as rack of lamb and T-bone steaks. Open daily; no dinner Tuesdays and Wednesdays. Reservations advised. Major credit cards accepted. *Sands Hotel*, 3355 Las Vegas Blvd. S. (phone: 733-5292). Expensive to moderate.

Savoia – Operated by the owners of *Pamplemousse* (see above), this large, bright, attractive place features first-rate fare. A specialty of the ever-changing menu is hobo steak (New York sirloin sliced thin and served with a sauce of Dijon mustard, shallots, cognac, and herbs). A small band provides live music on the weekends. Open daily; no lunch on weekends. Reservations advised. Major credit cards accepted. 4503 Paradise Ave. (phone: 731-5446). Expensive to moderate.

Alpine Village Inn – Best are the portions of good Swiss and German food — the wurst plates of all varieties, and the huge kettles of thick, dark German chicken soup that are meant for two but could actually feed the entire Swiss Family Robinson. The bright, gaily decorated restaurant also features a rathskeller with a piano player and lots of German beers. Open for dinner nightly. Reservations advised. Major credit cards accepted. 3003 Paradise Rd. (phone: 734-6888). Moderate.

Andiamo – A highly regarded northern Italian restaurant in the *Las Vegas Hilton*. The location is well away from the casino, so the atmosphere is quiet and formal; one of the menu's outstanding pasta dishes is *fettuccine all'aragosta e gamberi* (egg noodles with lobster and shrimp in a creamy white wine sauce). Open for dinner nightly. Reservations advised. Major credit cards accepted. In the *Las Vegas Hilton*, 3000 Paradise Rd. (phone: 732-5454). Moderate.

Antonio's – Flowers brighten the rooms of this hotel dining room featuring well-prepared Italian fare. The staff is friendly and attentive; some of the dishes they might recommend are the osso buco and the veal marsala. Accompanying dinner are fresh-baked, warm breadsticks dipped in olive oil. Dinner only. Closed Sundays and Mondays. Reservations advised. Major credit cards accepted. *Rio Hotel*, 3700 W. Flamingo Rd. (phone: 252-7777). Moderate.

Battista's Hole in the Wall – Plentiful Italian pasta for dinner, helped along by all the wine you can drink, and an occasional Italian aria by Battista himself, to create the proper mood. Open daily. Reservations unnecessary. Major credit cards accepted. 4041 Audrie, across from *Bally's* (phone: 732-1424). Moderate.

Benihana Village – The unusual ambience of this restaurant is as much of a draw as its traditional Japanese fare. This is actually a complex composed of *Hibachi* and *Robata*, two eateries built around a re-creation of a small Japanese village, including a 3-story imperial palace, lush gardens, running streams, and even a simulated tropical rainstorm. Open for dinner nightly. Reservations advised. Major credit cards accepted. In the *Las Vegas Hilton*, 3000 Paradise Rd. (phone: 732-5454). Moderate.

Bootlegger – Cozy, nestled in a quiet area about 3 miles from the Strip, and specializing in southern Italian dishes. The homemade pasta is especially good; be sure to try the lasagna or the lobster *fra diavolo*. The sunken-pit lounge area is a good place to relax after a day at the casinos. Closed Mondays; no lunch on weekends. Reservations advised. Major credit cards accepted. 5025 S. Eastern Ave. (phone: 736-4939). Moderate.

Café Michelle – A sidewalk café would seem a bit out of place amidst the flashy casinos of Las Vegas, but this place managed to find its niche. The bistro's menu changes daily, but the seafood and Italian dishes are always worth trying; the Greek salad is also a good bet. Open daily. Reservations unnecessary. Major credit cards accepted. 1350 E. Flamingo Rd. (phone: 735-8686). Moderate.

California Pizza Kitchen – Informal and friendly, this is a pizza place with a twist: Instead of pepperoni and anchovies, the pies here are topped with the likes of duck sausage, artichoke hearts, and baby shrimp. Though priced higher than the usual pizza, they're still relatively reasonable. Open daily. No reservations. Major credit cards accepted. In the *Mirage Hotel*, 3400 Las Vegas Blvd. S. (phone: 791-7111); and the *Golden Nugget Hotel*, 129 E. Fremont St. (phone: 385-7111). Moderate.

Caruso's – Northern Italian dishes prepared with veal and seafood are the mainstays at this hotel dining room. Elegant ambience and impeccable service make this place an especially popular setting for a romantic rendezvous. Dinner only. Closed Sundays and Mondays. Reservations advised. Major credit cards accepted. In *Bally's Hotel*, 3645 Las Vegas Blvd. S. (phone: 739-4111). Moderate.

China First – More elegant than the typical Chinese restaurant, this is one of the city's most popular dining spots. One of the main reasons is well-prepared dishes such as crystal shrimp (glazed and served with stir-fried vegetables) and Szechuan chicken. Dinner only. Closed Mondays. Reservations advised. Major credit cards accepted. 1801 E. Tropicana Ave. (phone: 736-2828). Moderate.

Claudine's – This posh room is part of *Harrah's*, and a welcome relief from the gaudy atmosphere of much of the rest of the hotel. Specialties such as escargots *bordelaise*, and shrimp scampi *dejonge* precede the excellent charcoal-broiled steaks. Closed Tuesdays and Wednesdays. Reservations advised. Major credit cards accepted. 3475 Las Vegas Blvd. S. (phone: 369-5000). Moderate.

DiNapoli – A first-rate Italian eatery, with attentive service and paintings of old Italy on the walls. Its homemade pasta is delicious, as are the osso buco and *rollatine di melanzane con ricotta* (eggplant slices stuffed with ricotta and baked with marinara sauce and mozzarella). Dinner only. Closed Tuesdays. Reservations advised. Major credit cards accepted. In the *Showboat Hotel,* 2800 Fremont St. (phone: 385-9123). Moderate.

Ferraro's – This comfortable, Italian-style family restaurant boasts the best osso buco in town, plus homemade bread and desserts. Open for dinner nightly. Reservations advised. Major credit cards accepted. 5900 W. Flamingo Rd. (phone: 364-5300). Moderate.

Flamingo Room – A large, attractive, Art Deco room, dominated by a savory salad bar, overlooking the hotel pool and the "Bugsy Siegel" gardens. The extensive menu features American dishes. Open daily from 7 AM to 2 PM, and from 5 to 11 PM. Reservations advised. Major credit cards accepted. In the *Flamingo Hilton Hotel,* 3555 Las Vegas Blvd. S. (phone: 733-3111). Moderate.

Golden Steer – In a town that has to revise the phone books twice a year just to keep up with the comings and goings of things, 20 years in the same place attest to a strong tradition. The decor is luxurious western and the offerings topnotch, from the steaks (try the Diamond Lil prime ribs) to the toasted ravioli, as well as the extensive wine list. With a day's notice, they'll serve up a special delicacy: pheasant, goose, quail, chukar (partridge), or roast suckling pig. Open for dinner nightly. Reservations advised. Major credit cards accepted. 308 W. Sahara Ave. (phone: 384-4470). Moderate.

Manfredi's Limelight – A lively family-run Italian establishment, serving such specialties as chicken Florentine, veal scaloppine marsala with demi-glaze, and sea bass poached with chablis, leeks, and cream. Open for dinner nightly. Reservations advised. Major credit cards accepted. 2340 E. Tropicana Ave. (phone: 739-1410). Moderate.

Marrakech – Authentic Moroccan fare, including couscous, lamb en brochette, and chicken baked with turmeric and served over rice. Diners sit on cushions in an informal, exotic setting, and a belly dancer provides entertainment. Open for dinner nightly. Reservations advised. Major credit cards accepted. 3900 Maryland Pkwy. (phone: 736-7655). Moderate.

Piero's – Offering northern Italian cooking with an emphasis on veal, the dishes change regularly, but recurring favorites are *vitello del chef* (veal scaloppine sautéed in egg batter and topped with bell peppers and cheese) and *zuppa di pesce* (a stew of lobster, clams, mussels, shrimp, scallops, and calamari). A selection from the restaurant's large wine cellar enhances the dining experience. Open for dinner nightly. Reservations advised. Major credit cards accepted. 305 Convention Center Dr. (phone: 369-2305). Moderate.

Rafters – San Francisco–style restaurant, with some of the best seafood in town. Joe Thompson, a native of the Golden Gate city, has shipments flown in daily from Fisherman's Wharf. Try the splendid bouillabaisse, which comes topped with a whole soft-shell crab. Open for dinner nightly. Reservations advised. Major credit cards accepted. 1350 E. Tropicana Ave. (phone: 739-9463). Moderate.

Skye Room – Perched on the 28th floor of *Binion's Horseshoe,* the view of the glittering lights of Las Vegas is a lovely counterpoint to the fine preparations of beef, veal, and seafood. Open for dinner nightly. Reservations advised. Major credit cards accepted. 128 Fremont St. (phone: 382-1600). Moderate.

Steak House – In the *Circus Circus* hotel, this is the place for steaks. Generous portions of sirloin are served in such a quiet, pleasant atmosphere, you could easily forget that the casinos are right nearby. Open for dinner nightly. Reservations advised. Major credit cards accepted. 2880 Las Vegas Blvd. S. (phone: 794-3767). Moderate.

Tillerman – This pleasant place off the Strip serves dishes featuring fresh fish and seafood flown in daily — and the prices are reasonable. The friendly, attentive staff can provide lots of information about the area along with your meal. Open for dinner nightly. No reservations. Major credit cards accepted. 2245 E. Flamingo Rd. (phone: 731-4036). Moderate.

Tony Roma's – Among the best rib joints in the city, this informal eatery with several branches offers meaty slabs of pork and beef coated with a spicy barbecue sauce. Try the onion rings on the side. Open daily. Reservations unnecessary. Major credit cards accepted. *Stardust Hotel,* 3000 Las Vegas Blvd. S. (dinner only; phone: 732-6500); *Fremont Hotel,* 200 Fremont St. (dinner only; phone: 385-6257); and at 620 E. Sahara Ave. (lunch and dinner; phone: 733-9914). Moderate.

Venetian – The oldest Italian restaurant in town (established in 1955) features hearty veal chops, sautéed greens, and (unlikely sounding but delicious) pork neck bones on its extensive menu. Dinner only. Closed Mondays. Reservations advised. Major credit cards accepted. 3713 W. Sahara Ave. (phone: 876-4190). Moderate.

Waldemar's – In a setting reminiscent of a German grotto, chef Waldemar prepares goulash, beef shashlik, and other Yugoslavian specialties. Open daily for lunch weekdays, and dinner nightly except Sundays. Reservations advised. Major credit cards accepted. 2202 W. Charleston Blvd. (phone: 386-1995). Moderate.

Ralph's Diner – Right out of *American Graffiti,* here's a diner that serves burgers, meat loaf, and chocolate malts. The employees sometimes interrupt their duties to sing 1950s hits with a vintage jukebox as backup. Open daily. No reservations. Major credit cards accepted. At the *Stardust Hotel,* 3000 Las Vegas Blvd. S. (phone: 732-6330). Inexpensive.

Vineyard – On the exterior of the *Boulevard Mall,* one of Las Vegas's three enclosed shopping malls, this quaint Italian eatery offers a fine antipasto salad bar and specialties such as chicken cacciatore and veal cutlet *parmigiana.* Open daily. Reservations advised. Major credit cards accepted. 3630 S. Maryland Pkwy. (phone: 731-1606). Inexpensive.

If all-you-can-eat sounds good to you, you can spend all your time in Las Vegas filling your plate. Virtually every Strip hotel and most of the downtown hotels have buffet breakfasts, lunches, and dinners where, for a couple of dollars or more, you can have as much as you can handle from an array of salads, fish, chicken, pasta, occasionally roast beef, and dessert. Best bets are the *Golden Nugget* (129 E. Fremont St.; phone: 385-7111); the *Fremont* (200 E. Fremont St.; phone: 385-3232); *Caesars Palace*'s *Palatium* (3570 Las Vegas Blvd. S.; phone: 731-7110); the *Riviera* (2901 Las Vegas Blvd. S.; phone: 734-5110); the *Sahara* (2535 Las Vegas Blvd. S.; phone: 737-2111); *Harrah's* (3475 Las Vegas Blvd. S.; phone: 732-2411); *Frontier* (3120 Las Vegas Blvd. S.; phone: 794-8200); and the *Mirage* (3400 Las Vegas Blvd. S.; phone: 791-7111).

■ **BEST BRUNCH:** For something really special, try the weekend Champagne Brunch at *Caesars Palace* — a feast for the eyes as well as the taste buds with its beautifully arranged selections of fresh pastries, fresh melons, eggs, bacon, ham, sausage, and all the champagne you can drink (3570 Las Vegas Blvd. S.; phone: 731-7110). Inexpensive. The Sterling Brunch at *Bally's,* served in *Caruso's* restaurant for $22.95, is exceptional. The all-you-can-eat entrées are presented in silver chafing dishes, the champagne is poured by white-gloved waiters, sushi and omelettes are made to order, and the dessert display is exquisite (3645 Las Vegas Blvd. S.; phone: 739-4111).

DIVERSIONS

For the Experience

Quintessential Las Vegas

Las Vegas is not a city that even attempts to hide its essence. Step off one of the 200 or so daily flights at McCarran International Airport and the gleefully anarchic display of elevators, escalators, people movers, palm trees, and slot machines leaves no doubt that you've reached your destination. Debark from *Amtrak*'s Desert Wind (two arrivals daily — one from Los Angeles, the other from Salt Lake City) and you walk straight back from Union Station into the casino of the *Plaza* hotel. Drive into town, and you're surrounded by building-high signs, a cityscape of neon towers of Babel (even *McDonald's* is neon) whose vertigo-inducing patterns express in myriad different ways the single message: This is Las Vegas — a city like no other in the world.

But though the visitor may feel unsure about where to find the real Las Vegas, keep in mind that the city comes in two distinct flavors: Downtown and the Strip. The heart of Downtown is a 4-block stretch of Fremont Street beginning at Main Street, 5 blocks west and about 2 miles north of the Strip, the 30-block stretch of Las Vegas Boulevard that has its northern boundary at Sahara Avenue.

The history of the two areas is as different as cherries and lemons. Decades before the Civil War, cowboys could be found Downtown purchasing questionable pleasures in gaming houses with sawdust-strewn floors. The Strip, on the other hand, is no older than the new wealth created by the Second World War, and from the start it has lured those in search of luxury as well as thrills. But the underlying message is the same: The Downtown area speaks in the traditional voice of the American West — Take a chance and strike it rich! — while the Strip remains faithful to its new-money origins. But the city as a whole continues to keep its promises. One: Every pleasure is yours to buy (or at least rent). Two: If you've got it, flaunt it!

BRIGHT LIGHTS, SMALL CITY: "Glitter Gulch" is the wonderfully appropriate name of the Downtown bus route on Fremont Street. At one time, fake Old West façades hid the drab fronts of single-story gambling casinos along this street. But in 1946, Thomas Young, a wheeler-dealer from Salt Lake City, changed all that; he was peddling an advertising gimmick that had become famous in Los Angeles nearly 2 decades earlier: the neon sign. During the 1950s, thanks to Young's super salesmanship and the intense competition among the casinos, the inert gas caused a veritable explosion of visual wonders in downtown Las Vegas. The company Young founded —

Young Electric Sign Company (YESCO) — still flourishes; in fact, YESCO is responsible for virtually every neon sign in town. YESCO's headquarters, located off Tropicana Avenue about 2 miles west of Las Vegas Boulevard, is worth a look: Piled haphazardly in its backyard is a collection of discarded neon masterworks, an amazing fossilized neon jungle that looks like the set of a science-fiction movie.

All that glitters here is not neon, however: Alas, the *Golden Nugget* sign — pictured on several decades' worth of postcards and the archetype of the virtually seamless 4-block night-into-day display — is no more. (When hotelier Steve Wynn took over the casino, he decided that the sign was passé and abandoned it.) But no one can accuse Wynn of diminishing Las Vegas's overall spectacle: His *Mirage* hotel boasts the current centerpiece of the city's eye-popping displays, a block-long series of manmade waterfalls (through which 5,000 gallons of water are pumped every minute). Atop the tallest of these waterfalls, 54 feet in the air, is a 60-foot-high "active" volcano. Every 15 minutes after dark, steam spews, flames shoot into the sky, and imitation lava plunges into a reflecting pool 5 stories below. In 3 minutes it is over, leaving behind a miasma not of sulfur, but of piña colada. Honest!

But neon fans need not worry, as plenty of bright lights linger along the Downtown area. On the north side of Fremont and Main, Cowboy Vic still waves his arms atop the *Pioneer* hotel, and across the way, Sassy Sally of the sexy, bright blue legs invites Vic's attentions from her perch on the *Golden Gate*.

The presence of neon remains prominent on the Strip as well, except that it is distributed among 30 hotels along 3 miles rather than crammed together in 4 blocks as it is Downtown. The sign at the *Stardust*, built in 1967, is 188 feet tall and contains 26,000 bulbs and 30 miles of wiring. The *Sahara*'s sign (at 220 feet, it's the world's tallest freestanding neon sign) and the one at *Vegas World* are, in their way, wonders of modern creation. Taken together, Glitter Gulch and the Strip have nearly 20,000 miles of tubing, attended by a "Neon Patrol" who circle the city after dark recording burnout locations. The lights, voluntarily extinguished only when President Kennedy was assassinated (though they were dimmed for 5 months during the oil crisis of the Carter presidency and for a single night as a tribute to Sammy Davis, Jr.), really aren't the electricity hogs they seem. Only about one-quarter of a percent of Nevada Power's output is devoted to keeping the skies above Las Vegas lit. Given the impressiveness of the effect — which is visible even from space — it's more or less an energy bargain.

The only thing brighter than Glitter Gulch on a normal night is Glitter Gulch on *New Year's Eve,* when more than 150,000 people fill the streets for a nationally televised celebration. At the center of the action, the *Plaza* hotel supplies live bands and a ball where revelers can count down the hours (and minutes) to midnight, and it offers competition to the flashing signs on Fremont Street in the rare form of fireworks (set off at 8 PM in order to make the national TV news hookups). The spectacle is brighter than bright and, combined with the cheering crowds, utterly dizzying.

After midnight, all the hotels offer parties suited to a variety of tastes and pocketbooks. *Bally's* is the best bet, with a host of festivities ranging from a lavish dinner and superstar entertainment in its Grand Ballroom to a country-and-western show in its Garland Ballroom. Other hotels offer similar variety on a somewhat reduced scale for their end-of-the-year blowouts. Though hotels start taking reservations for parties at the beginning of December, it's advisable to make room reservations well before that — a 3-night stay is usually required — since accommodations for this time of year are invariably sold out early.

WHERE THE ACTION IS: Whether this is your first — or even your 50th — visit to Las Vegas, the moment you step into the casino you know that you've moved into another orbit. Unlike the elegant, sedate gaming rooms of Europe, Vegas casinos aim at stirring your spirit (and, hopefully, your wallet), offering you a cleverly designed dream world where anything seems possible. Go with it: Immerse yourself in the experience; try a slot — even a penny one — "c'mon," it beckons, "you only live once."

That's the lure — it's up to you to succumb only as much as your budget will allow.

The first assault on your senses is the noise — the clash of coins in the slot machines (some strategically placed at each entrance) — oh those glorious (especially if they're coming from your machine) slots bells, announcing a really big win; the clink of glasses, balanced on trays held by scantily clad waitresses; the whoosh of the roulette wheel as it spins round, and the plunk of the ball as it lands (hopefully) in the right slot; the staccato of cards being shuffled at the blackjack table; the flap-flap-flap at keno as the rubber brushes against the metal spokes of the wheel; the click, click, click of chips being set in place and the raucous shouting and cheering at the craps table — and the deadly silence when someone rolls boxcars. Add to this the lights — brighter than bright (psychologists claim that light puts people in good moods, and casino designers have taken their theory to the limit), some blinking, others glowing, others flashing in a dizzying array of perpetual motion that makes you want to scream "stop," but instead have you clamoring for more (those PhDs really know what they're talking about). And then there's the color — seemingly endless miles of bright green felt; candy-colored slot machines; and more neon-color polyester-clad patrons than you'll see in all of Miami Beach. Your local bingo game will never seem the same again.

REALLY BIG SHOWS: There are five major showrooms where Vegas-style superstars (such as Diana Ross, Frank Sinatra, Ann-Margret, and Bill Cosby) earn Vegas-style salaries (Cosby is said to earn more than any other Vegas regular: $500,000 a week; at ten performances, that comes to about $50,000 per show!) by strutting their stuff in front of wildly appreciative crowds. But many would choose one of the city's floor show extravaganzas as a more quintessential form of Las Vegas entertainment. The most expensive of these shows ($30 million to produce), and arguably the most impressive, is Siegfried and Roy's "Beyond Belief" at the *Mirage* hotel (for more about "Beyond Belief," see *Best in Shows*).

But other spectacles have their fans, too. The biggest and most extravagant is "Jubilee" at *Bally's* hotel and casino. Originally produced for the hotel when it was the old *MGM Grand*, the $10-million spectacle is mounted on a stage second in size only to the one at New York City's *Metropolitan Opera*. Playing to an 1,100-seat house, "Jubilee" features more than 100 singers and dancers, who cavort in topless Bob Mackie–designed costumes while wearing 40-pound feather headdresses.

There are nearly 80 set changes in the course of the Don Arden–produced extravaganza, and the special effects are amazing. When Samson brings down the "temple" the entire theater seems to rumble. (Loosely based on the movie *Samson and Delilah,* the show's music is the same as that used in the film.) And if all that's not enough, the climax of the evening is an eight-scene mini-epic concluding with the sinking of the *Titanic* — onstage. There's a "good old days" medley of songs associated with Eddie Cantor, Al Jolson, Bing Crosby, and Judy Garland; a ballet interlude set to Johann Strauss's music; and between the big production numbers, jugglers, magicians, and a variety of specialty acts do their thing in front of the curtains.

Intended by its colossal size to give the audience the sense of being on an MGM soundstage, for some, the extravaganza succeeds only too well: It's so big that there's not much of the up-close and live excitement many look for in a stage show. Still, with its unmatchable mix of bare breasts, biblical heroics, nostalgia, shtick, and maritime tragedy, it's the sort of entertainment that could exist only in Las Vegas. Presented twice nightly at $35 a ticket, it's the pulse of the city — vast, voluptuous, and yes, more than a tad vulgar.

REBELS WITH A CAUSE: Quite a different sort of show but a must-see for basketball fans takes place regularly during the season (February to April) at the University of Nevada–Las Vegas's *Thomas and Mack Center.* It is here that the *Runnin' Rebels,* the hated, feared Bad Boys of the Court, winners of the 1990 NCAA championship, strut their stuff. The just-this-side-of-legal recruiting practices of former coach Jerry Tarkanian have added to the *Rebels'* unsavory reputation — but this naughtiness only enhances the team's cachet. Tickets to the on-court mayhem (home games begin with a volley of fireworks) are the hottest in town. But if you plan far enough in advance, you too may be able to witness the in-your-face humiliations Las Vegas's favorite hoopsters regularly inflict on their opponents. Last year the team promised to start playing by the rules. *Rebel* fans hope losing its Bad Boy status won't affect its winning ways.

EAT, TOO, CAESAR: Like the neon signs and the wonders of the nighttime entertainment, food in Las Vegas is mostly a come-on for the casinos. And the variety of eating experiences is as vast as the variety of casino ambiences. There's merit to the claim that Las Vegas's amazingly low-priced buffets define its culinary soul. (*Circus Circus*'s is the busiest, the *Golden Nugget*'s the most expensive, and *Palace Station*'s the best.) On the other hand, the efforts of upscale Strip hotels to symbolize their "best of the best" status by presenting first-rate fare in opulent surroundings is an equally important facet of Vegas dining. *Palace Court* at *Caesars Palace,* where the cutlery is gold, the waiters dressed in white, the wine served in hand-blown crystal, and the food superb, is an unparalleled experience for those who can afford it. But at comparably excessive prices, *Caesars* offers an even more opulent feast. At the *Bacchanal,* a room guarded by a pair of stone lions and featuring a lighted reflecting pool with a statue in the middle, dining is reborn as spectacle. The pricey dinner is served in a convincing (if not historically accurate) re-creation of a Roman feast at a private villa. The menu announces: "I Caesar welcome you to the most resplendent arena of gustatory delights ... The Bacchanal." Toga-clad "wine goddesses" not only dispense unlimited libations, but also massage the neck and shoulders of male guests just before the dessert course. Fans say that the *Bacchanal* is a uniquely delightful dining experience, especially when shared with a group. We figure that Las Vegas is the logical place to come to find out how the Caesars would have dined if they'd had credit cards.

SLEEPLESS NIGHTS: Las Vegas prides itself on being the only city in the world that's truly open 24 hours a day. (Sorry, but Hong Kong shares that pride.) It's not just the casinos — even the supermarkets and convenience stores never close; and for many it's only between the hours of 2 AM and 10 AM that the city reveals itself. Certainly there are few sights so conducive to "Twilight Zone" fantasies as a nearly deserted casino just before dawn. If you've the stamina for it, by all means plan a graveyard-shift tour of the Strip. In the hours when the polyester-clad crowds are gone, you can wander through the casinos, taking the time to look up at the ever-vigilant "eye-in-the-sky" video cameras which the casinos use to guard against cheaters. With luck you may even get to see an exhausted-but-elated slot machine player who has won a large pot and now is waiting patiently (more or less) for someone from the hotel's publicity staff to be awakened for the necessary photographs. At the very least, you can watch the slot players watch casino employees empty the slot machines, on the lookout for the machines with the fewest coins (those are the "loosest," the ones with the highest payoffs). During this time some casinos relax the rules a bit, with a couple of blackjack tables using a single deck instead of the customary seven. For gamblers with a little card sense and a lot of NoDoz, may the odds be with you.

High-Rollin' Hotels

The flashy days of Las Vegas hotel room architecture and decor live on at *Circus Circus,* where bright red carpets, red chairs, pink walls and red-, pink-, and blue-striped wallpaper make it plain that the management would ever so much prefer that you be downstairs spending money in the casino. Happily, however, these tacky trappings are now becoming an exception: The recent trend is toward rooms that are actually livable, with TVs and clocks (two amenities Las Vegas hotels were notorious for omitting), and even Jacuzzis. Indeed, in recent years the city has been able to boast that among its 55 major hostelries many offer ambience, service, and food that are truly world class, while maintaining Las Vegas's well-deserved reputation for providing lodgings at astonishingly affordable prices. Here are a few of the best bets.

CAESARS PALACE: The *Mirage* may (for the moment) incarnate the Las Vegas spirit of reality as spectacle, but throughout its 25-year lifetime *Caesars Palace* (no apostrophe, since all guests are Caesars) has been universally acknowledged as the benchmark of fantastical luxury. A 20-foot statue of Julius Caesar (who appears to be hailing a cab) stands in the driveway, and behind it 18 fountains shoot columns of water 35 feet into the air. Fifty-foot-tall Italian cypresses flank the approach to the hotel's entrance, where a 4-ton gold-plated bronze Buddha (a gift to the hotel from a Thai businessman) ensures luck and prosperity.

Once inside the 1,420-room palace, the ambience is equally imperial. The recently constructed *Roman Forum Casino* offers $100 slot machines that feed on special tokens minted of 10-karat gold and silver plate. Cleopatra's Barge is a real barge floating in a real pool of water, and it's large enough to allow room for a live band and dancing. Not far away is an 18-foot-tall, 9-ton replica of Michelangelo's *David,* made of marble from the same quarry as the original (it took 18 months to sculpt). There is also "the Garden of the Gods," a 243,000-gallon swimming pool (whose water is completely filtered every 4 hours) modeled after the ancient Roman baths at Pompeii; the 8,000 tiles that line its sides were imported from Carrara, Italy.

In 1991, *Caesars*'s management plunked down $100 million to make sure that hotel guests would have a suitable environment in which to spend their casino winnings. The 240,000-square-foot *Forum Shops,* which opened last May, boasts a collection of ultrastylish, upscale emporia, including *Gianni Versace, Guess, Victoria's Secret, Louis Vuitton, Bernini,* and *Porsche Design.* For hungry shoppers, branches of LA's *Spago* and New York City's *Carnegie Deli* are also here. Elsewhere in the hotel are some of the finest local eateries: the superposh *Palace Court* (white-gloved waiters, gold cutlery, hand-blown crystal), the *Bacchanal* (toga-clad waitresses serving a modern version of an ancient Roman feast), *Empress Court* (a Chinese restaurant so good you'll feel you've died and gone to heaven), *Ah So* (with equally splendid Japanese food), and *Primavera* (where you can dine poolside on Caesar salad — what else! — and a variety of other semi-Italian specialties). Most of the Caesars — Julius, Augustus, even Sid — and just plain folk like us feel right at home here. Information: *Caesars Palace,* 3570 Las Vegas Blvd. S., Las Vegas, NV 89109 (phone: 702-731-7110 or 800-634-6661; fax: 702-731-6636).

DESERT INN: Its opening night in 1950 was timed to coincide with the atomic bomb test in the Nevada desert — and the owners spent $13,000 to fly in 100 high rollers for the big blast. In many ways (including its early associations with gangland money) the *Desert Inn* has remained faithful to Bugsy Siegel's low-rise, high-luxury dreams for the Strip (for the ultimate in very laid-back, un–Las Vegas luxury, try the Wimbledon townhouses, each with its own private swimming pool). Spread out over 2,000 acres, the 821-room complex boasts Southwestern-style decor and offers its guests a view of its golf course, which hosts three major annual events — the *Desert Inn LPGA International,* the *Las Vegas Senior Classic,* and the *Las Vegas Invitational.* It's a relaxing perspective that's remarkably effective in helping guests unwind from the frenetic pace of the Strip. Other soothing amenities include separate dining and lounging areas attached to many of the hotel's suites, and what are arguably the best spa facilities in all of Las Vegas.

Neophyte gamblers can brush up on casino basics by tuning in Channel 4 on their TV sets; those in search of top-drawer entertainment can find it at the *Crystal Room,* where superstars such as Frank Sinatra, Liza Minnelli, and Shirley MacLaine are the order of the night (except Mondays). There are three elegant (for Las Vegas) dining rooms — the French *Monte Carlo Room,* Italian *Portofino,* and Chinese *Ho Wan.* The *Deli* offers more casual dining, as does the promenade, which is open 24 hours. In all, it's a class act. Information: *Desert Inn,* 3145 Las Vegas Blvd. S., Las Vegas, NV 89109 (phone: 702-733-4444 or 800-634-6906; fax: 702-733-4774).

GOLDEN NUGGET: This is an exception to the rule that the Downtown area is no match for the Strip's excessive spectacle. When owner Steve Wynn took over the 30-year-old casino with its world-famous sign in the mid-1970s, the major gambling attraction still had sawdust on its floors. When the 579-room, $18-million tower opened in 1977, the extent of Wynn's plans for Downtown's upscaling was apparent. Today, with two high-rise extensions bringing the total number of rooms to 1,908, the *Golden Nugget* takes up 2 full blocks. The decorating scheme is gold, gold, gold, with some marble thrown in to hold the building up. Everything — the telephones, the slot machines, the abundant vases of fresh flowers, even the elevators — features virtually acres of gold plating (and then there's the casino's 63-pound gold nugget — the world's largest — mined in Australia). Though the lobby is impressive, with its red rugs over white marble floors, high white marble columns, etched glass windows, and stained glass panels, visitors are likely to be happiest with the Victorian-style decor of the large guestrooms with their four-poster beds and antique-looking mirrors and furniture. The 13 individually decorated suites are among the most inviting in town; some even boast a personal room service waiter. The health club features Jacuzzis and a steambath, as well as a fully equipped exercise room for working off the pounds gained at the hotel's two restaurants: *Stefano's* and *Elaine's.* This is the only Downtown spot that features superstar entertainment: the intimate 450-seat showroom here offers the likes of Kenny Rogers and Don Rickles. It's a long (and expensive) taxi ride to the Strip, so plan on spending most of your time (and money) here. Information: *Golden Nugget,* 129 E. Fremont St., Las Vegas, NV 89101 (phone: 702-385-7111 or 800-634-3454; fax: 702-386-8362).

MIRAGE: The 31-story, 3,000-room hotel opened in 1989 at a cost of $725 million (a record even for Las Vegas). From the block-long strip of waterfalls at the entrance — with a volcano that erupts every 15 minutes after dark and a tropical rain forest — to the 57-foot-long, 20,000-gallon saltwater aquarium (complete with sharks) behind the check-in desk, Steve Wynn's contribution to the Strip really makes a spectacle of itself. (The hotel consumes twice as much electricity as all of Carson City, Nevada's state capital.) Everything about the place is oversize. The Y-shape, 3-million-square-foot structure sits on nearly 100 acres of lushly landscaped lawns, planted with 3,000 tropical plants, including palm and banana trees. Near the swimming pool behind the hotel is a 1.5-million-gallon dolphin tank, where one of the dolphins has given birth — twice. Six white Siberian tigers, stars of Siegfried and Roy's nightly "Beyond Belief" extravaganza, roam in a habitat on one side of the building. Additional treats for families visiting with children include Action Jackson, an audiovisual creation of Siegfried and Roy's friend Michael Jackson, who stays in a lavish suite that bears his name when he drops by to play with his tiger buddies.

The hotel also boasts a staff of 6,000 — the population of a good-size Nevada town. The double rooms and 1- and 2-bedroom suites all feature tropical flowers, brightly colored fabrics, and elegant cane and rattan furniture. High rollers also can choose to stay in 1 of 260 superplush penthouse suites. In addition to eight international restaurants, the *Mirage* is home to the wildly popular *California Pizza Kitchen,* and there is a shopping center of fine boutiques, jewelry stores, and gift shops. It may seem like a mirage — but it looks quite real to us. Information: *Mirage,* 3400 Las Vegas Blvd. S., Las Vegas, NV 89109 (phone: 702-791-7111 or 800-627-6667; fax: 702-791-7414).

Vegas Victuals

As is the case with lodging and entertainment, dining is the beneficiary of the city's main money-maker: casino gambling. Not that big-hearted owners have been moved to return their patrons' losses in the form of subsidized fine dining. Rather, they want to keep their guests within easy reach of the gaming tables, not merely physically but in spirit. The idea is for folks to wine and dine on a scale that allows them to see themselves as real "players," capable of wagering large sums with equanimity. Hotels compete to provide their guests with high-quality eats at low prices (and to prove that there's more to Vegas fare than patty melts and pastrami), hoping to satisfy their hunger without depleting their bank accounts. After all, the less money spent on food, the more that can be spent at the gaming tables.

There are fine restaurants in Las Vegas that are not attached to casinos; and though they tend to be somewhat more expensive for comparable quality, they're worth visiting for the salutary purpose of introducing you to the world beyond your hotel.

LE MONTRACHET: With its fine linen, leather-upholstered booths, paintings of pastoral scenes, soft peach lighting, fresh flowers on every table, and location at the rear of the hotel, far from the casino's din, the featured dining room at the *Las Vegas Hilton* succeeds at temporarily sealing off the normally pervasive Vegas atmosphere. By the time diners have done justice to such specialties as veal chops with mussel purée or breast of duck with apricot sauce, the casino beckons, and visions of cherries — on the slot machines, that is — dance in their heads. This is the magic of Vegas at its most subtle. Information: *Le Montrachet, Las Vegas Hilton,* 3000 Paradise Rd. (phone: 702-732-5111).

PALACE COURT: The most universally recommended of Las Vegas's hotel dining rooms, this *Caesars Palace* place reflects its regal name. The circular room, lit from above by a stained glass skylight and filled with all kinds of trees, bushes, and flowers, is palatial by anyone's standards. Genuine 17th-century portraits of the 12 Caesars (by the Italian painter Procaccini) adorn the walls. White-gloved waiters, gold cutlery, and wines from a cellar as extensive as it is excellent add to the mood. Classic French specialties include scallops in white wine, crayfish in vermouth, fresh Maine lobster steamed or baked thermidor, veal Oscar (medallions of veal with crab legs and white asparagus), and quail baked in crockery. There are only two seatings for these royal repasts: 6 to 6:30 and 9 to 9:30 PM, and though a meal here costs a king's (or an emperor's) ransom, it's worth every lira. Information: *Palace Court,* 3570 Las Vegas Blvd. S. (phone: 702-731-7110).

PAMPLEMOUSSE: Despite its unromantic name (French for grapefruit), this small country inn (elegantly decorated in varying shades of red) located at the north end of the Strip is the most romantic restaurant in Las Vegas. It has no printed menu; recent specials have included roast duckling in red wine and banana rum sauce, Cajun-style salmon in lemon-butter sauce with a mild curry, and medallions of veal in cream sauce with Dijon mustard. Owner George de La Forge has only two seatings nightly (for 70 lucky diners at each seating), so it's best to reserve well in advance. Information: *Pamplemousse,* 400 E. Sahara Ave. (phone: 702-733-2066).

STEAK HOUSE: Locals and visitors alike line up here, amid the big-top craziness of *Circus Circus,* to get their red-meat fix. With its antique brass ornaments and wood paneling reminiscent of 1890s San Francisco, the split-level dining room is a welcome contrast to Las Vegas's far-from-sedate casinos. But the reason people come here is not the atmosphere, but the first-rate food that the restaurant's name promises — and delivers. Sides of beef are displayed as they age in a glass-walled meat locker to the side of the dining area, and portraits of cattle line the walls. But steaks (with an occasional surf and turf dish) are as adventurous as the menu gets; this is decidedly not the place for vegetarians. Information: *The Steak House,* 2880 Las Vegas Blvd. S. (phone: 702-794-3767).

TILLERMAN: Off the beaten track (3 miles east of Flamingo Road) geographically as well as conceptually, this place is one of the best seafood restaurants in the desert. Each day fresh catches from the Pacific — from tuna to shark — are flown in; then they are prepared and served by an extremely attentive staff. There's also an excellently stocked wine cellar (mostly bottles from California). Best of all, the prices here are reasonable enough to leave you some pocket money — but don't worry, the casinos will be glad to help you spend it. Information: *Tillerman,* 2245 E. Flamingo Rd. (phone: 702-731-4036).

■**Best of the Brunch:** On a Sunday in Rome you look for a church; on a Sunday in Vegas you look for brunch. Hands-down, the Sterling Champagne Brunch at *Bally's* (3645 Las Vegas Blvd. S.; phone: 702-739-4111 or 800-634-3434) is the best in town. Offering an abundance of food (this *is* the city of excess, isn't it?) — from smoked salmon to sushi, omelettes filled with anything your heart desires to roast leg of lamb, French pastries to hot fudge sundaes — and magnumsworth of champagne, it's a lovely way to pass a few hours before re-entering the fray at the casino. Alas, this fabulous feast is available only on Sundays.

Weekday brunchers would do well to sample the fare served up at the *Golden Nugget* (129 E. Fremont St.; phone: 702-385-7111 or 800-634-3454). Hearty, varied, and well-priced, dishes include roast beef, baked ham, shrimp and seafood salads, plus some diet-defeating desserts (you can count calories another day).

Best in Shows

As much part of the go-for-broke luxe of Las Vegas as the architectural excess of its hotels are its preferred forms of entertainment: Big, Bigger, Biggest. Multimillion-dollar showroom extravaganzas and superstar concerts attract those caught up in the city's megabuck mentality. And though many of the tickets are pricey, the shows are an integral part of the Las Vegas experience. Try to go to at least one — it's like nothing else you've ever seen.

There are five "big rooms" in town where the superstars perform: *Bally's, Caesars Palace,* the *Desert Inn,* the *Golden Nugget,* and the *Las Vegas Hilton.* Of the crowd-pleasers, some — like Bill Cosby and Diana Ross — can pack houses all over the world, while others are stars that twinkle only in the local neon firmament — Las Vegas favorites like Engelbert Humperdinck, Wayne Newton, and Paul Anka.

Not to be outdone, other showrooms offer Arthurian jousting contests, ships sinking onstage, and tigers treading the boards in larger-than-life productions that would make P.T. Barnum blush.

Procedures for getting into the shows are in a state of transition. Increasingly tickets and pre-assigned seats are the rule, but the old tradition of making reservations and preparing yourself to queue up for at least 30 minutes (unless you've wangled a "line comp") lingers on at several rooms. Where that's the case, it's worthwhile tipping the maître d' $10 to $25 on entering to ensure that you're seated at a booth rather than at long tables where you can end up having to shift your seat around and crane uncomfortably for a good view of the stage. Once you've found your seat, you'll be expected to pay your bill before the show (headliners like Liza Minnelli command prices in the $50-to-$75 range these days), which includes two drinks. Then sit back and enjoy the spectacle. After all, you're in the "Entertainment Capital of the World," and in fact the superstars here *can* be relied on to knock themselves out giving the audience its due. Below, some of the top tickets in town.

BEYOND BELIEF: And it is. Currently the hottest (and at nearly $70, the most expensive) ticket in town, this $30-million sensory blitz features master illusionists Siegfried (he's the blond, serious-looking one) and Roy (the dark-haired, playful one). These 7-year veterans of the strip prestidigitate at the *Mirage*'s 1,500-seat showroom, joined by 6 white Siberian tigers. The resulting extravaganza features "Mind Is Magic," a theme song by friend (and tiger companion) Michael Jackson, a 30-foot-tall mechanical dragon, a disappearing (real) elephant, and almost no dialogue. Its first half is a Wagnerian epic of good triumphing over evil played out against an eye-popping backdrop of pre-Christian Europe; the second half consists of a compendium of illusions from Siegfried and Roy's earlier, less symbolically weighted shows. The climax is the song "Bless the Beasts and the Children" and Siegfried's moving plea to help save endangered animals. (The pair has been cited by the National Geographic Society for their work in preserving the line of white Siberian tigers with whom they share their palatial Las Vegas digs.) Information: *Mirage,* 3400 Las Vegas Blvd. S. (phone: 702-791-7111 or 800-627-6667).

CITY LITES: The tribute to Broadway musicals mounted at Bugsy Siegel's old stomping grounds, the *Fabulous Flamingo* (now the *Flamingo Hilton*), features production numbers from such megahits as *42nd Street, Dames, New York, New York, Cabaret,* and *Lullaby of Broadway.* Its intimate and up-close (at least compared to most other Las Vegas shows) presentation is the most enjoyable of the basic showroom revues. At the finale, bare-breasted showgirls wearing towering pink headdresses (they appear earlier in the show in topless green kimonos) belt out the title song from *The Act.* Sound crazed? It is. But then, this is Vegas, where anything can happen — and usually does. Information: *Flamingo Hilton,* 3555 Las Vegas Blvd. S. (phone: 702-733-3111 or 800-732-2111).

JUBILEE: Don Arden's "Jubilee" at *Bally's,* with its 100-plus cast, Samson pulling down the temple, the *Titanic* sinking below the waves, and Bob Mackie–designed topless costumes and 40-pound feathered headgear, is for many the essential contemporary realization of the Las Vegas phantasmagoria. It's a little bit of Ziegfeld, some Cecil B. DeMille, and more than a touch of The Greatest Show on Earth — all rolled into one. (Also see *Quintessential Las Vegas.*) Information: *Bally's,* 3645 Las Vegas Blvd. S. (phone: 702-739-4111 or 800-634-3434).

KING ARTHUR'S TOURNAMENT: The newest spectacle in town is also one of the most unusual. Produced twice nightly in the showroom of the *Excalibur* hotel, this musical fulfills the promise of the fantasyland castle architecture of the hotel. A bit of medieval jousting, plus lots of costumed knights, beautiful ladies, and fast horses, figure in the retelling of the Arthurian legend. The show — a genuine bargain at $24.95 — has an engaging twist, however: Before the action begins, guests are served a medieval-style banquet — one that they're expected to eat medieval-style, with their fingers. The show is especially exciting for kids, but even adults get into the spirit of the games. Information: *Excalibur,* 3850 Las Vegas Blvd. S. (phone: 702-597-7777 or 800-939-7777).

SPLASH: Both the extravaganzas and the superstar shows à la Las Vegas are more or less known for their appeal to an older crowd. The *Riviera* hotel's "Splash" attempts to buck this trend. By relying on a Top-40 sound, producer Jeff Kutash deliberately aims at an audience more likely to relate to Madonna than to Mel Torme. In other respects, too, this show is something of a departure: Most of the "Splashgirls" are clothed — they appear elaborately costumed as clams, mermaids, crabs, and other denizens of the deep as they go through their paces in and out of a 65,000-gallon water tank on stage. (Be advised, the showgirls aren't the only ones who get wet: Front-row patrons are often drenched as well.) Besides the amphibious dancers, the extravaganza features Shimata the Magician and a finale saluting Broadway and Hollywood with a 23-minute medley of songs from *Cats, Little Shop of Horrors, A Chorus Line, Phantom of the Opera,* and *Dirty Dancing.* For the younger crowd, daredevil motorcyclists wheeling around inside a giant steel Globe of Death provide the show's best moments. Your clothes may get wet, but the heart-stopping action will keep your mouth dry. Information: *Riviera,* 2901 Las Vegas Blvd. S. (phone: 702-734-5110 or 800-634-6753).

ALSO SHOWING . . .: At the *Imperial Palace* hotel and casino, performers offer a different style of illusion. A troupe of talented impersonators bring to life such stars as Elvis Presley, Marilyn Monroe, Louis Armstrong, Buddy Holly, Judy Garland, and Hank Williams. Like being featured on a US postage stamp à la Elvis, death is the prerequisite to being one of the subjects of the show. In fact, it is "Elvis" himself — in the plump, white-jumpsuited person of Tony Roi — who belts out the show's closing number, "Viva Las Vegas." Information: *Imperial Palace,* 3535 Las Vegas Blvd. S. (phone: 702-731-3311).

In another, more specialized (and questionably tasteful) style of Las Vegas pageantry, the *Plaza* hotel and casino, Downtown, features a troupe of entertainers who, in *La Cage Aux Folles* tradition, concentrate on reminding audiences that boys will, if they put their minds to it, be girls. "Boy-lesque," which started its run 15 years ago at the *Sahara* hotel, moved to the *Stardust,* found its audience, moved again, and has prospered, becoming more or less a Vegas institution. If you're not put off by it, the show really gives you a good romp for your money. Information: *Plaza,* 1 Main St. (phone: 702-386-2110 or 800-634-6575).

Luck Be A Lady

If the lost city of Atlantis were to reemerge in modern times, it might resemble the shining oasis of Las Vegas. Nestled in the harsh Nevada desert, this haven for high rollers (and brainchild of notorious mobster Benjamin Siegel, portrayed by Warren Beatty in the recent film *Bugsy*) quickly developed a reputation for round-the-clock action. Once the domain of superstars such as Elvis Presley, Frank Sinatra, Barbra Streisand, Dean Martin, and Sammy Davis, Jr., today's casino nightclubs now headline Liza Minnelli, Harry Connick, Jr. — and yes, Wayne Newton. Though for a time Las Vegas's golden, burnished gleam had tarnished, the arrival of the multimillion-dollar *Mirage* and the eagerly awaited (later this year) billion-dollar *MGM Grand* have restored a considerable amount of glamour and gloss — in the form of velvet and crystal and silver — to a city immersed in glitz. All of which only serve to make the polyester-clad customers stand out even more than they did before.

While time might be considered a precious commodity on Wall Street, Las Vegas casinos are symbolic rivers of Lethe. Nary a clock is in sight, and the lack of windows helps players focus exclusively on the game at hand. Cocktail waitresses are only too happy to supply drinks (the more alcoholic, the better), and most establishments have numerous eateries where gamblers can refuel for the next round of wagering.

The Strip, bordered by Sahara Avenue to the north and Tropicana Avenue to the south, is a "stately pleasure dome" center for such monolithic properties as *Caesars Palace,* the *Mirage,* and the *Tropicana.* Downtown Vegas, dubbed "Action Avenue," stretches out along Fremont Street, and you can even gamble with pennies if that's the extent of your bankroll. Local joints, also referred to as "satellites," are situated off the main drag, and they are die-hard favorites of local citizens because frequent players are amply rewarded with perks.

Just about every type of game of chance known to man (and woman) is available here, from the ubiquitous one-armed bandits and basic games — blackjack, craps, roulette, Big Six (wheel of fortune), and poker — to parimutuel horse racing bets, bingo, and keno. In many casinos, "double exposure" blackjack, where the player sees both of the dealer's cards, livens up the table. There are forms of craps where odds are taken up to 12 times the amount of the bet. Poker has recently become permeated with Asian themes that mix the rules of different games. Pai Gow, Super Pan 9, Red Dog, and Caribbean Stud Poker take a little bit of time to learn to play successfully, but it's very exciting once you catch on to the rather confusing variations. House personnel can instruct you about the gaming rules, or you can consult the gaming guidebooks offered at the larger casinos. The legal age for gambling is 21.

Las Vegas offers state-of-the-art slot machines, keno machines, and video poker. Nevada is linked into its own inter-casino slot system called Mega-Bucks, which is played with $1 tokens; Quartermania, which uses 25¢ coins; and Nevada Nickels, which promises a jackpot of at least $200,000 if you plunk at least 5 nickels into a slot machine. You might even hear the jangling of the slot machines in your sleep, for the casinos stay open around the clock.

ODDS-ON FAVORITES

Odds are, though all casinos don't look alike, the payoffs to be gained (or lost) along the Strip or Downtown are similar. That said, pick the neon sign that most appeals to you, stroke your rabbit's foot, and let the good times roll.

110 DIVERSIONS / Gambling

Aladdin: Although this time-honored establishment has recently been put up for sale, players still flock here, hoping to strike it rich. Once the place where singer Wayne Newton held court, the casino strongly resembles an Arabian Nights' harem decor. As to the gambling, nonsmoking tables are scattered about the area, and table limits stretch from $2 to $1,000 per wager. Information: *Aladdin Hotel & Casino,* 3667 Las Vegas Blvd. S. (phone: 702-736-0111).

Bally's: Located in one of the largest luxury resort hotels in the world, the ample 50,000-square-foot gaming floor equals a football field in size. Minimum bets at the gaming tables are normally $3 on weekdays, $5 on Fridays and Saturdays. More timid players make a beeline to the 25¢ slot machines, although there are plenty of folks pulling on the $100 slots. Baccarat, blackjack, and roulette lessons are offered daily. Information: *Bally's Casino Resort,* 3645 Las Vegas Blvd. S. (phone: 702-739-4111).

Binion's Horseshoe: Owner Jack Binion frequently walks around the gaming floor, handing out bucks from a bucket. Each spring, the *World Series of Poker* is held here (see below). Serious gamblers usually spend some time here on high-roller junkets, and traffic is so heavy that there often is a line for the blackjack tables. Highlights of play include a 4% commission on baccarat (the norm is 5%), 10 times odds on craps, single-deck blackjack, and single-zero roulette. Information: *Binion's Horseshoe Hotel and Casino,* 128 Fremont St. (phone: 702-382-1600).

Caesars Palace: Beloved by celebrities and those who enjoy lots of glitz, its crowning glory is a huge fountain framed by rows of 50-foot cypress trees. Three casinos offer a wide variety of table games and slot machines, some unique to *Caesars.* New variations on blackjack include multiple-action wagering and over/under 13, where the wagerer bets whether the dealer's cards will be over or under 13. Needless to say, this game is ideal for card counters. Machines range from traditional nickel slots to chariot races and high-limit slots that accept specially minted $500 tokens. Information: *Caesars Palace,* 3570 Las Vegas Blvd. S. (phone: 702-731-7110).

Circus Circus: Circus performers, including trapeze artists, high-wire acts, daredevil acrobats, and clowns, perform daily from 11 AM until midnight under the circus tent adjacent to the casino. Not to be missed is the merry-go-round, where players ride on a revolving stage while assiduously playing slot machines. Bets usually don't go higher than $500, and lessons in roulette, blackjack, and craps are offered daily. Information: *Circus Circus Hotel & Casino,* 2880 Las Vegas Blvd. S. (phone: 702-734-0410).

Desert Inn: Considered one of the more tasteful casinos on the Strip. The upscale decor has a Southwestern theme. Minimum bets at the tables are usually $5, although there are some $3 table limits. Beginners also can pick up a lesson in poker. Information: *Desert Inn Hotel & Country Club,* 3145 Las Vegas Blvd. S. (phone: 702-733-4444).

Dunes: Neon lights in blue, green, and red illuminate the dim interior of red carpeting and dark wood. Quarters are readily eaten by the slot machines, and $2 minimums at the tables are lower than at most casinos. Stationed inside the main casino are new cars that lucky players can win by jerking the handle of a slot machine down at just the right time. Information: *Dunes Hotel, Casino, & Country Club,* 3650 Las Vegas Blvd. S. (phone: 702-737-4110).

Excalibur: For those who can think of nothing so pleasurable as placing bets in King Arthur's Court, this mock medieval castle, surrounded by a moat, is a veritable playground. As you might expect, the employees are clothed in period costumes, and there is an amusement area with a medieval theme. This casino tends to attract low-budget gamblers, and has $1 minimums on tables and poker video game machines. Information: *Excalibur Hotel & Casino,* 3850 Las Vegas Blvd. S. (phone: 702-597-7777).

Fitzgerald's: Leprechauns, four-leaf clovers, and a horseshoe from *Triple Crown* winner Secretariat may not improve your luck, but slot machines that supposedly offer a 101% payback might leave you with a few extra coins in your pocket. There's also a nonsmoking area on the second floor for devoted slots slaves. Information: *Fitzgerald's Hotel/Casino*, Third St. and Fremont (phone: 702-382-6111).

Golden Nugget: This luxurious establishment is renowned for having the "world's largest golden nugget," which is on display in all its 63-pound glory. Almost everything appears covered in gold, right down to the pay phones. You can wager up to $5,000 a hand at the tables, and there are plenty of other games to play, including Pai Gow, Red Dog, keno, and mini-baccarat. Information: *Golden Nugget Hotel/Casino*, 129 E. Fremont St. (phone: 702-385-7111).

Las Vegas Hilton: In the 1970s, Elvis Presley truly reigned as the casino's king. Now Wayne Newton has taken over as the big nightclub draw. High rollers still flock to the tables, which entertain bets of $3 to $5,000 a hand, and there are $1 slot machines. Information: *Las Vegas Hilton Hotel & Casino*, 3000 Paradise Rd. (phone: 702-732-5111).

Mirage: If white tigers, shark pools, and magicians performing elaborate acts of prestidigitation don't amuse you, then the exploding volcano, complete with flowing "lava," will probably stop you in your tracks. You can play the slot machines with everything from a nickel to a $500 token, and table limits start at $3 and soar to $5,000. A secluded casino for those who wish to bet pots of money in private ($1,000 minimum wagers are the norm) is cordoned off from the rest of the gaming floor. Information: *The Mirage*, 3400 Las Vegas Blvd. S. (phone: 702-791-7111).

Palace Station: Another joint habituated by the locals, you'll find the best bingo games here, as well as nickel slot machines and low table minimums (the highest bets are made with $100 chips). The hotel and casino resemble a turn-of-the-century railroad depot. Information: *Palace Station Hotel & Casino*, 2411 W. Sahara Ave. (phone: 702-367-2411).

Plaza: A favorite with low rollers. An *Amtrak* station is located in the hotel, and there's always a heavy flow of customers. Slot machines accept everything from pennies to $5 tokens, and table limits range from $2 to $1,000. Information: *Plaza Hotel & Casino*, 1 Main St. (phone: 702-386-2110).

Riviera: The largest casino in the world, this establishment is more for the middle-of-the-road gambler; minimum bets at the tables range from $3 to $5, and blackjack, craps, roulette, poker, and keno lessons are given daily. Catch a glimpse of the "Walk of Fame," modeled after the one at *Mann's Chinese Theatre* in Hollywood. Information: *Riviera Hotel & Casino*, 2901 Las Vegas Blvd. S. (phone: 702-734-5110).

Sahara: Recently renovated, this is another casino for middle-of-the-road rollers. It has the usual nickel slot machines, as well as more unusual games such as Red Dog and keno. Tables with a $2 minimum are predominant, and lessons are offered for baccarat and poker. Information: *Sahara Resort Hotel & Casino*, 2535 Las Vegas Blvd. S. (phone: 702-737-2111).

Sam's: This Wild West–looking establishment offers nickel slot machines and is heavily frequented by locals, who return again and again to wager at the $1 tables. Information: *Sam's Town Hotel & Casino*, 5111 Boulder Hwy. (phone: 702-456-7777).

Sands: In its heyday in the 1960s, headliners like Frank Sinatra and Sammy Davis, Jr. held center stage, and Joey Bishop (remember him?) kept the lounge packed with gamblers taking a respite from the tables. Today, neon lights delineate the different slots areas, and there are blackjack tables for nonsmokers. Any denomination from a nickel to $100 tokens is accepted by one-armed bandits, and table limits range from $2 to $2,000. Information: *Sands Hotel & Casino*, 3355 Las Vegas Blvd. S. (phone: 702-733-5000).

Vegas World: Space as the final gambling frontier is practiced here; while the "astronaut" suspended from the ceiling, along with spaceships, meteors, and planets, may seem frivolous, the betting definitely is not. Other highlights are the largest wheel of fortune in the world (it has a diameter of 25 feet), crapless craps (where players cannot lose on the first roll of the dice), double-exposure blackjack, and high slot payouts. Owner Bob Stupak keeps a million dollars on display in a glass case in the lobby to whet impatient appetites. Information: *Vegas World Hotel & Casino,* 2000 Las Vegas Blvd. S. (phone: 702-382-2000).

■ **World Series of Poker:** Jack Binion's *Horseshoe* hotel on Fremont is the only casino in Las Vegas where high rollers have no upper limit on wagers. Also at the *Horseshoe,* you can watch (or play in) the *World Series of Poker.* Players from around the globe, including a minor celebrity or two, ante up $10,000 to take part in this contest of luck and card-sense that can last 21 days and bring a $1-million payoff — that is, if your money (and cards) holds out.

The annual event has its origins in a high-stakes marathon poker competition Binion set up in 1949 for the famous gambler Nick "The Greek" Dandalos. When the smoke cleared 5 months later, Nick was $2 million poorer — and a Las Vegas tradition had been born. If you're in town during late April and early May, even if you don't have a spare $10,000, it's worthwhile dropping by just to see what a roomful of poker faces looks like.

PLAYING BY THE RULES

Any discussion of gambling (and it would surely be perverse to visit Las Vegas without doing *any* gambling) must start with the fact that gambling is not a way to make money — not even a very very chancy way to make money. Gambling is a way to *spend* money. The annual gross profits of Las Vegas's gambling industry are over $4 billion. This amounts to losses at the tables of more than $1,000 a second, every second, every day of the year.

Casino owners set the rules for the games, and they aren't risking their capital any more than any other successful entrepreneur. The goal is to buy cheap and sell dear. What they sell is the excitement of gambling (or "gaming," as some like to call it). You pay them for this excitement every time you place a bet. The rate at which you pay is called "the house advantage," or "edge" (more about learning the language later).

Roulette provides a relatively simple example of the way the house advantage works. The wheel is divided into 38 slots, numbered 1 through 36, plus 0 and 00. When you bet on a number to come up, the chances of the ivory ball finding its way to the slot you've put your money on are, pretty obviously, 1 in 38. But when you bet on a number and win in roulette, the house gives you only $35 for every dollar of your wager. The $2 that they hold back is their "edge." (Since 2 units of 38 are 5.26% of them, the house advantage is 5.26%).

Here's an even simpler way to look at it. Suppose you decided to amaze everyone by approaching the roulette table and betting $38 — $1 on each of the 38 possible positions. After your inevitable victory, you'd get back the $1 that happened to be on the winning number plus $35 more — a total of $36. So for your efforts (and in this case not very much fun or excitement), *you'd actually walk away from the table $2 poorer!*

There are folks who do leave Las Vegas richer than when they arrived, however. Not too long ago a man from Houston, Texas, spent $300 at one of the Mega-Bucks machines at the *Stardust* hotel and came away with $6 million. But in general, between the house advantage and the logical odds against you, the best attitude to take is that you've come to pay a fee for the thrill of gambling (another way of looking at losses is to factor them in as vacation expenses), and then look around for the games and bets that take the lowest bets.

LAS VEGAS SPEAK

In addition to sharing a general floor plan, casinos share a specialized lingo and etiquette. When it comes to trying to adopt the local idiom, few things are as frustrating

DIVERSIONS / Gambling

as having the natives laughing at you behind their hands. But just as becoming familiar with French is a good idea if you're going to Paris, it's also smart to learn the specialized slang of Las Vegas casinos. Even if you still deal in chips and tips, the croupiers (dealers) — who call chips "checks" and tips "tokes" — do expect you to understand them. More importantly, what in these parts is called "Las Vegas total" (the complete Las Vegas experience of gambling, food, entertainment, and so on) can't be totally appreciated unless you speak — or at least understand — the lingo. We haven't yet discovered the trick to beating the casinos at their own game, but at least now you'll know what they're talking about.

Certainly, it is to *your* advantage to understand what's meant by "the *house* advantage" (also "the edge," "the percentage," "P.C.," "vigorish" and "vig"). Discussed in detail above, this is the casino's "charge" to gamblers for the thrill of wagering.

"Juice" — as in "Frankie may have the juice to get tickets, but I don't" — might seem to the uninitiated to mean power or ability, but rather, the concept is linked to the *appearance* of power or ability based on another person's respect. People with juice get things done, but they don't actually do them — and probably couldn't if they tried. Rather, things are done for them by someone else who respects their juice. In other words, juice is the ability to make something happen because other people *think* you can make it happen — a power one possesses because others *believe* one possesses it. It's a deep idea — almost mystical — but there's no question that it's even more important to Vegas than neon.

Another piece of linguistic advice before listing a few technical terms you're likely to hear: No one except possible first-time visitors ever refers to the Strip's near-legendary founder as "Bugsy" — in death, as in life, the infamous gangster-visionary is referred to by those in the know as Benjamin, or Ben, or Mr. Siegel.

action	amount of money at stake
bankroll	amount of money available
book	room where bets on athletic events and horse races are placed
boxcars	pair of craps dice showing 12 (double sixes), an automatic loss
boxman	head dealer at the craps table
cage	main cashier at the casino
carpet joint	upscale casino catering to high rollers
comp	freebie
crossroader	casino cheat
drop	cash that's been traded in for chips
george	a gambler who treats a dealer well
grind	someone who plays for low stakes
hard count	the count of coins in the slots
high roller	a gambler ready and willing to spend at least $5,000 in the course of a weekend
hold	the casino's profit
jet	a group of high rollers, usually flown in by the casino and fully comped
ladderman	baccarat supervisor
low roller	someone who places $1 and $2 bets
Marryin' Sam	wedding chapel minister
pencil	anyone who has the juice to write comps
pit	area behind the table games reserved for casino employees
plunger	gambler who keeps playing to try to recover his losses

points	percentage in a casino
rfb	room, food, beverage — a full comp
sawdust joint	a place catering to grinds
soft count	counting the folding money
stickman	craps dealer who handles the dice
stiff	a winning gambler who doesn't tip the dealer
toking	tipping

TABLE MANNERS

Most dealers are paid near-minimum wages, so even though they work for the house, "toking" (that is, tipping) should be an active part of every casino winner's vocabulary. Dealers are not allowed to accept cash; the proper and acceptable form is to share one's winnings by passing the dealer a few largish chips. (Since dealers rarely stay at the same table longer than 20 minutes, the truly tacky simply linger at the table until the dealer leaves — not approved procedure by any means.)

The flip side of "toking" is "comping" — the house's way of expressing its gratitude to favored patrons. If your game plan includes risking $1,000 or so at the tables, be advised that you needn't wait for the pit boss to notice your "action." It's perfectly appropriate to approach house personnel (other than dealers), announce that you intend to be spending a hefty sum at the casino's tables, and see what sorts of freebies you can get. Such freebies range from the coveted "rfb" (everything except your gambling losses on the house) to free dinners and entertainments, to "line passes" to the hotel's showroom extravaganza (so that you needn't waste valuable gambling time waiting in line). It's pretty certain that you will get comped if you spend enough. And besides, no one will blame you for asking — hey, this is Las Vegas.

More casino dos and don'ts: If you're spotted with a camera in a casino, security will sternly admonish: "No photographs." Many visitors suppose that this is one of the hundreds of rules laid down by the Nevada State Gaming Commission. In fact, the no-photographs policy is simply a courtesy extended to players who might be distracted by flashbulbs or (a more suspicious-minded interpretation) who might not like their actions (or companions) to be recorded on film. There are, in fact, three Las Vegas casinos that do not adhere to this policy: the *Four Queens* and *California* (Downtown) and *Excalibur* (on the Strip).

Though the State Gaming Commission remains mute on the question of cameras, its views on casinos and minors are explicit: Anyone who's under 21 and attempts to gamble will be asked to leave the table by the house security forces. While minors are allowed to pass *through* casinos in the company of adults, an adult with a youngster in tow will not be allowed to pause for even a single pull at a slot machine. There are no exceptions.

Finally, some visitors may have heard that dealers are not allowed to speak to players at their tables. This is false. Your dealer should answer any questions you have about how the game is played. If he or she prefers not to, show your displeasure by moving to another table. It's unreasonable to expect the dealer to enlighten you about the fine points of the game if the table is busy, however. If you feel you need on-the-spot tutoring, if you're the sort who likes to ask questions, or, for that matter, if you'd just as soon do your wagering when the crowds are not madding, learn to take advantage of the daily rhythms that all casinos share. Action gets under way at 11 AM, builds steadily to 5 PM, remains constant till about 8 PM, then starts to intensify until it peaks between 11 PM and midnight.

If you're a novice, rising early not only increases your chances of a helpful chat with a dealer, it allows you to take advantage of the before-noon, hour-long gambling workshops offered by nearly all the casinos. Those who are flat-out ignorant are best

DIVERSIONS / Gambling

advised to read up on the basic rules of the games that attract them (pamphlets spelling out rules and strategies are readily available in casinos and hotel lobbies). But book learning usually isn't enough. Wake up early and attend a few lessons to gain some hands-on experience.

If you should (you really shouldn't!) go over your planned "gambling loss" limit, you'll find that casino management has made it dangerously easy for you to keep on betting by providing easy access to automatic teller machines. Be aware, however, that unlike those at banks, these ATMs levy a $1 surcharge on your transactions; a more economical strategy is to use a major credit card to get a cash advance at a local bank. A second advantage to this strategy: Leaving the frenzied atmosphere of the casino to pick up your money may be all that's needed to help you decide when enough is enough.

Though hotels will cash personal checks for some high rollers, most everyone else will have to search out a check-cashing service and pay the (generally high) fees they charge. For the truly desperate, *Capital Leasing* (2501 Meadow Ave.) and *Instant Auto Pawn* (1613 N. Boulder Hwy. in Henderson) take automobiles as collateral on personal loans. And, as might be expected, Las Vegas has its share of traditional pawnshops. *Stony's Lucky Money* and *John's Loan* (both on S. First and E. Carson) are Downtown, just across the street from the *Golden Nugget*. A third well-known shop (but nearly last resort) is *Pioneer Loan* (down First St. across Fremont). If worse comes to worst and you have to phone and have someone wire money to you, you're not alone: Open 24 hours, Las Vegas's *Western Union* office (517 Fremont Ave.; phone: 702-382-4322) is one of the busiest branches in the world.

Now that you're properly sobered by the specter of financial embarrassment, we can return to the visions of instant wealth that Las Vegas evokes. Here is a primer for players. Good luck!

THE NAMES OF THE GAME

SLOTS: The banks of whirring, chinking machines near the entrance to virtually every Las Vegas casino and in a variety of other less plausible locations (from laundromats to *7-Elevens*) around the city are among the most recognizable symbols of 20th-century gaming. Invented in the 1890s by Charlie Fey, a Bavarian immigrant, slots spread rapidly from their original habitat in San Francisco's Barbary Coast gambling halls to venues, legal and otherwise, throughout the US. Until the mid-1960s slots remained pretty much as Fey — who started out as a maker of scientific instruments — created them: a stiff handle, a single-coin fee, three revolving wheels marked with fruit symbols. They were largely condemned by "real" gamblers as an idle amusement fit only for the wives of craps shooters and $20 blackjack players. Though still a favorite of women and beginners, slots have gained considerably in prestige since Bally (they were in the game business before the hotel business) introduced electronic slots and, in the mid-1970s, a seemingly endless variety of computerized poker, keno, blackjack, even greyhound racing formats. Today, slots account for the biggest jackpots in the casinos (remember the Texan who walked off with $6 million), take up more than 60% of the floor space, and contribute more than half the gross profits.

The idea behind all slots is wonderfully simple and (for the house) wonderfully profitable: You put money in the machines, pull a handle or press a button, and get money back (or, more often, not). Then you repeat the procedure, over and over and over again. The machines are set up to return a certain portion of the money put in them (often the exact amount is posted right on the machine in the form of a legend reading "returns 96%" or some such). Generally speaking, the higher the denomination of the coins the machine accepts, the greater the percent of return. That's simple arithmetic from the house's point of view: It's all the same to the casino whether it keeps 20% of quarter wagers or 5% of dollar ones — a nickel is a nickel. Other things being equal, then, dollar slots are where to invest your money, and if the slot allows the option of putting in more than a single coin, put in the maximum to increase the percentage of return if you do get lucky.

Progressive slots — some, like Quartermania and Mega-Bucks, linked by telephone modems in networks throughout the state of Nevada — are the ones that offer astronomical jackpots. Each non-winning pull on any machine in the network increases the jackpot at all the machines by 5% or so. Since the rules for eligibility for the big prizes are often fairly complex, always read the instructions posted on the side of the machine you're playing; and if you're still unclear, ask an attendant. If you do win any substantial jackpot (even if it's not one of the astronomical ones and not on a progressive machine), not all of your winnings will come chittering out at you. Don't worry, and don't pull the handle a second time. Stay where you are — you don't have to search for someone to notify. The house will be aware that you're a winner and quite soon an attendant and a mechanic will show up. After the mechanic verifies that the machine has not been tampered with (that's no reflection on your honesty — they do this for every win), you'll be asked to provide identification and your picture may be taken. You'll be given a check or, if you wish, the money will be transferred to your bank account. In either case, if you've won more than $1,500, you'll have to sign a G-2 form for the IRS, recording the amount of your win. But it's up to you to settle with the government. Except for state-lottery-size Mega-Bucks wins where payments may be stretched out over a 10-year period, you'll acquire your new fortune immediately.

In the Downtown area, there is a thrifty remnant of the past — penny slot machines, 184 of them, distributed among the *Plaza,* the *Western,* the *Gold Spike,* and the *Nevada* hotels. Visitors are likely to turn up their noses at the cheap thrills penny slots offer, but the locals are loyal to the old machines, and their loyalty has been amply rewarded. Recently one Las Vegas resident won $95,172 from a progressive penny slot at the *Western,* and another won $76,800 from a similar machine at the *Gold Spike.* (It's a safe bet that these winners don't agree with those people who call for the abolition of the penny as an outmoded and useless piece of currency.)

A different sort of slot highlight in the downtown area can be found at the New Orleans-style *Four Queens* hotel and casino. Hardly missable, even amidst the distracting all-pink decor, is the Queen Machine, certified by the *Guinness Book of World Records* as the world's largest slot. The 7-foot-by-8-foot behemoth accommodates six silver-dollar players at a time, who try to match the pull from the casino's Elizabethan-robed player. Should all eight reels come up queens, the payoff is $300,000 (split among the players). Even if you're not inclined to climb aboard for a pull, this gargantuan engine of chance is a must-see on any tour of Downtown.

BIG SIX: Like slots, Big Six (the wheel of fortune) is especially popular with beginning gamblers and generally disliked by more experienced ones. The wheel is divided into 54 slots of different denominations: 24 $1 slots, 15 $2 slots, 7 $5 slots, 4 $10 slots, 2 $20 slots, and 2 joker slots marked with a special design. You play by placing your currency on a board marked with the denominations on the wheel; the payback corresponds to where you've placed your money. One dollar on a $1 square pays a dollar; place the same dollar on a $20 square and if it comes up, you've won $20. The joker slots pay $40. Though the spinning wheel makes a pleasantly old-fashioned sound as the leather flap at the top flicks against the nail studs separating the slots, there's little else to recommend this game to any but the terminally optimistic. The house advantage on the even money ($1 square) bets is 11.1% and increases all the way up to 24% on the joker bet (for suckers only).

Among the many outlandish attractions of the *Vegas World* hotel is its casino's bigger-than-big Big Six wheel — an 8-foot-diameter giant that weighs in at 2,000 pounds and rotates on a 4½-inch-thick steel bar. The device has to be set in motion by a motor. Minimum wagers at this wheel are $5, and there are those who claim that it's worth $5 just to watch the wheel go round while contemplating the fact that you've knowingly made what is, in more than one sense, the biggest sucker bet in town.

DIVERSIONS / Gambling

BINGO: Though it is one of the two casino games with the distinction of having a room of its own, isolated from the general mayhem (the far-more-upscale baccarat is the other), bingo — a direct descendant of the 16th-century Italian national lottery — is avoided by many casino visitors on the grounds that it's readily available in their hometowns. Certainly, bingo's 35 million or so US devotees (and almost everyone else) have had some exposure to the cards on which numbers from 1 to 75 are randomly distributed in 24 squares arranged in 5 rows of 5 (the center square is free). In case you've forgotten, this is the game: You may cover a square on your card when the corresponding number is chosen from among the numbered ping pong balls thrust up one at a time by an intricate blower apparatus. If you cover 5 squares across, down, or diagonally, then you win — up to $5,000 on a $1 card, up to $7,000 on a $3 card, and up to $10,000 on a $6 card — and it's customary to announce your victory with the cry of "Bingo!"

Most casinos require that you ante up at least $3 — for one $3 board or three $1 boards. Play is scheduled for 1-hour sessions between 11 AM and 1 AM. Free coffee and cocktail service is offered.

KENO: A sort of solitaire bingo which traces its lineage back to the Han Dynasty of China, keno came to Nevada in the 1860s with Chinese railroad workers. To play, purchase a keno ticket, on which are printed the numbers from 1 to 80 in lines of ten. You get to mark between 1 and 15 of the printed numbers, called "spots." After you've marked your ticket — the best way is to place an "X" over each of your selected numbers — write the amount of your bet in the upper right-hand corner of the ticket and the number of spots you've picked below your bet. Then take your ticket to the keno counter (or have a keno runner bring it there). At the counter, a keno writer will transcribe your choices onto a blank ticket, time-stamp it and your original, and mark it with the number of the next game to be played. Keep the duplicate ticket and wait for the drawing of 20 numbers. It'll happen soon: Most casinos run approximately 200 keno races per day. The results will be shown as they occur, simultaneously on electronic keno boards all over the casino.

If you paid $1 for your ticket, marked a single number, and it is among the 20 drawn during the keno race, you win $3. If you mark 15 numbers on your $1 ticket and all 15 are among the 20 drawn, you get to share $50,000 with the IRS (wins of $1,500 or more require that you sign a G-2 form).

Despite the formidable number of different bets (virtually ubiquitous keno instruction books explain an astonishing number of variations on the basic style of ticket-marking described here), keno is quite popular. One reason is the high payoffs on small investments. The fact that keno provides a low-stress break from faster, riskier games and can be played anywhere in the casino is a second source of its popularity. On the other hand, be aware that canny gamblers resist the temptations of keno: the house advantage for the average bet is about 28%.

ROULETTE: The roulette wheel is one of the most familiar and potent symbols of high-stakes gaming. For many, a visit to a casino would be incomplete without joining the ranks of those who have been wagering on the vagaries of the wheel's spin and the ball's roll for nearly 4 centuries. You can buy into one of the six seats at the roulette table, where as many as 90 games whiz by in the course of an hour, for as little as $20 worth of chips.

The value of the chips (their colors represent the different players, not the denominations of the bet) is fixed by each player — for example, if you give the dealer $10 and tell him you want each of your chips valued at $1, he will pay you — or collect from you — accordingly. Chips can be assigned values of from $1 to $100 (although some casinos allow wagers as low as 25¢). Since they have no fixed dollar value, wheel chips (as they're called) must be cashed in when you leave the table: they're worthless elsewhere in the casino.

In addition to betting on individual numbers, roulette players can wager that six, four, three, or two connecting numbers (at odds of 5 to 1, 8 to 1, 11 to 1, and 17 to 1, respectively) will include the particular dot where the ball ends up. Also possible are wagers on whether the lucky number will be even or odd, black or red, among the first 18 numbers or the second. These are even-money bets. Other, more *recherché* sorts of bets — also made by placing chips in the "outside" area of the game board — include wagering which 12 numbers will include the lucky one. The payoff on these is $2 for every $1 wagered.

Traditional European roulette wheels (descended from those used in games called in different locales *bocca, boule,* and even-odd) differ from US ones. Our wheels have, in addition to the numbers 1 through 36, a single 0 and a double 0; European wheels have only a single zero. Since the payoff remains the same ($35 for every dollar bet on an individual number), while the chance of winning is 2 in 37 rather than 38, European casinos make considerably less money from roulette than casinos on this side of the Atlantic.

The strange-sounding names of wagering systems for roulette include the Martingale (which counsels doubling one's bets after a loss), the reverse Martingale (which counsels the opposite), the D'Alembert, the Biarritz, Cuban, and the Third Column. (Unfortunately, no matter what system or strategy you choose, it's no good unless your number comes up.)

CRAPS: Though it lacks the panache of roulette, baccarat, or even blackjack, craps is *the* game in the opinion of many casino gamblers. A casual tour of any casino shows that the craps table is where bettors are at their noisiest, as they frantically try to decide among a bewildering variety of wagers concerning the outcome of the next roll of the dice.

Though the origins of dice are shrouded in antiquity, the game of craps is an easily recognizable descendant of *hazard,* introduced into Europe in the 8th century by the Saracen conquerors of Corsica. *Hazard,* the French name of the game — which came to mean "chance" in that language (and "danger" in this one) — is derived from *az-zahr,* the Arabic word for dice. *Hazard* retained its grip on the gaming spirit of the Continent long enough to reach New Orleans in the 19th century, where its popularity among Southern slaves helped it spread outward from the Mississippi Delta. Modern craps is the result of an innovation by John Wynn, a turn-of-the-century dicemaker, who for a commission of half a percent per wager allowed players to bet against the house rather than each other. Today's craps retains the relative generosity of its founder. It's one of casino gambling's best bargains, offering a variety of bets on which the house advantage is only 1% to 2%.

In the modern casino, craps is managed by a "boxman," who watches over the game, and two dealers, who stand on either side of the boxman, paying out the winnings and raking in the losses. On the players' side of the table, opposite the boxman, the "stickman" makes sure that all bets are down and then begins play by passing several sets of dice to the shooter (one of the players). The shooter selects one pair of dice and rolls them across the table so that they bounce off the opposite wall, thereby accomplishing one of three things. If on the first roll the shooter's dice total 7 or 11, a "natural" has been scored and the shooter collects even money for the chips he or she has placed on the pass line. If on the first roll, the shooter's dice equal 2, 3, or 12, that's "craps" — an immediate loss for the shooter. If on the first roll the shooter gets a 4, 5, 6, 8, 9, or 10, the "box point" has been established. The shooter continues to roll the dice until the box point is matched or a fatal 7 comes up; the other players at the table bet for or against the shooter with each roll of the dice.

More than a little study and a considerable amount of practice are required to feel comfortable at the craps table. (By all means take advantage of the hotel's free lessons.) The good news, though, is that most of the more complex wagers — hard ways, any craps, seven, eleven, and horn — are bad bets, in which the house edge ranges between

11% and 17%. If, in relative ignorance, you play the line and either "pass" (bet with the person rolling the dice) or "don't pass" (bet against the roller), you'll be bucking a house advantage of less than 2%. Further advice: When you bet the pass line, always take the full odds in back of your pass line bet. (A few casinos offer triple odds — a four-tenths of a percent house edge, and the Downtown *Horseshoe* has gained a worldwide reputation by offering 10-times odds, in effect charging you only two-tenths of a percent to win.)

All this is as confusing as it sounds. Still, as you can easily find out, craps is a wonderfully exciting game. As long as you resist the temptation to demonstrate your increasing knowledge by making fancy bets, it's a relatively inexpensive way to get in on the hottest action in any casino.

BLACKJACK: Casino craps is the game of choice for those who like their excitement fast, noisy, and extroverted. The quiet, the cerebral, those who pride themselves on being guided by intellect rather than instinct, inevitably gravitate to the blackjack table, where the venerable French game of *vingt-et-un* (21) is pursued with irresistible intensity. The name "blackjack" originated in racetrack gambling dens in turn-of-the-century Evansville, Indiana, where players whose opening cards consisted of an ace and a black jack (of spades or clubs) received a $5 bonus for their winning hands.

To play casino blackjack, first find a table where the minimum bets are within your price range. Some casinos have $3 and even $2 or $1 blackjack tables, and that's where novices will want to sit. Once seated, purchase chips from the dealer (when you're finished playing, you'll get cash for chips at the cashier's window; the dealer cannot redeem them) and make an initial bet by stacking your chips neatly in the playing area directly in front of your seat. The dealer (on the opposite side of the table) shuffles the cards and invites one of the players to cut the deck. Then the dealer discards the top one, two, or more cards from the top of the deck. When the top cards have been "burned" (Vegas lingo for discarding them), cards are dealt around the table from the dealer's left. If play is at a 1- or 2-deck table, players' cards will be dealt face down. If 4 or even 6 decks are in use, players' cards will be dealt face up from a plastic "shoe" (card holder). In either case, the dealer's first card will be face down, the second one face up. After the players have received their two-card initial hands, they calculate its point value: Kings, queens, and jacks are each worth 10; other cards are worth their face value (deuces are worth 2 points, threes 3 points and so forth); aces are worth either 1 or 11, as the player chooses.

Since the object of the game is to obtain a hand totaling as close as possible to 21 points without going over, inspection of your first two cards tells you how to proceed. If you're holding an ace and any card worth 10, you win (at a rate of $3 for every $2 you've wagered) unless the dealer has a similar hand (in which there's a tie and no money is lost or gained — called a "push"). If you don't have 21 but have close to it (16 or 17), you'll likely decide not to receive any further cards, or "stand." If your first two cards bring you to a low total (remember the ace can count as 1 *or* 11), you can choose to be "hit" — that is, dealt more cards. After each subsequent card is dealt, you're faced with the same choice until you decide to "stand" or your hand totals more than 21. If the latter happens, you've "busted" — and have no choice but to turn your cards face up and forfeit the money you've bet.

The players have several options, which include variations such as splitting (doubling the amount at stake by electing to use one's initial cards as the basis for two hands to be played simultaneously), buying insurance (making a side bet equal to half the original wager that pays double if the dealer has blackjack), and surrendering (forfeiting half your wager after seeing the first two cards). The dealer has considerably less freedom. If the dealer's initial hand is 16 or below, he or she must take additional cards until the total reaches or exceeds 21. If the dealer's initial hand is 17 or more, he or she must stand.

The fact that the players' choices are so much more varied than the dealer's is one of the sources of blackjack's attraction. But there is a much more important factor at work. *Unlike every other casino game,* the outcome of any particular hand in blackjack depends on the hands that have preceded it. For instance, in roulette, even if 36 has come up three times running on the roulette wheel, the chances of its coming up a fourth straight time remain 1 in 38, neither more nor less — despite the well-known, tempting, but ultimately disastrous tendency to think otherwise. On the other hand, in this card game, if the dealer has gotten blackjack twice in a row, it's a pretty safe bet he or she won't get it the next hand — two of the four aces in the deck (if this is a one-deck game) have already been used. It's the elaboration of this basic idea that makes blackjack uniquely winnable by the employment of betting strategies. There are a dozen or so different systematic strategies which, by assigning point values to different cards being played, fulfill the impossible dream of gaining an advantage over the house.

Obviously, casinos are less than happy to surrender their profits to players who use counting strategies. Tactics for players to disguise — and casinos to detect — card counting are in constant development. The simplest and most effective tactic for the house is to increase the number of cards in play (hence the existence of 4- and even 6-deck blackjack tables) and the frequency with which they are shuffled. Burning the top cards also helps sabotage card-counting strategies.

Even those on the sidelines of the ongoing struggle between casinos and card counters can profit from the use of basic, easily mastered strategies. Spend a day or two learning them and you can reduce the house advantage to as little as one-half of a percent, savoring a small taste of what it would be like to beat the house at its own game.

BACCARAT: Nevada-style baccarat is an adaptation of the blackjack-like French card game *chemin de fer.* Fifteen bettors wager on which of two hands — the "player's" or the "banker's" — drawn from an 8-deck shoe passed around the table will be closer to nine. Tens and picture cards are valued at zero, other cards at face value. The payoff is even money. Baccarat differs from blackjack in that receiving additional cards is never a matter of choice. There are no decisions to be made other than how much to wager and whether to bet on the player or the banker — and the outcome of the game is purely a matter of chance. Nevertheless, baccarat is extremely popular for two reasons: First, the house advantage is low. With a commission of only one-half of a percent on winning bank bets (collected after the finish of a shoe) and no commission on winning player bets, the edge is a modest 1.37%. More important, perhaps, is the fact that from the moment the *Stardust* hotel introduced baccarat, shortly after its 1958 opening, the game has been merchandized as the *ne plus ultra* in glamour. High minimums are imposed, play is with cash rather than chips, and tuxedoed dealers guide the action in hushed pits conspicuously segregated from the hurly-burly of the main casino. Though in recent years mini-baccarat (played just like the original except with smaller minimums) has begun to find its way onto the edge of blackjack pits, the cachet with which the *Stardust* invested the game has remained. It's definitely an upscale thrill to play your hunches in the baccarat room.

Vegas Vows: Winning Weddings

The same 1931 law that saved Nevada's economic future by legalizing gambling in the state established liberal divorce and marriage laws with a similar hope of ensuring a steady flow of tourists. The strategy succeeded: The possibility of divorce granted after a mere 6-week residency (Reno is still the divorce stop of choice) and of marriage for

DIVERSIONS / Winning Weddings   121

those over 18 requiring only a license and a willing minister continues to lure visitors to Las Vegas. Every year 75,000 marriage ceremonies — 200 a day — are performed here. Some feature big names (the recent past has seen nuptials celebrated between Bruce Willis and Demi Moore, and Richard Gere and Cindy Crawford) but mostly it's ordinary people who plight their troths where the neon is brightest. Drive along the Strip any Saturday afternoon and you'll see movie-theater-length lines of couples patiently waiting to exchange vows in the high-turnover chapel of their choice. Only in Las Vegas . . .

If you and your companion are of a mind to join the lines, the procedure is simple enough. Proceed to the Clark County Marriage License Bureau (200 S. 3rd St.; phone: 702-455-3156; after 5 PM, on Saturdays, and holidays, 702-455-4145). The office is open 8 AM to midnight Mondays through Thursdays, and 24 hours Fridays, Saturdays, and holidays. Both of you must appear in person to get a license. Those 16 to 18 must bring along a parent or an affidavit from one (under 16, a court order is needed). The license costs $35; arrive without cash and you'll run into a hitch in your hitching plan: Neither check nor credit card is accepted.

Once you've a license, you can look around for a place to have the ceremony performed. No-frills, justice of the peace nuptials are performed at the office of the Commissioner of Civil Marriages, a block away from the license bureau (136 S. 4th St.; phone: 702-455-4415), during office hours (8 AM to midnight Mondays through Thursdays, and then from 8 AM Friday all the way to midnight Sunday). You don't have to make a reservation, and except for *New Year's Eve* and possibly *Valentine's Day,* you won't have to wait in line.

Fancier ceremonies in more traditional settings complete with flowers, organ music, photographs, and a minister don't take much longer to arrange. There are a dozen chapels competing for your nuptial attentions in the 10-block stretch of Las Vegas Boulevard South between Downtown and Sahara Avenue. Most charge between $40 and $60 and expect a $35 cash donation to the minister. If you want, pile on the extras — a $5 silk boutonniere for the groom, $50 worth of snapshots, live organ music, a videotape of the ceremony, rented gowns and tuxedos, wedding cakes, and the like. Perhaps you'd like a limo ride back to your hotel? It's easily arranged, and a $25 "toke" to the limo driver ensures some of the funniest wedding stories you've ever heard.

The most popular chapel is the *Candlelight* (2855 Las Vegas Blvd. S.; phone: 702-735-4179), right in the heart of the Strip. Getting married here is a 24-hour-a-day business. Even more intensely efficient is the drive-through window (no kidding) at the *Little White Chapel* (1301 Las Vegas Blvd. S.; phone: 702-382-5943). The *Riviera, Circus Circus, Imperial Palace, Excalibur, Bally's,* and the *Plaza* hotels offer the services of an in-house chapel to their guests. *L'Amour Chapel* (1901 Las Vegas Blvd. S.; phone: 702-369-5683) features red velvet love seats, and *Weddings on Wheels,* a 36-foot RV, makes it possible to get married right in front of the *Mirage* hotel, to the accompaniment of the hotel's erupting volcano. Ain't love grand?

There's a somewhat more traditional atmosphere at the genuinely pretty *Little Church of the West* (3960 Las Vegas Blvd. S.; phone: 702-739-7971), a half-size replica of a Columbia, California, church from the Gold Rush era. This chapel enjoys not only the distinction of being the oldest extant, but also a unique association with master eccentric Howard Hughes. In the early 1980s, when the reclusive billionaire bought the *Frontier* hotel, where the chapel had stood since 1942, he decided he didn't want it there anymore and arranged to have it trucked south along the Strip to its present location. The *Chapel of Love* (1431 Las Vegas Blvd. S.; phone: 702-387-0155) books only one of its four rather elegant rooms at a time, so you won't be rushed out the door in order to make room for the next anxious couple.

For the genuinely romantic, the best advice is to drive 35 miles to Mount Charleston, where amidst the beautiful mountain scenery you can be married at the *Mount Charleston Lodge* (a traditional favorite; Kyle Canyon Rd.; phone: 702-386-6899 or 702-872-5408) or the *Mount Charleston Inn* (newer with beautiful, rustic-style guest rooms; 2 Kyle Canyon Rd.; phone: 702-872-5500). Also see *Tour 3: Mt. Charleston.*

Wherever you tie the knot in Las Vegas, you can hope to emulate the lucky couple from Santa Rosa, California, who decided to stop at the slots in one of the casinos after their wedding. The bride, who'd never before gambled, deposited her coins and pulled the handle. When the noise and confusion subsided, she was informed that she'd just won $126,000. That's some wedding gift!

A Shutterbug's Las Vegas

Perhaps no place on the planet seems so posed for the camera as Las Vegas. Virtually anywhere you look you'll find a subject that seems to exemplify the local penchant for spectacle. And within less than an hour's drive of the city lie natural vistas that rival the neon ones for drama and interest. Capturing the excitement of your visit on film should be a snap.

Even a beginner can achieve remarkable results with a surprisingly basic set of lenses and filters. Equipment is, in fact, only as valuable as the imagination that puts it into use. (For further information on equipment, see *Cameras and Equipment* in GETTING READY TO GO.)

Don't be afraid to experiment. Use what knowledge you have to explore new possibilities. At the same time, don't limit yourself with preconceived ideas of what's hackneyed or corny. Because the volcano at the *Mirage* has been photographed thousands of times before doesn't make it any less worthy of your attention.

In Las Vegas, as elsewhere, spontaneity is one of the keys to good photography. Whether it's a look of ecstatic wonder on the face of an 8-year-old watching the animated dinosaurs at Las Vegas's *Museum of Natural History* or a group of business-suited executives at McCarran Airport studiously ignoring an off-work showgirl playing the slots, don't hesitate to shoot if the moment is right. If photography is indeed capturing a moment and making it timeless, success lies in judging just when a moment worth capturing occurs.

A good picture reveals an eye for detail, whether it's a matter of lighting, of positioning your subject, or of taking time to frame a picture carefully. The better your grasp of the importance of details, the better your results will be photographically.

Patience is often necessary. If you'd like a shot of newlyweds leaving the *Little White Chapel*'s drive-up window, it's worth waiting for just the right couple in just the right vehicle. A herd of nondescript rental cars blocking your shot of the statue of Caesar at *Caesars Palace?* Reframe your image to eliminate the obvious distraction. People walking toward a scene that would benefit from their presence? Wait until they're in position before you shoot. After the fact, many of the flaws will be self-evident. The trick is to be aware of the ideal and have the patience to allow it to happen. If you are part of a group, you may well have to trail behind a bit in order to shoot properly. Not only is group activity distracting, but bunches of people hovering nearby tend to stifle spontaneity and overwhelm potential subjects.

The camera provides an opportunity, not only to capture the nowhere-else-on earth glitz of Las Vegas, but to interpret it. What it takes is a sensitivity to the surroundings, a knowledge of the capabilities of your equipment, and a willingness to see things in new ways.

LANDSCAPES AND CITYSCAPES: Las Vegas's neon signs are most often visiting photographers' favorite subjects. But hotel façades, lobbies, and even the upscale restaurants provide numerous photo possibilities as well. And don't neglect the city's natural — if not native — wonders. At the *Mirage* hotel, for example, a wide variety of exotic flora and fauna, including banana trees, dolphins, and white tigers, are there for the photographing. Even without taking to the road, where the scenic wonders of the desert landscape await, photographers can find dramatic vignettes as close as the local golf courses.

Color and form are the obvious ingredients here, and how you frame your pictures can be as important as getting the proper exposure. Study the shapes, angles, and colors that make up the scene and create a composition that uses them to best advantage.

Lighting is a vital component in landscapes. Take advantage of the richer colors of early morning and late afternoon whenever possible. The overhead light of midday is often harsh and without the shadowing that can add to the drama of a scene. This is when a polarizer is used to best effect. Most polarizers come with a mark on the rotating ring. If you can aim at your subject and point that marker at the sun, the sun's rays are likely to be right for the polarizer to work for you. If not, stick to your skylight filter, underexposing slightly if the scene is particularly bright. Most light meters respond to an overall light balance, with the result that bright areas may appear burned out.

Although a standard 50mm to 55mm lens may work well in some landscape situations, most will benefit from a 20mm to 28mm wide-angle. The neon signs of Downtown's Glitter Gulch, for example, form a panorama that fits beautifully into a wide-angle format, allowing not only the overview, but the opportunity to include people or other points of interest in the foreground. A mother and father guiding their starstruck kids across Fremont Avenue, for example, can add a charming sense of perspective to a shot of the neon signs overhead.

To isolate specific elements of any scene, use your telephoto lens. Perhaps you'd like a photo of just one of the statues in front of *Caesars Palace* or the interplay of light and shadow on a crenelated corner of the *Excalibur*'s fantasy castle. The successful use of a telephoto means developing your eye for detail.

PEOPLE: As with taking pictures of people anywhere, there are going to be times in Las Vegas when a camera is an intrusion. In fact, with the exception of the *Excalibur* on the Strip and the *Four Queens* and *California* hotels Downtown, Las Vegas's casinos assume that cameras of any kind are always an intrusion where people have come to gamble. In the three rooms where you can memorialize the excitement of gaming, you should, however, be aware that your photographic interest may still be irritating to some. Your approach is the key: Consider your own reaction under similar circumstances, and you have an idea as to what would make others comfortable enough to be willing subjects. Gamblers, especially those focused on whether the next roll of the dice, spin of the wheel, drop of a coin, or turn of a card will bring a change of fortune, are often sensitive to having a camera suddenly focused on them. A polite request, while getting you a share of refusals, will also provide a chance to shoot some wonderful portraits that capture the spirit of the gaming. For candids, an excellent lens is a zoom telephoto in the 70mm to 210mm range; it allows you to remain unobtrusive while the telephoto lens draws the subject closer. And for portraits, a telephoto can be used effectively as close as 2 or 3 feet. Both lenses, indeed all lenses, are inappropriate in any of the Las Vegas showrooms. Though it would be nice to capture some out-of-towners in rapt contemplation of their superstar idols or the spectacle of an eye-popping extravaganza like *Bally's* $10-million "Jubilee," please note: While there are exceptions to the cameras-in-casinos etiquette, photographs are *always forbidden* in Las Vegas showrooms. Enjoy the show, and enjoy the audience enjoying the show — but leave your camera behind.

For authenticity and variety, select a place likely to produce interesting subjects. Glitter Gulch is an obvious spot for visitors, but if it's local color you're after, you might want to visit a laundromat or convenience store to photograph the locals in their native habitat, complete with the ubiquitous slot machines that are so closely associated with their town. When taking outdoor portraits, say of a happy couple patiently waiting in line at one of the wedding chapels on the Strip, remember that morning or afternoon light will add richness to skin tones, emphazing tans. To avoid the harsh facial shadows cast by direct sunlight, shoot in the shade or in an area where the light is diffused.

SUNSETS: Most hotels on the Strip have hallways with picture windows, so an elevator ride is all that's needed to position you for impressive overhead shots of the sun setting on the tropical surroundings of the *Mirage* or the beautiful golf course behind the *Desert Inn.*

When shooting sunsets, keep in mind that the brightness will distort meter readings. When composing a shot directly into the sun, frame the picture in the viewfinder so that only half of the sun is included. Read the meter, set, and shoot. Whenever there is this kind of unusual lighting, shoot a few frames in half-step increments, both over and under the meter reading. Bracketing, as this is called, can provide a range of images, the best of which may well be other than the one shot at the meter's recommended setting.

Use any lens for sunsets. A wide-angle is good when the sky is filled with color-streaked clouds, when the sun is partially hidden, or when you're close to an object that silhouettes dramatically against the sky.

Telephotos also produce wonderful silhouettes, either with the sun as a backdrop or against the palette of a brilliant sunset sky. Bracket again here. For the best silhouettes, wait 10 to 15 minutes after sunset. Unless using a very fast film, a tripod is recommended.

Red and orange filters are often used to accentuate a sunset's picture potential. Orange will help turn even a gray sky into something approaching a photogenic finale to the day. If the sunset is already bold in hue, the orange will overwhelm the natural colors. A red filter will produce dramatic, highly unrealistic results.

NIGHT: It's only as the sun goes down that the neon lights come on, so Las Vegas is one city where after-dark photography is not something you'd want to leave exclusively to the professionals. Here's something to think about: Look at the photo postcards that hotels circulate of their own neon signs. You may be surprised to find that the sky in the background is blue, not black. The trick to incorporating both the bright colors of the signs and a photogenic blue sky into a single photograph is to plan your shots for just after sunset when the signs will be on, and behind them, against the still-blue sky, you'll see the desert haze, streaked with strands of yellow and red. Choose 100 ISO print film rather than 400 or 1000, and aim for exposures no briefer than half a second. Otherwise you'll find the colors of the neon weak and the effect bland.

For other nighttime shooting in Glitter Gulch, say of the barkers along the streets, remember that a flash used too close to a subject may result in overexposure, resulting in a 'blown out" effect. With most cameras, strobes will work with a maximum shutter speed of 1/125 or 1/150 of a second. If you set the exposure properly and shoot within range, you should come up with pretty sharp results.

CLOSE-UPS: Whether of people or of objects such as the gold-plated pay phones in the lobby of the *Golden Nugget* or the fresh flowers in your hotel room, close-ups can add another dimension to your photography. There are a number of shooting options, one of which is to use a 70mm or a 210mm lens at its closest focusable distance. Unless you're working in bright sunlight, a tripod will be worthwhile. If you are very near your subject and there is a good deal of reflective light, it may pay to underexpose a bit in relation to the meter reading.

If you do not have a telephoto lens, you can still shoot close-ups using a set of magnification filters. Filter packs of one-, two-, and three-time magnification are available, converting your lens into a close-up lens. Even better is a special macro lens designed for close-up photography.

The following are some of Vegas's best vistas.

A SHORT PHOTOGRAPHIC TOUR

GLITTER GULCH: Among favorite Downtown shots are the larger-than-life Cowboy Vic and Sassy Sally (atop the *Pioneer* and *Golden Gate* hotels, respectively). By standing in the street (while the traffic's stopped at a red light) at the corner of Fremont and Third, you can get both into a single shot. At the same location, you can also get a shot of the *Horseshoe* hotel's neon sign. Walk down the street toward the *Four Queens* sign. Along the way, the variously costumed barkers offering freebies make good subjects. When you arrive at the *Four Queens,* go inside and attach a flash — you're at one of the few casinos that permits the taking of photographs. Just up the street is another favorite Las Vegas photo-op: the world's largest gold nugget (63 pounds) at (where else?) the *Golden Nugget.*

THE STRIP: Though it's an initially tempting project, there's simply no way of getting all the neon lights of the Strip into one photograph unless you're prepared to rent a helicopter and go airborne.

In fact, many of the signs on the Strip are so large that they don't make very good photos. Still, it's hard to pass up such "naturals" as the *Circus Circus* display: a nude dancer and the 125-foot-tall Lucky the Clown. Even more tempting to those who want a filmed record of the Strip is an eruption of the volcano atop the waterfalls fronting the *Mirage* hotel (which happens every 15 minutes after dark). The pink and blue lights and fountains of *Caesars Palace* next door are equally irresistible.

Even in a town where every few steps seems to reveal a fresh piece of kitsch crying for memorialization, the fountain across from the entrance of *Bally's* has achieved near-legendary status among photographers. "Neptune and the Sirens" is the name of this monument to bad taste, a magnet to thousands of male shutterbugs who just know that the folks back home will need evidence that the sirens actually gush streams of water from their nipples.

Equally kitschy, though considerably less offensive, is the 4,032-room *Excalibur* hotel. It's not its bigness, however, but its architectural motif — a pastiche European castle — that makes this a natural subject for photographers. Day or night, its turrets framed against the sky look splendidly dramatic on film. Inside, at the 23-shop medieval village, strolling performers in elaborate costumes are eminently photogenic. Inside is another one of the casinos that allows photographs.

OUT OF TOWN: As impressive as the city's photographic opportunities are, they're easily equaled or surpassed by those that nature provides just a short drive from the strip. Superb landscape shots are possible at Red Rock Canyon, only 15 miles west on Charleston Boulevard. The best time for photographs here is just before sunset when, amid the long shadows, the colors come alive. The dramatic rock formations at the Valley of Fire State Park (55 miles northeast of the city on I-15) are capable of inspiring photographs that look as if you took them during a vacation on Mars. It's hard to imagine that anyone would visit the park without a camera. Finally, Boulder Dam has, over the years, provided millions of tourists with memorable souvenirs of their Western vacations. Take the informative tour that begins atop the dam, and be sure to bring your camera.

For the Body

Great Golf

With its average of 320 sunny days a year and 21 championship courses from which to choose, it's little wonder that visiting golfers are likely to find that green in Las Vegas is more than just the color of money. Armed with an adequate supply of liquids and sunscreen, anyone can enjoy the greens even during the hottest months (early mornings and late afternoons are recommended in summer, however, when midday temperatures can soar to a sizzling 110° — and higher). But be aware that the desert air's lower humidity also means lower air resistance. Drives travel farther, but then again, so do putts.

ANGEL PARK COUNTRY CLUB: Established in 1989, this two-course club, only a few miles northwest of the city, has gained an enviable reputation among local and visiting golfers. Its Arnold Palmer–designed championship courses — the 6,743 yard, par 71 *Palm* and the 6,772-yard par 71 *Mountain* — both feature a natural desert canyon as a hazard. The *Palm* course, well-bunkered with elevation changes and fast, bent-grass greens, provides impressive views of the city. Golfers face challenges from desert areas and, on five holes, water. The greens fee, including a mandatory cart, is $70. Sporting severely undulating greens as well as stunning views of Red Rock Canyon, the *Mountain* course has water hazards on four holes. The fee here, also with mandatory cart, is $60. Club rentals for both courses are $25. Call at least 30 days in advance to reserve tee times. Facilities offered at the year-round club include a lighted driving range, pro shop, bar, restaurant, snack bar, and refreshment cart. To help hone your putting skills, an 18-hole putting course and a putting green are available. Information: *Angel Park Golf Club,* 100 S. Rampart Blvd. (phone: 702-254-4653).

DESERT INN COUNTRY CLUB: The 18-hole, 7,111-yard, par 72 course that's part of the *Desert Inn* hotel-casino complex is, in a city of golfers, the recipient of respect approaching veneration. The well-kept, long, undulating greens designed by Lawrence Marion Hughes in 1952 host three annual tournaments: the *Desert Inn LPGA International* in March or April, the *Las Vegas Senior Classic* in late April or early May, and the *Las Vegas Invitational* in October. Hotel guests usually reserve tee times along with their rooms; greens fees are $62.50 on weekdays, $112 on weekends. Carts are mandatory and cost $12.50 per person; club rentals are $18. Non-hotel guests must reserve at least 48 hours in advance; the greens fee is $137.50. There's a pro shop, a driving range, a putting green, a deli, a snack bar, and a bar. Information: *Desert Inn Country Club,* 3145 Las Vegas Blvd. S. (phone: 702-733-4290).

DUNES COUNTRY CLUB: Challenging Las Vegas golfers since 1964, this 7,078-yard, par 72 William Francis Bell–designed championship course features desert terrain, palm trees galore, and one of the longest layouts in the state. Located directly behind the *Dunes* hotel, it charges $60 to hotel guests on weekdays, $70 on weekends. The fee includes a mandatory cart (club rentals are $15); non-guests pay an additional $20. There's a pro shop, driving range, putting green, restaurant, snack bar, bar, and beverage cart. Convenient location, reasonable fees, and never-less-than-exciting play have ensured the course an enduring place in the hearts of Las Vegas golfers. We've heard, however, that the *Dunes*'s prolonged transition in ownership has left the course in somewhat less than top condition. Ask around or take a look before you decide to play through. If management has gotten its act together, you're in for a treat. Information: *Dunes Country Club*, 3650 Las Vegas Blvd. S. (phone: 702-737-4747).

LEGACY GOLF CLUB: The 15- to 20-minute drive southeast of the city required to reach this relatively recent addition to area courses, as well as the advisability of reserving at least 2 months in advance, seem daunting at first. But this home of the *Nevada Golf Hall of Fame* and (since 1990) the *US Open Regional* qualifying course offers interesting play. Designed by Arthur Hill, the championship 7,150-yard, links-type, par 72 course demands extra-long drives to carry the ball over the natural desert landscape. Holes 11, 12, and 13 are reminiscent of those on the traditionally long, rolling courses in Scotland. The greens fee, with a mandatory cart, is $75; it costs an additional $25 to rent clubs. There's a driving range, putting green, and the usual amenities, including a beverage cart. Information: *Legacy Golf Club*, 130 Par Excellence Dr., Henderson (phone: 702-897-2187).

SAHARA COUNTRY CLUB: Host to the PGA *Tournament of Champions* from 1962 to 1967 and to the LPGA *Tournament of Champions* in the late 1970s, this Bert Stamps–designed course is a well-bunkered 6,815-yard layout made more challenging by its many tough pin placements. The maturity of the par 71 course is attested to by its abundance of towering pine and palm trees. The course's Las Vegas location (a short distance from the major Strip hotels) is one of its pluses. On the excellent par 5 18th hole (one of the best in the state), you can bet on reaching the green in two shots. Clark County residents pay only a $50 greens fee; non-residents pay $70 (*American Golf Club* members get discounts). Carts are mandatory, club rental is $25, and the driving range is lighted at night. Information: *Sahara Country Club*, 1911 E. Desert Inn Rd. (phone: 702-796-0013).

Tennis

The same sunny climate that makes Las Vegas a year-round pleasure for golfers provides a welcoming environment for tennis enthusiasts from around the country. And though the city is more intimately associated with rackets than racquets, lovers of the game should draw some inspiration from the fact that Andre Agassi, tennis's current bad boy, learned his craft (if not his attitude) on the courts of the old *MGM Grand,* where his father was a showroom maître d'. Pancho Gonzales, the resilient and redoubtable comeback king of professional tennis in the late 1950s, put in his time in Las Vegas too, serving for years as the tennis pro at *Caesars Palace*. Somewhat more important than these bits of lore are the general cautions about playing in the desert's dry heat: Drink plenty of fluids and wear sunblock. (But you probably already knew that.)

Most hotels on the Strip offer their guests at least a couple of outdoor courts, but even moderately serious players will want to choose from among the following quartet, all of which offer lessons and have pro shops.

BALLY'S: All ten courts are hard-surface; five are lighted. The fee is $10 an hour for hotel guests, $15 for non-guests. Information: *Bally's,* 3645 Las Vegas Blvd. S. (phone: 702-739-4598).

CAESARS PALACE: Caesars offers four hard-surface, unlighted courts. Guests pay $15 an hour; non-guests, $25. Information: *Caesars Palace,* 3570 Las Vegas Blvd. S. (phone: 702-731-7786).

DESERT INN: The ten courts here are considered by tennis aficionados to be the best of the Las Vegas hotel set-ups. In addition to nine hard courts (five of them lighted), the hotel coddles tender-ankled players with a special "sponge" surface court. Hotel guests play free, non-guests are charged $10 per hour. Information: *Desert Inn,* 3145 Las Vegas Blvd. S. (phone: 702-733-4577).

FLAMINGO HILTON: All four hard-surface courts here are lighted. Local residents as well as hotel guests play for an extremely reasonable $5 an hour; guests staying at other hotels pay $12. Information: *Flamingo Hilton,* 3555 Las Vegas Blvd. S. (phone: 702-733-3344).

Tennis buffs in search of the city's best venue might want to check into the availability of the dozen lighted courts at the University of Nevada–Las Vegas. 4505 S. Maryland Pkwy. (phone: 702-739-3150).

Build a Lake and They Will Come

There's not much from which to choose in the way of venues for boating and fishing in Las Vegas — this is, after all, the desert. On the other hand, the one option — the 115-mile Lake Mead, created in the 1930s when the Hoover Dam backed up the waters of the Colorado River — more than satisfies its 6 million annual visitors. Only 25 miles from the city, the largest artificial body of water in the US provides 500 miles of shoreline, luring anglers in search of striped and largemouth bass; rainbow, brown, and cutthroat trout; channel catfish; and black crappie. Best bets are the striped bass: their popularity (those taken are mostly in the 2- to 5-pound range, though the lake record is held by a 50-pound leviathan) has provided the opportunity for the lake's largemouth bass, nearly fished out in recent years, to stage an impressive comeback.

Non-residents wishing to get their hooks into Lake Mead's scaly inhabitants can choose between a 3-day ($17.50) and a 10-day ($30.50) permit, both issued by the Nevada Department of Wildlife (phone: 702-486-5127) and obtainable at any of the five marinas located around the lake.

These marinas — *Callville Bay Resort and Marina* (phone: 702-565-8958), *Cottonwood Cove Resort and Marina* (phone: 702-297-1464), *Echo Bay Resort* (phone: 702-394-4000), *Lake Mead Resort and Marina* (phone: 702-293-3484), and *Willow Beach Resort and Marina* (phone: 800-845-3833) — serve the recreational needs not only of fisherfolk, but also of anyone who'd like to ply the waters, offering a variety of fishing craft and powerboats. Jet skis, wet bikes, and inflatable craft can be rented from *Fun n' Sun Rentals* (Henderson Industrial Park; phone: 702-564-54520), and canoes and jet skis from *Wilderness Outfitting* (205 Rainer Ct., Boulder City; phone: 702-293-7526).

For a leisurely treat, many of Lake Mead's inland sailors recommend houseboat odysseys. Models that sleep six to ten people are rented by *Echo*

Bay Resort (Overton; phone: 702-394-4000), *Lake Mead Resort* (322 Lakeshore Rd.; phone: 702-293-2074), *Temple Bar Resort* (Temple Bar, Az; phone: 602-767-3400), and *Forever Resorts* (Box 100 HCR-30; phone: 702-565-7340 or 800-255-5561). If you prefer a professional hand on the tiller, sightseeing cruises on Lake Mead and around Hoover Dam are the province of *Lake Mead Cruises* (W. Lake Mead Dr., Henderson; phone: 702-293-6180). A more intimate exposure to Lake Mead's pleasures can be had through the day-long raft trips down the Colorado River from the base of Hoover Dam offered by *Black Canyon Tours* (1417 Pueblo Dr., Henderson; phone: 702-293-3776).

Lake Mead also offers a variety of opportunities for below-the-surface sightseeing. Scuba divers will revel in the 30-foot-visibility; wet suits are needed only in the winter. There, lurking underwater just waiting to be explored, are the yacht *Tortuga,* near the Boulder Islands; the submerged factory where the asphalt for Hoover Dam was manufactured; and the old Mormon town of St. Thomas, which became the Atlantis of Nevada when the rising waters of Lake Mead finally covered it in the mid-1930s.

Diving equipment can be rented from *Blue Seas Scuba Center* (4661 Spring Mountain Rd.; phone: 702-367-2822) and *American Cactus Divers* (848 E. Lake Mead Rd.; phone: 702-564-6810).

For those ready to abandon the oasis of their desert hotels, this virtual water wonderland awaits less than a 40-minute drive south of the Strip.

DIRECTIONS

Introduction

Even to the uninitiated, the mere mention of Las Vegas conjures up images of endless miles of neon lights, flashing signs, feather-clad (if clad at all) showgirls, and countless casinos, their tables covered in enough green felt to carpet the *Astrodome*. Most people think of Las Vegas as a *Disneyland* for gamblers. And they're right. So if someone advised you to bring along comfortable walking shoes or even skis, you'd laugh. But you'd be wrong.

For just beyond the glaring glitter of the Strip are natural and manmade wonders that surprise and delight — easy drives and scenic hikes that make for a welcome respite from the frenetic pace within the hotels.

The first, and only, walking tour in this section starts in the city, taking in the sights along the Strip. Although Las Vegas is not generally regarded as a pedestrian-friendly town, sincere efforts have been made to make it more so, and the Strip, in particular, is surprisingly navigable on foot. Sidewalks are plentiful, and, as is the case in most western cities, pedestrians always have the right of way. But until the wizards who have created such marvels as a piña colada–spewing volcano and a casino with a flying circus within its walls can work their legerdemain on Mother Nature, the desert heat will always be a definite deterrent to walkers. A 2-mile stroll along the Strip in the dog days of summer will easily convince you of the absolute necessity of air conditioning and cars. Best to plan this walk for early morning or even better, at dusk, when the neon lights are lit against a still startlingly blue sky.

In addition to the Strip walk, we offer three easy day trips, well worth the short drive, and three longer drives — ones that require more time and a suggested overnight stay. In all, these seven tours take you through and beyond the desert fairyland that is Las Vegas. Boating, skiing, hiking, golfing, even an alternative gambling destination — they're all just down the road apiece, back in the real world.

Only 20 minutes west of town is Red Rock Canyon, its pristine beauty silently and majestically contrasting with the glaring glitz of the nearby city. A little farther, Valley of Fire State Park and the adjacent *Lost City Museum*, less than 50 miles out of the city limits, are reminders that millennia before there was a Las Vegas there existed in the area an amazingly sophisticated Native American civilization. The Pueblo Anasazi people who inhabited much of the region left behind cryptic petroglyphs on the face of the red sandstone that later societies have been puzzling over for years. Nearby Hoover Dam, a relatively recent historical development, certainly should be on any Las Vegas visitor's must-see list. The formidable manmade structure that changed the course of the mighty Colorado River also created Lake Mead, with more than 500 miles of shoreline and opportunities for a host of water-related activities.

Also within a day's drive of the city is the Mount Charleston recreation area, a boon for Vegas residents in the summer, with its cool pine forests and alpine scenery, and in the winter, as it claims its place as southern Nevada's only fully equipped ski resort.

And there's more. Three hours south of the city (and the driving is easy) on the Colorado River is picturesque Laughlin, Nevada's fastest-growing community and a popular gaming town in its own right. Not only is it a pleasant respite from the Strip's often impersonal, always crowded casinos, but it also offers a glimpse of what Las Vegas looked like some 30 years ago.

Farther afield, but at 140 miles away still a feasible 1-day drive, is California's redoubtable Death Valley. A remarkable sight, much of it resembling a bizarre lunar landscape, it also recalls the indomitable spirit of America's early pioneers and miners, many of whom lost their lives crossing the merciless, parched valley.

Heading in another direction about 3 hours from Las Vegas, in neighboring Utah, is Zion National Park — part of the vast terrain that geographically comprises the Grand Canyon — with its dramatic, rainbow-colored canyons. The region also includes Bryce Canyon, about a 2-hour drive from Zion. Bryce's breathtaking, pink-and-white-limestone chasms, some as deep as 1,000 feet, have made it one of the world's most-photographed natural wonders.

More than a desert with a megawatt metropolis plopped down in its center, Las Vegas offers visitors the chance to explore some of the most spectacular scenery the American southwest has to offer. And every site's a winner.

Tour 1: The Strip

Las Vegas has taken its place in the collective world consciousness as an entirely synthetic monument to excess and hedonism, and to many its name evokes images of an unfettered, consummately "American" free-market mania run amok. Vegas's Strip, with its seemingly infinite array of mind-boggling choices, best embodies this spirit. A walk along the 4-mile Strip — technically, Las Vegas Boulevard South — is like nothing else in the world precisely because of this hyperbole, the never-ending search to outglitz the competition. Indeed, the blocks upon blocks of hotels and casinos are engaged in a constant, upwardly spiraling contest of one-upmanship. All this is a real boon for the visitor: Every place wants your business, and each will go to great lengths to win you.

In recent years, the family resort theme, as begun by such hotels as *Circus Circus,* and followed by the *Tropicana,* the *Excalibur,* and the soon-to-open *Treasure Island, MGM Grand,* and *Luxor,* provides yet another element of entertainment for visitors of all ages. And in fact, the magic show, the animal act, and the midway are becoming just as much the symbols of the Strip as are the showgirl, the cocktail waitress, and the blackjack dealer.

Nearly every complex on the Strip is its own self-contained miniature city; you could easily spend an entire day in, say, *Caesars Palace* or the *Mirage* without feeling that you have missed part of the Las Vegas experience. But only by looking at the entire Strip — and exploring the interiors of its variety of hotels, casinos, shopping complexes, and museums — can you get a total perspective of not just the lavish excess of one resort but, rather, the sometimes outré effects that decades of constant anything-you-can-do-I-can-do-bigger have wrought.

This competitive environment even extends to the city's dining spots. Many restaurants, especially those in the hotels, subscribe to the "bigger is better" school of thought, as evidenced by the gargantuan all-you-can-eat buffets that add a whole new set of superlatives to the list (the *Circus Circus* buffet, for example, serving over 12,000 customers a day, claims to be the largest commercial dining establishment in the world). The Strip presents the visitor with a bewildering variety of non-buffet culinary experiences as well, from haute cuisine to hot dogs, from *boeuf bourguignon* to *Burger King* and *Baskin Robbins.* So put on your walking shoes, pocket a little spare change to test the spinning gaming wheels, and enjoy your visit to one of the most dynamic — and most unusual — cities in the world.

■ **Hot Flash:** This walk is *not* recommended during the mid-afternoon summer heat, when the mercury can soar to over 110F. Thankfully, most of the sites and sights mentioned below have ample parking facilities; so if it's too hot, you can drive this walk.

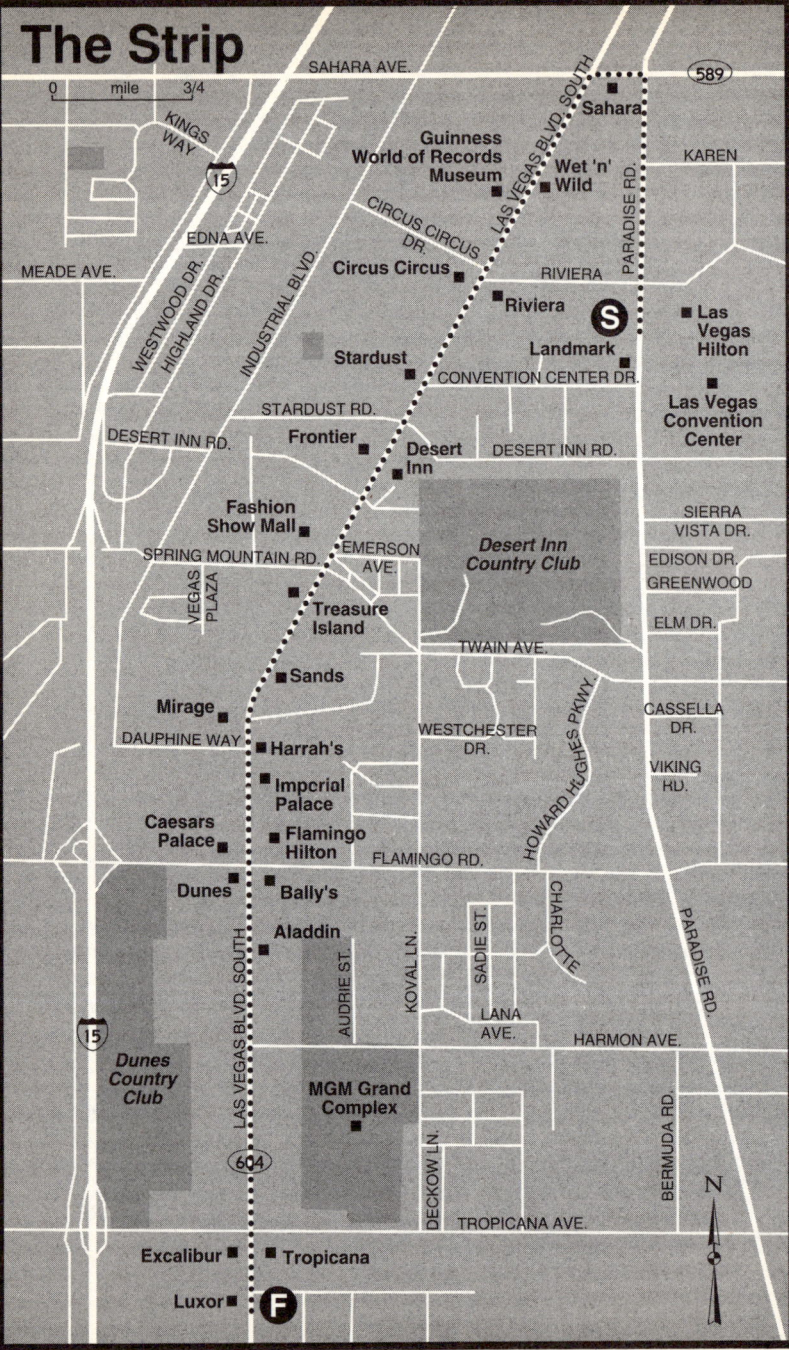

This tour begins 1 block east of the Strip, between Sahara Avenue and Desert Inn Road. The towering, streamlined structure looming before you is the *Las Vegas Hilton* (3000 Paradise Rd.; phone: 702-732-5111). With 3,100 rooms, this hotel held claim to the title of the city's largest for many years, and it brings in more money than any other in the worldwide Hilton chain. To get a visual perspective of the Strip before you set out, take a ride in the glass-enclosed elevator on the north side of the hotel to the 29th floor. Elvis fans, take note: The *Hilton* is the site of Presley's 1970s Las Vegas digs — he occupied the Penthouse Suite, still nostalgically known as the Elvis Suite.

The *Hilton*'s casino is well-known for its $17-million sports book, which accepts bets on football, basketball, baseball, and horse racing. Bettors track the progress of their wagers on any one of the 46 giant video screens that line the walls of the 30,500-square-foot "Superbook" room. There is an alcove devoted to sports memorabilia and, for true followers of the track, a life-size statue of famed racehorse Man O' War, which cost a reported $150,000.

Extending from Paradise Road to the Las Vegas Strip (and hard to miss) is the *Wet 'n' Wild* water park (2600 Las Vegas Blvd. S.; phone: 702-737-3819; admission charge), open daily from early April to early October. The 26-acre family-oriented aquatic playground has a surf lagoon, rapids, water flumes, a 70-foot water slide called Der Stuka, and the Banzai Boggan water roller coaster; a new attraction is added almost every season.

Just north of *Wet 'n' Wild* is the towering marquee — Las Vegas's tallest — of the *Sahara* hotel (2535 Las Vegas Blvd. S.; phone: 702-737-2111). Its desert theme is reflected in the brightly colored tableau to the right of the hotel — two life-size, blue-and-pink Arabian sheiks, complete with mustard yellow camels. The *Sahara*'s New York–style *Turf Deli* (phone: 702-737-2825) serves up such distinctively non-Nevadan fare as hot pastrami sandwiches and matzo ball soup. The large vacant lot across the Strip from the *Sahara* was the site of the legendary *El Rancho Vegas,* the Strip's first hotel-casino, which opened in 1941. In its heyday, the place attracted visitors with such celebrity headliners as Joe E. Lewis and Sophie Tucker. The resort burned down under mysterious circumstances in 1960.

Stop in next at the *Guinness World of Records Museum* (2780 Las Vegas Blvd. S.; phone: 702-792-3766; admission charge), a hall of hyperbole perfectly appropriate to this city of superlatives. Open daily, the museum is divided into six sections. "Amazing Humans" has a model of the world's tallest man (8 feet 11 inches); "Nature's Wonders" includes exhibits on Death Valley (which holds the record for the highest temperature sustained over a long period of time — 120F or more for 43 consecutive days) and the Grand Canyon (the world's largest land gorge). Also covered are the world of sports; performing arts; amazing animals; and buildings and structures. There are also videos of records as they were being set (many of the food-gorging variety) and a special display focusing on Las Vegas.

A half-block south looms what appears to be a massive pink-and-white-striped big top. It's actually the concrete roof of the casino of *Circus Circus* (2880 Las Vegas Blvd. S.; phone: 702-734-0410), whose white towers, emblazoned with enormous neon letters, announce the hotel's presence with a lack of modesty worthy of P.T. Barnum. As you walk up the sidewalk to the entrance, take a look at the white plaster statues of circus denizens — tightrope walkers, jugglers, and even gorillas — along the way. While skeptics predicted an early demise to this, the first Vegas hotel to cater to families with children, not only has the resort been successful, but the company has expanded to include four other properties on the Strip (*Silver City, Slots of Fun, Excalibur,* and *Luxor*). From 11 AM to midnight, trapeze and high-wire artists, clowns, acrobats, and dancers perform to the accompaniment of a brass band in the tent-shape casino, and the observation gallery at circus level is lined with food and carnival stands. Children are permitted in the gallery but not on the casino floor. In the heart of the hotel is a wildly popular, no-frills breakfast, brunch, and dinner buffet; typical dinner entrées are American (barbecued ribs, fried chicken), Italian, and Oriental dishes. Other dining options are the *Circus Pizzeria* (phone: 702-734-0410), with both deep-dish and thin-crust pizza, and the *Steak House* (phone: 702-794-3767), one of the best in town (see *Vegas Victuals* in DIVERSIONS). For those seeking a more familiar ambience, *McDonald's* is located on the carnival midway.

Across the Strip from *Circus Circus* is the block-long, curving façade of the nearly 40-year-old *Riviera* hotel (2901 Las Vegas Blvd. S.; phone: 702-734-5110). Over the multicolored neon display for "Splash," the hotel's main extravaganza, are huge glittering stars, and all that's not covered with neon or mirror is plastered with billboard-style signs promoting the *Riviera*'s other revues. The hotel boasts the world's largest casino, plus the *Mardi Gras Food Court,* at the south end of the building; easily accessible from the street, it offers a wide range of international fast foods — from gyros and falafel to Chinese egg rolls and French pastries. One block south of *Circus Circus* is the *Stardust* hotel (3000 Las Vegas Blvd. S.; phone: 702-732-6111), whose brilliant marquee, with a riot of multicolored stars that are visible for blocks, is one of the most attractive (and famous) on the Strip. The many fountains on the sidewalk outside the *Stardust* provide a welcome cooling respite from the stifling summer heat. If you're in the mood for a quick burger, a chocolate malted, or just some nostalgia, stop in at the 1950s-style *Ralph's Diner* (in the south end of the hotel; phone: 702-732-6330). The employees sometimes break into dance, accompanied by music from the vintage jukebox.

A few blocks south of the *Stardust* is the *Flame* (1 Desert Inn Rd.; phone: 702-735-4431), whose nondescript blue-and-white wall and relatively unassuming yellow sign make the place easy to overlook. It's worth a visit, though; charcoal-broiled steaks are served round-the-clock, and its walls are covered with framed, autographed photos of many of the celebrities (but not the reputed mobsters) who have counted themselves among its clientele. The restaurant has been in continuous operation since 1961 — longer than any other on the Strip.

One block south is the gleaming 20-story black glass tower of the *Desert Inn* (3145 Las Vegas Blvd. S.; phone: 702-733-4444), at 43 years of age one of the oldest on the Strip. Over the decades, it has hosted hundreds of luminaries, from presidents Lyndon Johnson and John F. Kennedy to entertainers Frank Sinatra and Jerry Lewis. Across the street is the *Fashion Show Mall* (3200 Las Vegas Blvd. S.; phone: 702-369-8382), Vegas's venue for the so-called carriage trade. Be sure to check out the Hall of Fame sidewalk in front of the mall, where the handprints of favorite Vegas celebrities — including Johnny Carson, Wayne Newton, Siegfried and Roy, the Smothers Brothers, and Neil Sedaka — have been pressed into the concrete. The 34-acre shopping center houses 145 stores — high-fashion retailers such as *Neiman Marcus* and *Saks Fifth Avenue* plus specialty stores, including *Marshall-Rousso, Abercrombie and Fitch,* and *Black, Starr and Frost. Chin's* (phone: 702-733-8899), one of the city's better upscale Oriental restaurants, is located in the mall. Other places worth investigating are the *Gallery of History* (phone: 702-731-0785), which displays autographs and letters written by every US president, and *Minotaur Fine Arts Ltd.* (phone: 702-737-1400), where major art exhibits — ranging from Rembrandt to Rockwell — are mounted.

The relatively old-fashioned marquee of the *Sands* hotel (3355 Las Vegas Blvd. S.; phone: 702-733-5000), visible across the Strip and a few blocks south, displays a virtual encyclopedia of information pertinent to the hotel (including a dinner menu). During its historic 40-year tenure, the *Sands* gave a new meaning to the word "publicity." The most widely covered marriage of the 1950s — that of movie star Rita Hayworth to singer Dick Haymes — took place here. Later the same year (1953), the hotel sponsored the high-profile, star-studded assembly of a "time capsule," into which celebrities placed their personal effects. Tallulah Bankhead, for instance, offered a photo of herself; Bing Crosby handed over his pipe; Sugar Ray Robinson donated his boxing gloves; and Jimmy Durante contributed a wax impression of his nose. (The capsule was unearthed during a construction project in the late 1970s, but was replanted.) In 1960, when members of the "Rat Pack" — Frank Sinatra, Sammy Davis, Jr., Dean Martin, Peter Lawford, and Joey Bishop — were on location in Las Vegas to film *Ocean's Eleven,* legendary press agent Al Freeman used the opportunity to create "Sinatra's Summit Meeting." He invited world leaders such as Dwight Eisenhower, Winston Churchill, and Nikita Khrushchev to attend the group's performances at the *Sands,* once again attracting the attention of the world press — but apparently not that of the world leaders, who didn't show up. Although the halcyon days of the *Sands* are long gone, the hotel is the site of the posh *Regency Room* (phone: 702-733-5292), one of the oldest hotel restaurants in the city. The very reasonably priced Italian luncheon buffet is delicious (though it may weigh you down for the rest of the walk!).

What looks like a massive riverboat south of the *Sands* is actually the colorful façade of *Harrah's* (formerly the *Holiday Inn/Holiday Casino;* 3475 Las Vegas Blvd. S.; phone: 702-369-5000). On the grounds is the charming *Jackson Square* shopping arcade, designed to resemble a typical New Orleans street, plus *Joe's Bayou,* an informal Louisiana-style dining room serving up southern fare — hush puppies, gumbo, and corn bread (phone: 702-369-5000).

A step south of *Harrah's* is the *Imperial Palace* (3535 Las Vegas Blvd. S.; phone: 702-731-3311), whose Oriental-theme architecture is best appreciated from across the street. From there, you can see its giant, royal blue pagoda roof, ends curling upward in true Eastern style. At night, pastel blue floodlights bathe the entire building in an azure glow, colorfully complementing the green lighting of *Harrah's* to the north and the pink neon of the *Flamingo*

Hilton to the south. The *Imperial Palace* houses one of the largest (over 200) and most expensive (valued in excess of $10 million) antique-car collections in the world. Located on the fifth floor of the 2,700-room resort, the collection is rated among the world's ten best by *Car and Driver* magazine. Among the "star cars" here are the 1947 Tucker and Al Capone's custom-built 1930 V-16 Cadillac, plus a number of the late entertainer Liberace's glitzy vehicles and a 1939 armored parade car that once belonged to Adolf Hitler. Other awesome autos on exhibit include one owned by the Rockefellers and the personal cars of Mrs. Henry Ford I, Howard Hughes, and Cecil B. DeMille. Should you have exceptional luck at the tables, you might want to price some of the autos here — they sell for five, six, and seven figures. On the casino floor of the *Imperial Palace* is *Betty's Diner and Ice Cream,* which serves up typical snack food (shakes, pizza, nachos, hot dogs, and the like). The *Pizza Palace,* on the fourth floor, and the *Burger Palace,* on the third floor (opposite the sports book), are both handy eating spots.

A few hundred yards south of the *Fashion Show Mall,* across the Strip from the *Sands,* is the tropical garden that surrounds the spectacular *Mirage* resort (3400 Las Vegas Blvd. S.; phone: 702-791-7111). The brainchild of hotel entrepreneur Steve Wynn, this 3,000-room property cost $725 million to build — Las Vegas's most expensive price tag to date. The main entrance of the gold-and-white Y-shape edifice dazzles visitors with a sensory overload of towering palms, cascading waterfalls, pools, tropical banana trees, and orchids. Its most outrageous feature is unquestionably a 60-foot volcano, which erupts every 15 minutes after dark, filling the air with the faint aroma of piña coladas. To the right as you walk in is the registration desk, which fronts a 20,000-gallon aquarium swimming with sharks, rays, and angelfish weaving between the buildings of a sunken undersea city. The *Mirage* casino sports a Polynesian theme; gaming areas are sheltered under thatch roofs to create an impression of intimacy. Under the casino's 90-foot-high, glass-enclosed atrium is a lush tropical garden, with waterfalls, orchids, elephant ears, banana trees, and canary palms. The spectacular outdoor pool area features a series of inlets, waterfalls, and lagoons, with two tropical islands in the center. Ensconced within this megalith is the *California Pizza Kitchen* (phone: 702-791-7111), whose avant-garde creations sport such toppings as duck sausage, artichoke hearts, and baby shrimp. Another dining option in the resort is their colorful *Bermuda Buffet;* it offers breakfast, lunch, and dinner, as well as a Sunday champagne brunch.

The *Mirage* is the home to two unique habitats. The first is the domain of master illusionists Siegfried and Roy's rare white tigers, which are kept behind a glass wall just inside the south entrance of the hotel, where they pace, swim, yawn, and flex their muscles, seemingly oblivious to the crowds watching them. Next to the hotel swimming pool is a 1.5-million-gallon water tank, which serves as a habitat for playful dolphins. There is no charge to see the tigers; there is a charge to see the dolphins.

Right next to the *Mirage,* a decidedly anachronistic spectacle is taking place: a battle between two ships, one a British frigate and the other flying the Jolly Roger. What appears to be a Vegas version of street theater, however, is actually a staged contest devised by the owners of the *Mirage,* who are promoting their *Treasure Island* property as a less expensive alternative to its flamboyant cousin. About every half hour, the two ships sail from the corners of the property, captained by actors and stuntmen in military dress. The British ship then engages the pirate ship in a special-effects skirmish (this being Las Vegas, the pirates always win). The hotel is scheduled to open this year on November 22, the fourth anniversary of the *Mirage*.

Just a few feet south of the *Mirage* complex is a massive Roman arch — "guarded" by costumed Roman legionnaires — through which you enter an aboveground moving walkway, covered on top but open on the sides. Called a "people mover," it transports visitors past the stately fountains and graceful Italian cypress trees decorating the grounds. This grandiose approach is but a prelude to the interior of the 240,000-square-foot *Forum Shops,* the newest attraction of *Caesars Palace* (3750 Las Vegas Blvd. S.; phone: 702-731-7110). *Caesars Palace* has become nearly synonymous with the city in which it's located, and a stroll inside this most sybaritic of resorts quickly reveals why. The theme of the *Forum Shops* is — you guessed it — ancient Rome, and the space is filled with immense columns and arches, central piazze, ornate fountains, and replicas of classical statuary. The Festival Fountain is the site of a bizarrely robotic bacchanal, as disconcertingly lifelike, animated statues of Plutus, Venus, and Bacchus converse and sway to the music of Apollo, who strums the lyre (the sound effects are provided by lasers). About 70 retailers and restaurateurs are housed here, including branches of *Gucci, Louis Vuitton,* and *Victoria's Secret,* a branch of Los Angeles's *Spago,* New York City's *Carnegie Deli,* and the *Palm,* the well-known New York and Los Angeles steakhouse.

The second entranceway to *Caesars Palace,* 200 yards south of the first one, features another moving walkway affording views of fountains, marble and gold statuary, and sentries in ancient Roman garb; on the way to the Roman-theme *Olympic Casino,* the people mover passes through a "temple" whose dark interior is filled with small holograms of cavorting Roman figures. The casino itself is peopled by mimes, Roman soldiers, and goddesses, all attired in ancient Roman garb; a stunningly dressed Caesar and Cleopatra stroll the casino area, offering words of encouragement to the guests. The main entrance to the hotel boasts a pink-lighted porte cochere — the largest cantilevered structure of its kind in the world. If you're here on the weekend, you might want to try the hotel's reasonably priced Champagne Brunch (all you can drink) — it's one of the best in the city. Keep in mind, though, that alcohol and searing summer heat do not a good combination make; champagne will only exacerbate the dehydration brought on by the sun. (In case you were wondering, the giant golf ball projecting from outside the north side of the hotel is actually the 57-foot-high *Omnimax,* where 70mm films are screened.)

Across the street, the dazzling, pink-flamingo-colored marquee of the *Flamingo Hilton* (3555 Las Vegas Blvd. S.; phone: 702-733-3111) is hard to miss — it boasts the most neon in all of Las Vegas. The hotel has been enjoying a surge of popularity following the release of the movie *Bugsy.* Seen from the Strip, today's *Flamingo Hilton* bears no resemblance to its 1946 prototype. Benjamin "Bugsy" Siegel's ambitious 105-room resort, built on what was then a dusty dirt road, was dismissed as a grand folly, and indeed, the first incarnation of the *Flamingo* — his nickname for his flamboyant girlfriend, Virginia Hill — went under almost immediately (as did Siegel). The property passed from owner to owner until 1971, when the Hilton group took it over; fortunately, they followed the lead of previous owners in leaving the original "Bugsy Siegel Suite" intact. Those who have a desire to view the famous suite at close range, including the trapdoor escape routes and secret passageways, can rent it — for a mere $400 a night. If you still haven't had lunch, stop in at the *Flamingo Room* (phone: 702-733-3111), the hotel's Art Deco–style restaurant, which has a great salad bar and moderately priced American fare. Another worthwhile spot is *Hamada of Japan* (phone: 702-733-3111), one of the only places on the Strip where you can have sushi for lunch.

Across Flamingo Road, covered by a massive porte cochere, is the entrance to *Bally's* resort-casino (3645 Las Vegas Blvd. S.; phone: 702-739-4111). The imposing fountain fronting the hotel is home to a bronze statue — "Neptune and the Sirens" — perhaps best known for the anatomical liberties the sculptor took in creating it (the maidens' nipples spout water). On the casino level is *Grapes,* a pleasant sidewalk-style café, but the hotel's biggest culinary attraction is its Sunday champagne brunch, held in *Caruso's* restaurant, where white-gloved service prevails.

If your feet are still willing, 1 mile south of *Bally's,* at the corner of the Strip and Tropicana Avenue, is Las Vegas's answer to *Disneyland:* the mammoth *MGM Grand* complex, scheduled to open late this year. The billion-dollar mega-resort — all designed around an MGM movie theme — boasts 112 acres of entertainment facilities, including 2 theaters and a 15,000-seat sports arena. The hotel's *Wizard of Oz* motif includes an "Emerald City Casino." Touted as the biggest hotel in the world (5,000-plus rooms), once the *Grand* is in operation, Las Vegas will be able to add yet another superlative to its long list of biggest and best: The city will have the world's ten largest hotels.

Visitors to the resort's theme park enter through an 88-foot statue of the MGM lion, endowed with piercing laser eyes. Attractions in the theme park include the "Over the Edge" flume ride, a spiraling water trip through a logging camp; and the "Grand Canyon Rapids Ride," which barrels passengers along exhilarating rapids through a flooded Old West town and a gold-mine tunnel.

Across Tropicana Avenue from the *MGM Grand* is the "Island of Las Vegas" — the *Tropicana* hotel (3801 Las Vegas Blvd. S.; phone: 702-739-2222). Two giant, 20-foot-high, stone heads of the variety found on Easter Island guard the entrance to the hotel; visitors walk across a bridge between them to reach the front steps. The *Tropicana*'s 5-acre water park features one of the world's largest swimming pools, with swim-up blackjack tables and poolside video poker. Inside is a promenade-level walkway lined with exotic birds (including talking parrots) and lush aquariums; the casino is best known for its magnificent stained glass ceiling.

The colorfully turreted façade of the *Excalibur* (3850 Las Vegas Blvd. S.; phone: 702-597-7777), across the Strip from the *Tropicana,* looks like a massive castle, with colorful spires and even a moat and drawbridge. The medieval-theme hotel boasts 4,032 guestrooms — for the moment it's the largest in the world, at least until construction is completed at the *MGM Grand*. The jugglers, magicians, minstrels, and sword swallowers — all dressed in period costume — perform on the second floor near the restaurants, whose whimsical nomenclature complements the medieval motif. You can have a bite or dine at *Lance-a-Lotta Pasta; Sir Galahad's* (which serves thick slices of prime rib, carved at the table); the *Robin Hood* snack bar, built around two large sycamore trees that extend through the roof; or the romantic *Camelot* dining room, in a castle-like setting on the third level. There are also magic-motion machines, which enable guests to experience thrills like riding in a runaway train and slaloming in an *Olympic* bobsled without leaving their seats, along with a children's arcade with games of skill and prizes.

Just south of the *Excalibur* is the Circus Circus corporation's newest tribute to imaginative design, the Egyptian-theme *Luxor* resort, scheduled to open this fall. Designed as a 30-story pyramid, it includes the "River Nile," complete with barges that transport guests from the registration desk to the hotel tower elevators. Featured in the structure is a 90,000-square-foot casino, decorated with replicas of artifacts, columns, and tombs found in the temples of Luxor and Karnak.

And there you have it. Some 75,000 hotel rooms, thousands of miles of neon tubing, and billions of dollars later — what an oasis!

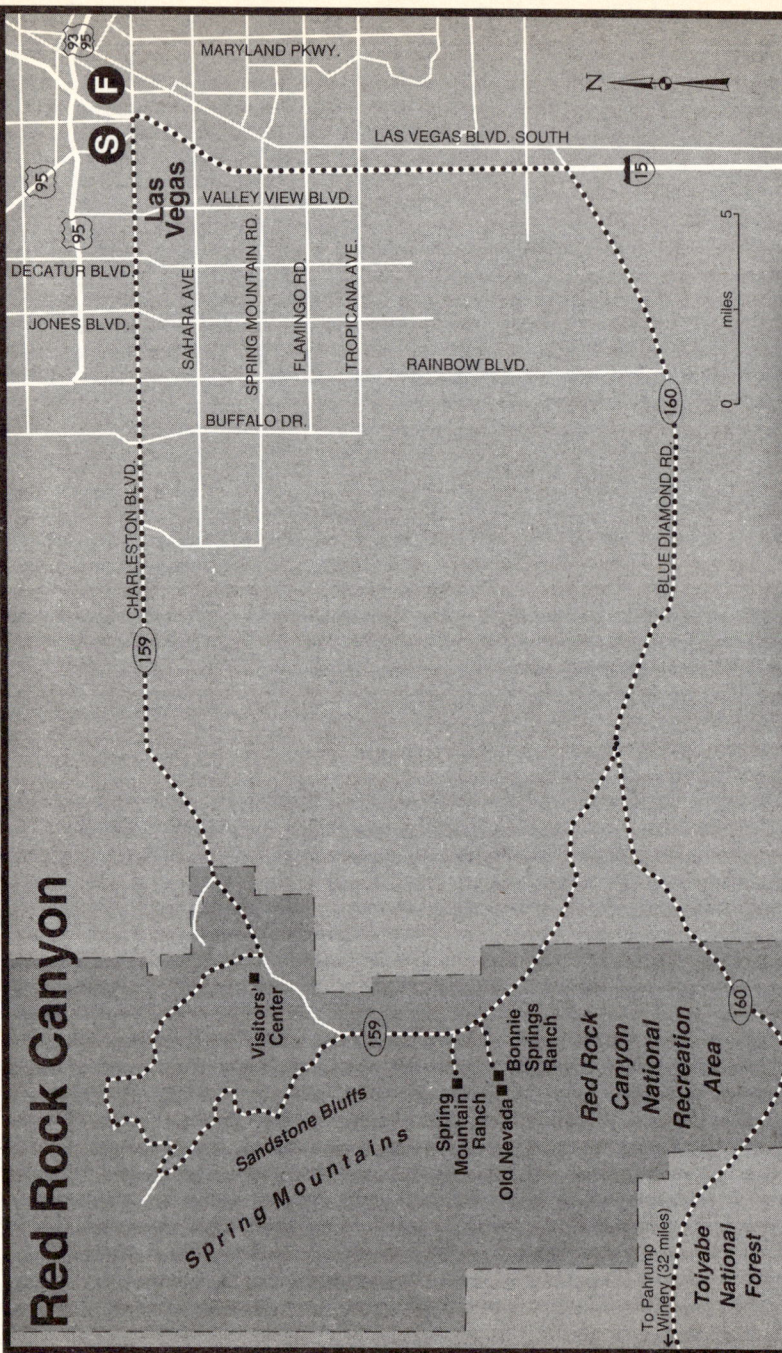

Tour 2: Red Rock Canyon, Pahrump Winery

This tour leads to one of Nevada's most awe-inspiring sights — and it's only a 20-minute drive west of the city. Covering 62,000 acres, Red Rock Canyon is a stunning showcase of colorful red sandstone, craggy mountains, and steep valleys. The entire canyon is ringed by a 13-mile loop road, considered the most scenic drive in the Las Vegas area. (It's also a very popular biking route.) Visitors take note: As Red Rock Canyon is a national conservation area, all of its flora and fauna are protected; it's against the law to damage or remove plants. Only 4 miles from Red Rock Canyon, and offering a totally different landscape, is the gorgeous 528-acre Spring Mountain Ranch, whose lush green lawns and New England–style architecture are a welcome break from the sometimes overwhelming barrenness of the desert. Right next to the ranch are *Old Nevada* and *Bonnie Springs Ranch,* two commercial establishments especially appealing to children (but popular with adults as well).

Oenophiles and gastronomes will definitely want to make a side trip to Pahrump, the site of Nevada's only winery. A soothing respite from the unrelenting energy of the city, it's also the site of an unexpectedly elegant restaurant where complimentary wines can be sampled. This drive, allowing time for leisurely nature walks and a picnic lunch, should take about 4 hours. Add at least another 3 hours if you plan to visit Pahrump.

From Las Vegas, take Charleston Boulevard, one of the city's major east–west arteries, west for 15 miles. On the way out of town, it becomes clear how quickly the residential area of Las Vegas has developed: Most of the homes on the west side of town were built only in the last few years. Unlike the neon-saturated city, the route has few signs, and the 2,500-foot-high ruby-colored canyon clearly dominates the view.

Red Rock Canyon was created about 65 million years ago when two of the earth's crustal plates collided so forcefully that part of one plate was wedged over another, younger one. This impaction created the Keystone Thrust Fault, which extends from the Cottonwood Fault, a few miles south, all the way through Red Rock Canyon. The best evidence of the fault in Red Rock Canyon is the clearly discernible contrast between ancient gray limestone and the younger tan and red Aztec sandstone underneath it.

The 130-square-mile Red Rock Canyon area varies in elevation from 3,500 to 7,500 feet, accounting for the great variety of plant life found here. At the lower elevations are spiny yucca plants; at intermediate elevations, shaggy-looking Joshua trees; and at the highest, towering, rough-barked ponderosa pine. The silence of the place is deafening; even birdcalls and twitterings stop when you approach a stand of brush. The area is also home to a wide variety of fauna, including bighorn sheep, antelope, wild horses, and a small population of wild burros. The US Bureau of Land Management, author of a pamphlet entitled "Please Don't Feed the Burros," warns visitors that these animals bite and kick when frightened. Perhaps the pamphlet's strangest feature is the section detailing how an individual can go about adopting a wild burro (for more information, call 702-646-8800). Well, it would make an offbeat souvenir!

At the entrance to the 13-mile scenic loop, make sure to stop at the Red Rock Canyon Visitors' Center (phone: 702-363-1921), where you can pick up a wealth of free brochures, maps, and other literature, as well as visit the bookstore and peruse excellent exhibits relating to the area's geological history. (The visitors' center is also the only place along the 13-mile drive that has drinking water.) There are several scenic spots along this route, perfect for photographing the dramatic sandstone. The first overlook is the Calico Hills Vista, which affords an exceptional panorama of the massive red cross-etched hills. A mile farther is the Sandstone Quarry turnoff, a cul-de-sac parking area where huge blocks of white and deep red sandstone remain as a testament to turn-of-the-century quarry activity. The stone formations appear deceptively easy to climb, but be forewarned: Many people have lost their lives falling from the rock surfaces here.

Near the apex of the scenic loop is Willow Spring, a picnic area with tables and an opportunity to relax and take in the panoramic view of sheer peaks and the gradual change in vegetation zones, from desert scrub to piñon pine. The mysterious-looking ring of fire-cracked and whitened limestone visible behind the restrooms at the base of the sandstone cliffs here was used by ancient Native American peoples to roast indigenous plants such as agave hearts and animals such as desert tortoises. One of the largest roasting pits in southern Nevada, it's considered an important historical artifact.

On the way back to the main road (Rte. 159), the scenery on the right side of the valley — high craggy escarpments and rainbow-colored pinnacles, rising precipitously above you — provides a dramatic contrast to that on the left — the desert landscape of the Cottonwood Valley. The setting may seem familiar: This area has been used as the backdrop for many a Hollywood western. Along this road are several perfect spots to leave the car in the designated parking areas and hike up into the canyons. The 2½-mile round-trip trek to Ice Box Canyon (so called because the canyon is so narrow that the sun's rays hardly ever penetrate it) ends up at a seasonal waterfall, reached by boulder hopping. The Pine Creek Canyon trail, 4 miles round-trip, takes the hiker downhill to the ruins of an old homestead near a running creek surrounded by mighty ponderosa pines; the pines thrive here because of the moisture and cooler temperatures. The 13-mile scenic loop road is open daily from 8 AM to 6 PM; no admission charge.

Continue on West Charleston Boulevard (Rte. 159) about 4 miles to Spring Mountain Ranch. This beautiful 510-acre estate in the desert has an interesting history: Once owned by Vera Krupp of the German munitions family, for a short time it was also home to the famous Krupp Diamond. Howard

Hughes even owned it briefly (although he never took up residence here). The red main house and barnlike east wing, complete with gambrel roof, are more reminiscent of a New England farm than of a southwestern ranch. With its white picket fence surrounding the entire complex, long green lawns and vast meadows, and tall cottonwoods, the ranch blends harmoniously with its brilliant backdrop of towering red-and-white cliffs. The ranch is the site of musical productions with picnic dinners in the summer. Visitors are welcome to tour the house, which is open daily from 8 AM to 6 PM (hours vary with the seasons; admission charge; phone: 702-875-4141).

About a half-mile west of Spring Mountain Ranch on Charleston Boulevard is *Old Nevada,* a re-creation of an old western mining town, complete with (staged) shoot-outs, hangings, and wooden sidewalks. The little village boasts many quaint shops (such as an old western trading post and a jewelry store selling silver and turquoise pieces), plus a theater and a museum with a mine-shaft setting. (Open daily from 10:30 AM to 5 PM; admission charge; phone: 702-875-4191.) Right next to *Old Nevada* is the *Bonnie Springs Ranch* (phone: 702-875-4300), a children's delight, with a petting zoo — with everything from reindeer to llama — a large animal zoo, a duck pond, an aviary, and horseback riding. The *Bonnie Springs Ranch Restaurant* (phone: 702-875-4300) is a great place to stop for a burger.

Two miles southeast of Bonnie Springs is Route 160; take a right and follow it for 32 miles to Pahrump.

Pahrump Valley Vineyards (phone: 702-727-6900), the only winery in Nevada, rests against the jagged western slope of Mount Charleston in the mainly agricultural community of Pahrump. The design of the place is modern Spanish, with rounded arches, sparkling white walls, and cobalt blue tile roofs. Its centerpiece is its 3-story bell tower, whose cocktail lounges afford visitors a panoramic view of the entire valley, with alfalfa fields, clumps of sagebrush, spiny mesquite trees, solitary houses, and lush green golf courses. Free tours and wine tastings are conducted daily from 10 AM to 4:30 PM. Unfortunately, attempts at raising vines on the property have been thwarted by the grazing of wild horses, and most of the grape juice is now imported from California and only processed at the winery. "Symphony," a white varietal, was entered in Reno's Ninth Annual West Coast Wine Competition in 1991 and won silver and bronze medals; other wines are worth trying and can be sampled in a separate tasting room.

Also on the grounds of the winery is *Tastings,* a cozy, 40-seat restaurant. The ambience is one of quiet elegance — unusual in these parts — with comfortable, high-backed wing chairs and wraparound floor-to-ceiling windows. Diners are encouraged to try several complimentary wines before choosing the variety that will accompany the meal. Reasonably priced specialties include beef tournedos Rossini (marinated in madeira wine and served with mushrooms, foie gras, and béarnaise sauce), lemon chicken Marco Polo, and duck *à l'orange.* Also in Pahrump is the *Saddle West* hotel and casino (Rte. 160; phone: 702-727-5953), which offers 60 rooms at modest prices, as well as access to a swimming pool and a hot tub.

Take Route 160 east, in the direction of *Bonnie Spring Ranch,* for 53 miles to US 15. Follow US 15 north for 9 miles back to Las Vegas.

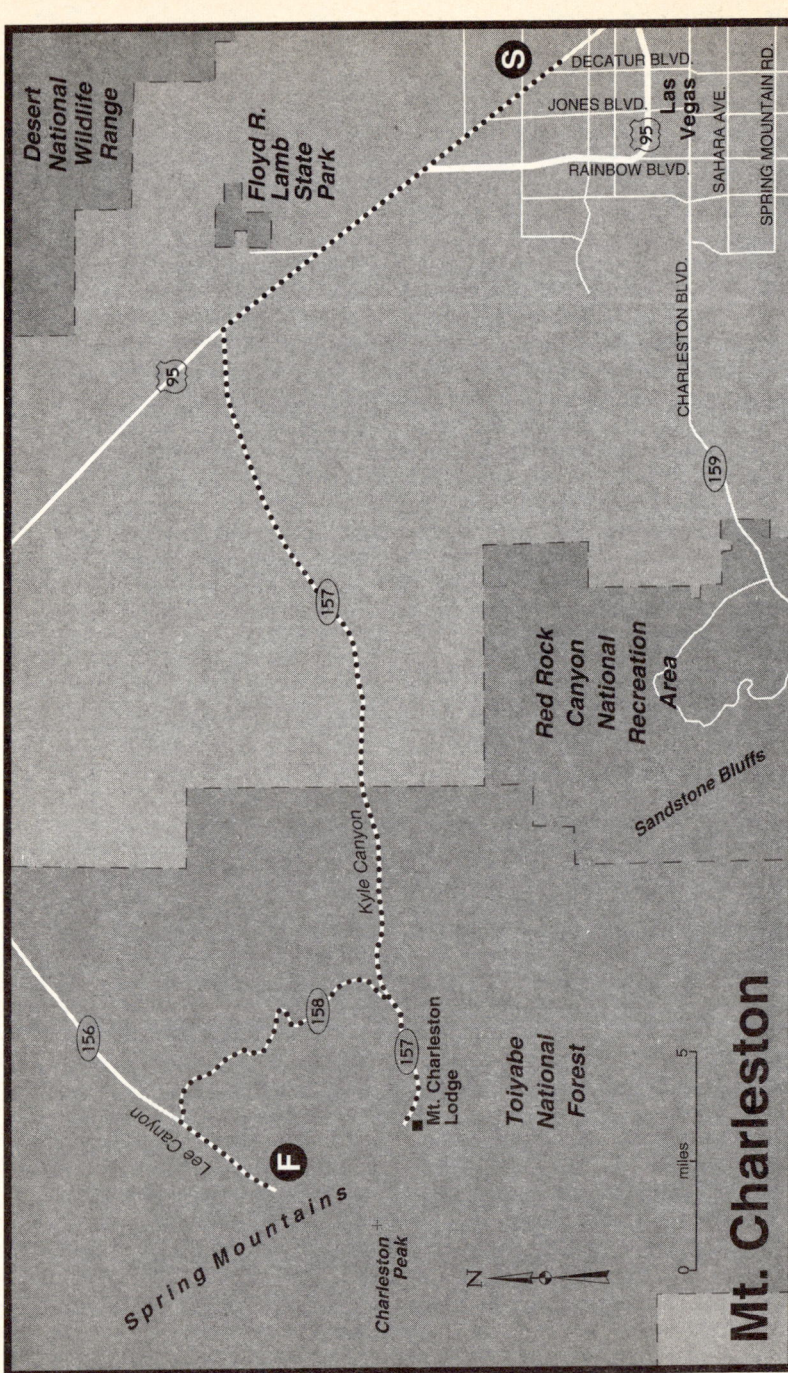

Tour 3: Mt. Charleston

It's hard to imagine a fully equipped skiing area only 45 minutes from the shimmering desert oasis of Las Vegas, but the Mt. Charleston area offers just that, in the form of *Ski Lee,* at Lee Canyon. If you happen to be here during snow season (from about *Thanksgiving* to *Easter*), you could conceivably enjoy the novelty of skiing all morning, sunning by the hotel pool in the afternoon, and topping off the experience by playing the slots on the Strip into the wee hours of the morning. At *Ski Lee Rentals* in Las Vegas (2395 N. Rancho Rd.; phone: 702-646-0008), skiers can rent equipment and even purchase lift tickets.

Kyle Canyon, about 10 miles from Lee Canyon, is one of the area's most popular spots for picnicking, hiking, and camping, with average summer temperatures 15 to 20° cooler than those in the city. Among the trails here are two that lead all the way to the top of nearly-12,000-foot Mt. Charleston, the third-highest peak in Nevada. The hike is arduous, but well worth the incredible view: On a clear day, you can see for more than 200 miles! Part of the 100-mile-long Spring Mountain Range, Mt. Charleston is the home of the bristlecone pine (*Pinus aristata*), the oldest tree in the world (some are estimated to be more than 4,000 years old), and it's also rich in piñon pine, juniper, mountain mahogany, ponderosa pine, aspen, and fir. Native fauna — deer, elk, antelope, mountain sheep, wild turkey, coyote, bobcat, fox, and chipmunks — abound.

Depending on how much you want to see (or do), expect to spend about 6 hours on this tour; if you plan to ski at Lee Canyon, consider staying overnight at *Mt. Charleston Lodge* or *Mt. Charleston Inn* (see below for address and phones for both) or at one of the designated campgrounds in the area.

Take US 95 for 15 miles; along the way, the suburban shopping centers and fast-food restaurants lining the road eventually give way to barren desert terrain, dominated by thorny mesquite trees and spiky yucca plants. Turn left at the intersection with Route 157 toward Kyle Canyon. On this 21-mile stretch of the drive, there are no gas stations, restaurants, or crap games to mar the beauty of the mountain scenery. As the road climbs gently, the air gradually thins out and the desert heat gives way to the cool mountain breeze, heady with the scent of pine. The highway leads up through a winding canyon with interesting wind-carved rock formations. Craggy peaks surround the narrow canyon, with majestic Mt. Charleston towering over the foliage. (Confusingly, Mt. Charleston is also the name of the recreation area that comprises the mountain, Kyle and Lee canyons, and their surroundings.)

Your first stop along the ascent into Kyle Canyon should be the ranger station, right past the intersection with Deer Creek Highway (Rte. 158). Nestled among towering 30- and 40-foot ponderosa pines, it provides useful area maps and brochures. About a mile farther, the road splits. To the right is Echo Road; take a left to stay on Kyle Canyon Road (Rte. 157). At the end of the road, at an elevation of about 8,500 feet, is cozy *Mt. Charleston* restaurant and lodge. If you want to linger a while, its restaurant offers first-rate fare; there also are 24 cabins. The dinner menu focuses on wild game (rabbit, venison) and poultry (quail, pheasant); hearty breakfasts and lunches are also available. The comfortable lounge — with a big circular fireplace — is a perfect place to relax over some "Mt. Charleston Coffee," a soporific concoction of coffee, Drambuie, brandy, ice milk, whipped cream, nutmeg, and cinnamon (phone: 702-386-6899 or 702-872-5408).

The area attracts hikers — both day-trippers escaping the sultry desert heat and overnight campers seeking a more long-term return to nature — on its two strenuous trails that lead all the way up to the peak of Mt. Charleston. The South Loop begins at Cathedral Rock picnic grounds, past the lodge, near the end of Kyle Canyon Road; the North Loop begins on the Deer Creek Highway. Both trails cover 9 miles in either direction (most hikers camp at the top and return the next day). The trails traverse several climatic zones, so that you pass through stands of massive ponderosa, with fragrant pine needles blanketing the path, up to grassy meadows, and finally, past the tree line to an alpine ridge environment. The top of the mountain offers views that more than compensate for the physical effort spent reaching it: The 360° vista takes in Telescope Peak to the northwest in Death Valley, with the magnificent Sierra Nevadas beyond; Lake Mead and much of Arizona to the east; the Nevada Test Site to the north; and (on a clear day) the huge cloud of smog blanketing the Los Angeles region to the southwest.

For those less inclined to stay overnight, there are plenty of shorter hikes scattered throughout the area, and all the trails are well marked, with rocks on either side. The difficult 2-mile round-trip Cathedral Rock trail (entrance at first parking lot at picnic area near the end of Kyle Canyon Rd., near the entrance to South Loop; admission charge for parking) passes through stands of large pines and white fir. Hikers are rewarded at the very abrupt end of the trail (there is a precipitous drop of several hundred feet) with a breathtakingly vertiginous close-up view of Kyle Canyon from the vantage point of the zenith of Cathedral Rock's gothic cliffs. Echo Cliff Loop (entrance at Cathedral Rock trailhead), 2 miles round-trip, ascends through ponderosa pine and white fir and descends by crisscrossing a snow avalanche path. Upper Kyle Canyon, accessible via the gravel Echo Road, boasts vertical cliffs and bucolic waterfalls. The trail to Mary Jane Falls and Big Falls is about 3 miles round-trip; note, however, that this hike should not be attempted during heavy rains, as flash flooding is common.

There are several campgrounds in the Kyle Canyon area (see below for information); camping is limited to 5 days, and there is a daily fee. In addition to the campsites, there are numerous picnic areas scattered throughout the grounds. All campsites provide parking, tents, picnic tables, and firepits or grills. In the summer horseback riding is possible here, while the winter brings skiing and horse-drawn sleigh rides.

To get to Lee Canyon and the *Ski Lee* area, backtrack on Kyle Canyon Road past the ranger station; turn left on Deer Creek Highway. Along this

9-mile route are several scenic overlooks and easy walking trails, with spots along the side of the road for parking. From Deer Creek Highway is a short (.2-mile) stroll to Robber's Roost, a cave-like limestone overhang reportedly used by Mexican horse thieves as a base from which to launch their raids. A bit farther down the road is a paved trail leading to Desert View, an easy walk (.1 mile) that rewards hikers with a magnificent vista of parched lake beds languishing in the desert below. To the north one can see the Nevada Test Site — this was the very spot from which the first photographs of the awesome mushroom-shape atomic clouds were snapped.

At the end of Deer Creek Highway is Lee Canyon Road (Rte. 156); turn left. As the road rises to an altitude of 8,500 feet, it passes through several elevation zones, from stands of small piñon pine and blue-green juniper at 5,000 feet to quaking aspen and white fir at 8,000 feet. The huge ponderosa pines gracing the canyon can grow to be 4 feet thick and 100 feet high.

Ski Lee has three double chair lifts and 40 acres of maintained slopes (phone: 702-872-5462; ski report, 702-646-3805). There's also a ski shop with complete rentals available, and a coffee shop and cocktail lounge. Unfortunately, Lee Canyon offers no overnight accommodations; skiers usually make this a day trip; stay at *Mt. Charleston Lodge* (see above) or the more expensive *Mt. Charleston Inn* (2 Kyle Canyon Rd.; phone: 702-872-5500); or camp in the area. For more information on hiking or camping in the Mt. Charleston area, contact the US Forest Service (phone: 702-873-8800).

The quickest way back to Las Vegas is via Route 156, 21 miles to US 95; Las Vegas is 15 miles southeast.

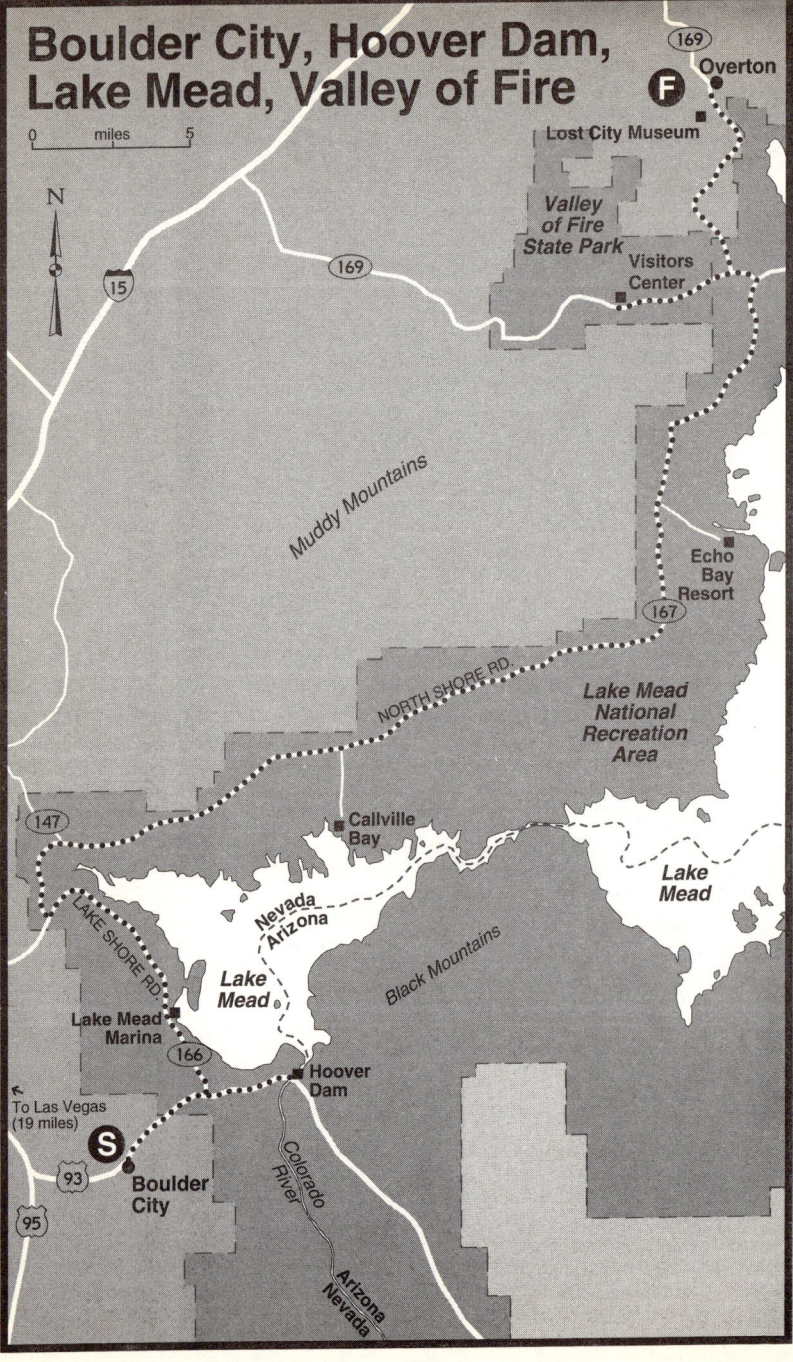

Tour 4: Boulder City, Hoover Dam, Lake Mead, Valley of Fire

This tour begins at the planned community of Boulder City, created in the 1930s as housing for the more than 5,000 workers who built Hoover Dam. The unusual community — the only one in Nevada that *prohibits* gambling — has retained its small-town charm, though it's now more of a Las Vegas suburb than a Depression-era "ghost town." From Boulder City, it's an easy 15-minute drive to 726-foot-high Hoover Dam, one of the most awesome engineering feats ever accomplished. A testament to man's ability to harness nature, the dam not only diverted the mighty Colorado River, but also created massive Lake Mead; with more than 500 miles of shoreline, it is one of the largest manmade lakes in the world and a major attraction in its own right.

From Hoover Dam, the tour winds east and then north along the shoreline of Lake Mead to the spectacular Valley of Fire State Park, famous for its garishly colored rock formations. The compelling etchings and pictures on the rocks are believed to have been the work of the ancient native civilizations that inhabited the nearby Muddy River area. From Valley of Fire, the tour continues to the *Lost City Museum,* which provides insight into those ancient cultures through its displays of artifacts of the enigmatic Anasazi civilization.

Plan on a full day for this trip, allowing for a lunch stop at Lake Mead Marina or *Echo Bay Resort.* Note that there are not many gas stations along the route; it's best to fill your tank in Las Vegas before you leave.

From the Strip, take any major east–west artery (Sahara Ave., Desert Inn Rd., Flamingo Rd., or Tropicana Ave.) east to the junction with US 93/95 (Boulder Hwy.); turn right. From downtown Las Vegas, follow Fremont Street east; at Charleston Boulevard, Fremont Street becomes Boulder Highway. Take Boulder Highway for 23 miles to Boulder City.

In 1928, after Congress approved the construction of Hoover Dam, the government was faced with the dilemma of housing what would turn out to be the more than 5,000 workers involved in the project. Rather than erecting a temporary construction camp, planners had the foresight to create a permanent community to accommodate those involved in post-construction administration of dam-related business, utilities, and activities. And so Boulder City was born.

At the time — during the throes of the Great Depression — Boulder City was intended as a model community, a place that symbolized America's hope for a better future. City fathers (mostly Mormons), hoping to steer dam workers away from the lure of the nearby bright lights and big city, deliberately created a blandly pleasant community, in which gambling and drinking were illegal. The city had a self-contained social and civic infrastructure — churches, schools, and fraternal groups — and, in the words of President Roosevelt, was a "cactus-covered waste" turned into lush green lawns and gardens. It was mapped out in a fan shape, with clearly separated and delineated commercial and residential zones radiating outward from the civic area. The homes were fairly simple, boxy affairs, with well-manicured lawns.

Though most of the homes remain intact, the construction workers are long gone. Some federal agencies related in one way or another to the project, such as those responsible for the distribution of the electrical power generated by the dam, still live in the district; the rest of the population (total 13,000) consists primarily of retirees. Although the drinking of alcoholic beverages is no longer illegal here, it's still the only town in Nevada that prohibits gambling.

The *Boulder City Museum* (444 Hotel Plaza, Boulder City; phone: 702-294-1988), established to preserve the historical artifacts relating to the construction of Hoover Dam, has exhibits chronicling the workers' lifestyle during the time the dam was being built (1931 to 1936). A film detailing the process of building the dam is shown several times a day. Open daily from 9 AM to 5 PM. Admission by donation. For more information about Boulder City, contact the visitors bureau (phone: 702-293-1202).

Follow US 93 along the Lake Mead National Recreation Area for 11 miles to Hoover Dam.

With its massive, stark white surface reflecting the desert sun, Hoover Dam is an awesome sight. Seven hundred and twenty-six feet high (the equivalent of 70 stories) and, at its base, 660 feet thick (wider than 2 football fields), the entire concrete megalith weighs nearly 4.5 million tons. (To put that figure in perspective, Las Vegas's McCarran International Airport's expansion and improvement activities, ongoing through the year 2000, are projected to require only 100,000 tons of concrete.) If stretched out on a 4-inch-thick, 10-foot-wide highway, the concrete used to construct the dam would cover more than 68,000 miles. Nine million tons of rock were excavated from the Black Canyon to make way for the dam — enough to build the Great Wall of China.

Contrary to popular belief, Hoover Dam was intended not as an electrical project but as a hydro-engineering one: Historically, after heavy snow seasons, spring and summer runoff would transform the 1,400-mile-long Colorado River into a rampaging torrent that flooded farm fields and carried away millions of tons of topsoil. In dry years, the flow would shrivel to a useless trickle. In the early 1900s, when the Colorado River wreaked unusually massive destruction in California, Arizona, Nevada, and New Mexico, the government finally took action to harness it.

Construction of Hoover Dam — then called Boulder Dam — was authorized by Congress in 1928 and completed in 1936. The enterprise eventually required the services of six construction companies, which took 5 years to complete the job at a cost of $60 million (about $1.5 billion in 1993 dollars).

The dam was dedicated in 1935 by President Franklin Delano Roosevelt (its name was officially changed to Hoover Dam — named for President Herbert Hoover, not the FBI director, J. Edgar Hoover — in the 1940s). The hydroelectric power generated by the dam — a felicitous, yet secondary, result of its creation — is now measured at 4 to 5 billion kilowatt-hours annually. Marketed to Arizona, California, and Nevada, this energy has more than paid back the original cost of its construction and maintenance.

Guided 35-minute tours take visitors deep inside the bowels of Hoover Dam for a complete explanation of its history, purpose, and inner workings. Reflecting its Depression-era construction, the interior of the dam was designed in the Art Deco style; at night, the entire structure is lit by a tiny fraction of its generated power, and giant floodlights play on its surface. The tour includes vivid descriptions of the hardships the builders had to endure toiling in the 100° heat of the Black Canyon (tours given daily, except *Christmas,* from about 9 AM to 4 PM; times vary slightly with the seasons; admission charge). For the more adventurous, day-long rafting trips down the Colorado River are offered at the dam. For more information about the dam and nearby attractions, contact the Hoover Dam Visitor Center (phone: 702-293-1081).

As you drive across the dam, notice Black Canyon on one side — through whose narrow walls trickles a modest flow of water from the once rambunctious Colorado River — and Lake Mead on the other. Formed when completion of Hoover Dam backed up the Colorado River, Lake Mead is one of the largest manmade lakes in the world, with more than 500 miles of shoreline. From the dam, take Lake Shore Road northeast for 5 miles to Lake Mead Marina (phone: 702-293-3484), one of several such facilities along the lake. If you haven't had lunch yet, the marina's nautical-theme restaurant is a good place to stop; once you reach Valley of Fire, there aren't many dining spots.

Fishing boats, motorboats, and water skiing equipment can be rented at the marina, as can houseboats (there is a 3-day minimum). *Echo Bay Resort* (near Overton; phone: 702-394-4000) and *Callville Bay* resort and marina (23 miles north of Lake Mead Marina; phone: 702-565-8958) offer rental facilities similar to those at Lake Mead Marina. Fishing permits are easily procured at any marina and at most bait shops; the most prevalent types of fish are striped and largemouth bass, bluegill, crappie, catfish, and trout. Lake Mead Marina is also the departure point for cruises on the 150-ton riverboat *Desert Princess* (phone: 702-293-6180). Breakfast, daytime, and dinner-dance cruises chug around the lake, affording a spectacular view of Hoover Dam. Swimmers can take a refreshing dip at the Boulder Beach swimming area, right next to Lake Mead Marina. For those who really want to test the waters, there are a host of scuba-diving clubs in the area. And for campers, there are six developed campgrounds along Lake Mead. For more information about the lake, contact the Lake Mead National Recreation Area (phone: 702-293-8907).

From Lake Mead Marina, continue northeast on Lake Shore Road for 3 miles to North Shore Road, which follows Lake Mead all the way to Overton, at the upper end of the lake. The drive winds through long stretches of desert landscape, sporadically broken by glimpses of the lake and of the hills. In the spring and early summer, brilliant red and yellow cactus blooms dot the sides of the road. About 40 miles along North Shore Road is *Echo Bay Resort* (phone: 702-394-4000), a 52-room motel whose restaurant serves light lunches of the soup-and-sandwich variety. Five minutes south of Echo Bay is Cathedral Cove, surrounded on three sides by rock walls that thrust up dramatically from the water to soar hundreds of feet into the sky. Quail Bay, across from Echo Bay, is a great bird watching spot.

From Echo Bay, continue west for 2 miles on Route 169 to Valley of Fire State Park, a surreal, painted landscape with red, gray, and ocher limestone wind-carved cliffs.

This 56,000-acre preserve of unusual, even grotesque rock formations was, many millennia ago, a region of sand dunes and flat, sandy plains. The sand eventually petrified into stone, which in turn was buried under layers of the earth's crust and later uplifted by seismic activity. Wind and water then took over, eroding the stone and creating the bizarre formations visible today.

The Valley of Fire got its name from the fiery color of its rocks, which range from lavender to tangerine to the predominant bright red hue (attributable to the high iron, or rust, content of the rock). At certain times of day, the valley bears an eerie resemblance to Mars; in fact, its unusual formations have served as the backdrop for many science fiction movies (and westerns).

Before exploring the park, stop at the visitors' center (phone: 702-397-2088) for park regulations, information, and maps. While the center has water coolers and a soda machine, no other concessions are offered in the park, so bring plenty of extra water.

Wandering about the valley, notice the mysterious-looking signs and symbols — petroglyphs and pictographs, respectively — etched into or painted onto the surface of the rocks. The legacy of the enigmatic Basketmaker and Anasazi Pueblo civilizations, who lived here between 300 BC and AD 1150, the carvings and pictures are believed to be records of hunting forays. The ancient pictures afford valuable clues to the culture of these peoples. Atlatl Rock (near the west end of the park), for instance, depicts hunters employing a rudimentary spear launcher (*atlatl* in Aztec), basically a stick with a cup on one end, which acted as a lever to launch the spear.

Throughout the valley are wind-sculpted formations named for just what they resemble. Elephant Rock, accessible via a short trail from the east entrance, requires no description. One of the valley's better-known areas is Mouse's Tank, a hidden canyon marked with ancient petroglyphs. Mouse, a renegade Paiute Indian who hid from local lawmen by seeking out water-collecting basins in the sandstone, was finally apprehended. His hiding places still attract attention, as they evoke the era just before the West was "tamed." Typical desert wildlife inhabits the valley: Coyote, kit fox, spotted skunk, jackrabbits, antelopes, roadrunners, and the rare desert tortoise can all be seen here. Typical desert flora include creosote bushes and deceptively cuddly-looking cholla cacti. The park is open year-round daily from 8:30 AM to 4:30 PM.

Take Route 169 east for 8 miles; then make a left at the "T" crossing for another 8 miles to the *Lost City Museum of Archaeology.*

This area — now the Moapa Valley — was once home to waves of Pueblo, Native American civilizations each superseded by other, more advanced ones.

Around AD 500, farmers settled in the area, planting maize, beans, squash, cotton, and tobacco. Their homes were shallow pits surrounded by rock walls plastered with sunbaked mud (adobe).

The highly advanced Anasazi Pueblo created a 5-mile-long settlement (*pueblo*) along the Muddy River, grouping their homes around central courtyards. They buried their dead under the floor of the house with his or her personal effects — a custom that would later allow archaeologists to unearth significant clues to the amazingly sophisticated Anasazi culture. The civilization mysteriously disappeared around AD 1150, probably due to famine or disease. (It is believed that some Pueblo migrated to what is now Arizona or New Mexico.) In the 1920s, their ancient village — Pueblo Grande de Nevada — was discovered and excavated. About 10 years later Hoover Dam was constructed, creating Lake Mead, which in turn unfortunately buried all vestiges of the original Indian homesites.

The *Lost City Museum* features full-scale, walk-in replicas of the adobe dwellings that sheltered the Anasazi, plus some of their tools and artifacts, and examples of their basketry and pottery. Other exhibits depict the evolution of ancient civilizations that successively inhabited the area. Also on display are farm tools used by the Mormons, who settled in the area in the mid-1880s. For more information, contact the *Lost City Museum* (open daily from 8:30 AM to 4:30 PM; phone: 702-397-2193; admission charge).

To return to Las Vegas, take Route 169 west for 10 miles to I-15. Once there, turn left; Las Vegas is 55 miles to the south. Note that there are no facilities on the return route until the first Las Vegas exit on the freeway.

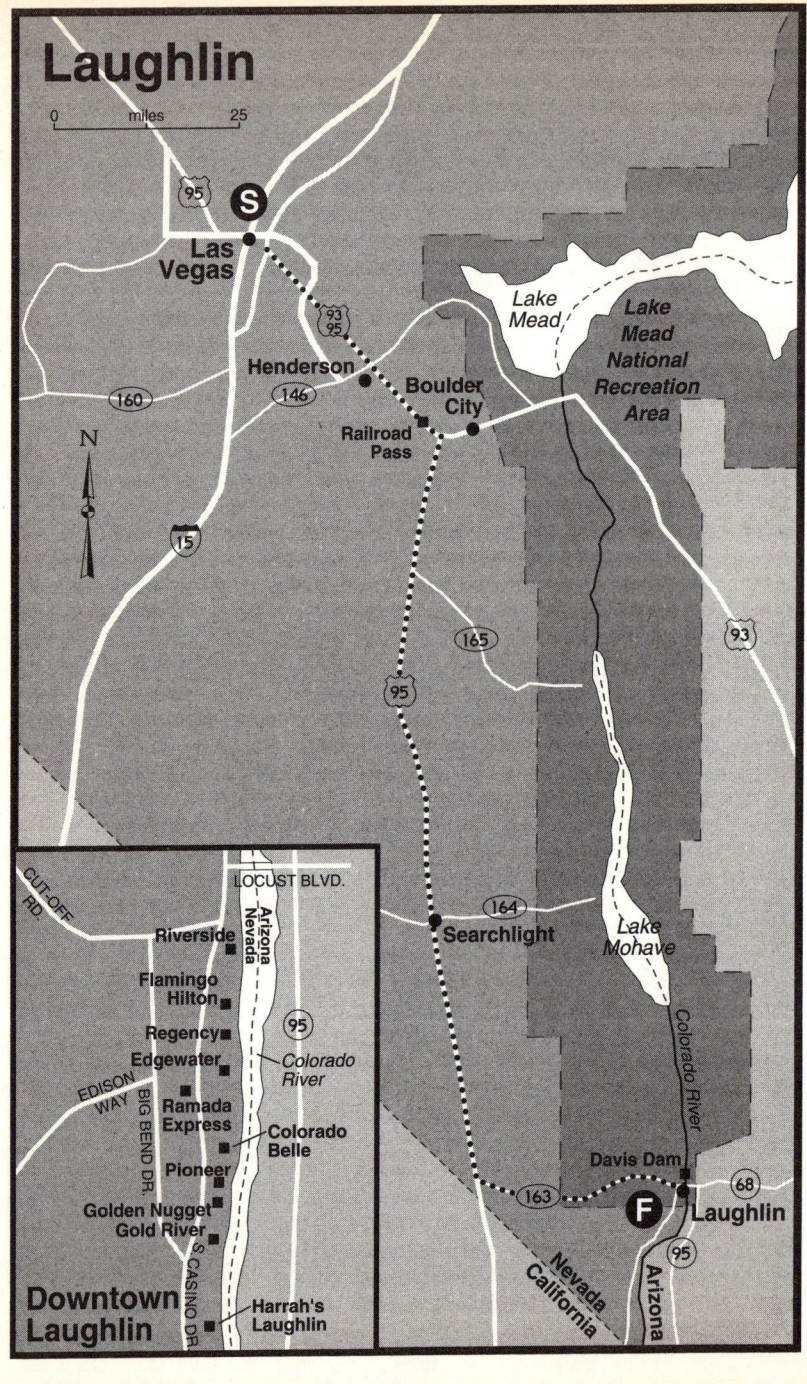

Tour 5: Laughlin

Located on the bank of the swift-moving Colorado River 100 miles from Las Vegas, the picturesque boomtown of Laughlin, Nevada's fastest-growing community, has become the state's new "in" gaming destination. Its friendly hotel-casinos attract not only visitors from California and Arizona — Bullhead City is right across the river from Laughlin — but even native Las Vegans, seeking a break from the relentless activity and crowds that are endemic to their city. On the way to Laughlin is the community of Searchlight, 60 miles south of Las Vegas; harking back to the turn of the century, it's noteworthy primarily as a typical example of the ghost towns so prevalent in this area.

Don't expect beautiful scenery along the fairly stark, 3-hour trek from Las Vegas; the drive through the hot desert, offering few facilities along the way, can be monotonous and even downright exhausting. (Most visitors break up the 200-mile round trip by staying overnight in Laughlin, whose hotels offer great bargains, excellent food, and amenities competitive with those in Las Vegas.)

From Las Vegas take US 93 (Boulder Hwy.) southeast for 25 miles to *Railroad Pass* (phone: 702-294-5000), a casino and restaurant that offers a large buffet at moderate prices — it's the last chance for food and drink until you reach Searchlight. From *Railroad Pass,* take a right onto US 95. Follow this route south for 35 miles to Searchlight.

It's hard (if not impossible) to imagine that at its apogee (1907) the sleepy backwater town of Searchlight was home to more than 5,000 residents, 2 weekly newspapers, 12 saloons, and 44 working gold and silver mines. The mines closed years ago; remnants of their headshafts are visible on the surrounding hills. Searchlight's historic buildings peacefully coexist with modern structures, and a small population of about 600 — mostly retirees — lives here, perhaps waiting for the next big "strike." If you have time, stop in at the *Searchlight Museum* (open weekdays from 9 AM to 5 PM; Saturdays, from 9 AM to 1 PM; 200 N. Michael Wendell Way; phone: 702-455-7955). Through photos, artifacts, and exhibit text, the museum relates the history of the town. Searchlight's few modern facilities include a couple of rustic coffee shops, a general store, and a casino.

From Searchlight, take Route 163 south for the remaining 40 miles to Laughlin.

Rising unexpectedly from the floor of the barren desert, Laughlin's towering hotels — some as high as 20 stories — come as a surprise to many visitors, especially in contrast with the stark monotony of the surrounding terrain. The scene is dominated by the fast-moving Colorado River and, shimmering alongside it, Casino Drive, along which all ten of the city's hotels are situated (another half-dozen hotels are in the planning stages).

Laughlin's brief history began in 1966, when rancher and developer Don Laughlin — then 35 years old — bought a bankrupt bar and restaurant at the end of a dirt road on the banks of the Colorado River. Since he had obtained a gaming license in the Las Vegas area, he was able to acquire an unrestricted gaming license for his casino, and he could offer as many slot machines as he wanted. At the time, he had only eight motel rooms: four for his family and four that he rented. (This still-growing property — the *Riverside* — has expanded to comprise 660 rooms and 5 restaurants.) Recognizing the town's strategic location — on the border of Arizona, where gambling was (and still is) illegal — other enterprising folk followed suit, and large casino-hotels were soon springing up along the main street. Their foresight paid off: Today, Laughlin is the fastest-growing place in Nevada. Indeed, the town is so new that its "founding father" is still an active businessman in the community.

Besides its casinos, Laughlin has two chief tourist attractions. One, its clement weather — the average winter temperature is 72F — draws "snow birds" from the cooler surrounding states. The town's other major draw is the picturesque Colorado River. The diminutive ferryboats that ply the river, shuttling visitors from one hotel-casino to another, are a popular attraction. In addition, two paddlewheelers, the *Little Belle* and the *Fiesta Queen,* and the the cruiser *Riverside* take visitors on cruises along the river as the ships' captain narrates the history of the area. The late-afternoon sails often feature live music. Tickets can be purchased at the ships' docks (the *Little Belle* leaves from the *Edgewater* hotel-casino; the *Fiesta Queen,* from *Harrah's Laughlin* and the *Gold River;* the *Riverside,* from the *Riverside* hotel).

Less than 5 minutes from Laughlin is the manmade Lake Mohave, Lake Mead in miniature (Lake Mohave was created by the Davis Dam, 2 miles north of Laughlin). Its more than 200 miles of fantastic shoreline feature sheer, dramatic rock cliffs and sandy beaches. To get there, cross the Laughlin Bridge into Arizona and turn left at the first light; Lake Mohave is 3 miles north on Route 68. Katherine's Landing (phone: 602-754-3245), about 15 minutes north of Laughlin on Route 68, is the closest marina to Laughlin; here, you can rent everything from houseboats, fishing boats, and power boats to water skiing equipment. The marina has a restaurant and a convenience store, and there's a beach nearby.

If you find yourself riding the momentum of a lucky wave — or if the prospect of the long drive back to Las Vegas sends you reaching for the blackest cup of coffee you can find — consider staying overnight in Laughlin. All ten hotel-casinos offer rates significantly lower than those in Vegas. (The five discussed here get our nod for best in town.) Also, because of the stiff competition among them, prices don't vary much from one to the next, about $25 to $50 for a double room — with the one notable exception of the *Flamingo Hilton,* which costs $90 to $110. The 1,238-room *Colorado Belle* (2100 S. Casino Dr.; phone: 702-298-4000 or 800-458-9500) is designed like a riverboat; the pricey (by Laughlin standards) *Flamingo Hilton* (1855 S. Casino Dr.; phone: 702-298-5111 or 800-HILTONS) offers 2,000 rooms, each with a river view, plus 3 lighted tennis courts, an 1,800-square-foot swimming pool, and a Jacuzzi on the premises. With 1,005 rooms, the *Gold River* (2700 S. Casino Dr.; phone: 702-298-2242 or 800-835-7903) boasts Laughlin's only comedy club, plus a resident troupe of vaudevillian characters who hold forth in the hotel's revamped casino. *Harrah's Laughlin* (2900 S. Casino Dr.; phone: 702-298-4600 or 800-447-8700), a south-of-the-border-theme hotel, boasts the only private beach in town. One section of its large casino is nonsmoking — the only one of its kind in Laughlin. The relatively small (406 rooms) *Ramada Express* (2121 S. Casino Dr.; phone: 702-298-4200 or 800-272-6232) was designed with a railroad motif; guests can take a ride on the narrow-gauge steam locomotive that circles the property.

Also appealing are the hotel dining rooms, which are competitive with those in Las Vegas in terms of both quality and affordability. As is the case with Laughlin's hotels, the restaurants don't vary much in price. The *Gourmet Room* (in the *Riverside;* 1650 S. Casino Dr.; phone: 702-298-2535) is notable for its magnificent view of the river, along with its hearty selection of steaks, seafood, and veal; *Granny's* (in the *Pioneer,* 2200 S. Casino Dr.; phone: 702-298-2442) is especially recommended for its elegant Sunday champagne brunch, which includes caviar and lobster thermidor. For those seeking Mexican fare, *La Hacienda* (in *Harrah's Laughlin,* 2900 S. Casino Dr.; phone: 702-298-4600) is the place to go; their hedonistic desserts — Kahlúa flan and Ibarra tart (made with Mexican chocolate and pecans) — are knockouts. The *Hickory Pit* (in the *Edgewater,* 2020 S. Casino Dr.; phone: 702-298-2453) affords diners a wonderful vista of the Colorado River (and of the chefs in the kitchen, visible through glass windows); specialties include steaks and Australian lobster tails. For exotic pizza — with toppings such as chicken *fajitas* and ham and pineapple — try *Jane's Grill* (in the *Golden Nugget,* 2300 S. Casino Dr.; phone: 702-298-7111). The *Mississippi Lounge* oyster bar and adjacent *Orleans Room* restaurant (both in the *Colorado Belle,* 2100 S. Casino Dr.; phone: 702-298-4000) offer good seafood. And for steak-and-potatoes fare, plus salads tossed tableside, head over to the *Steakhouse* (in the *Ramada Express,* 2121 S. Casino Dr.; phone: 702-298-4200).

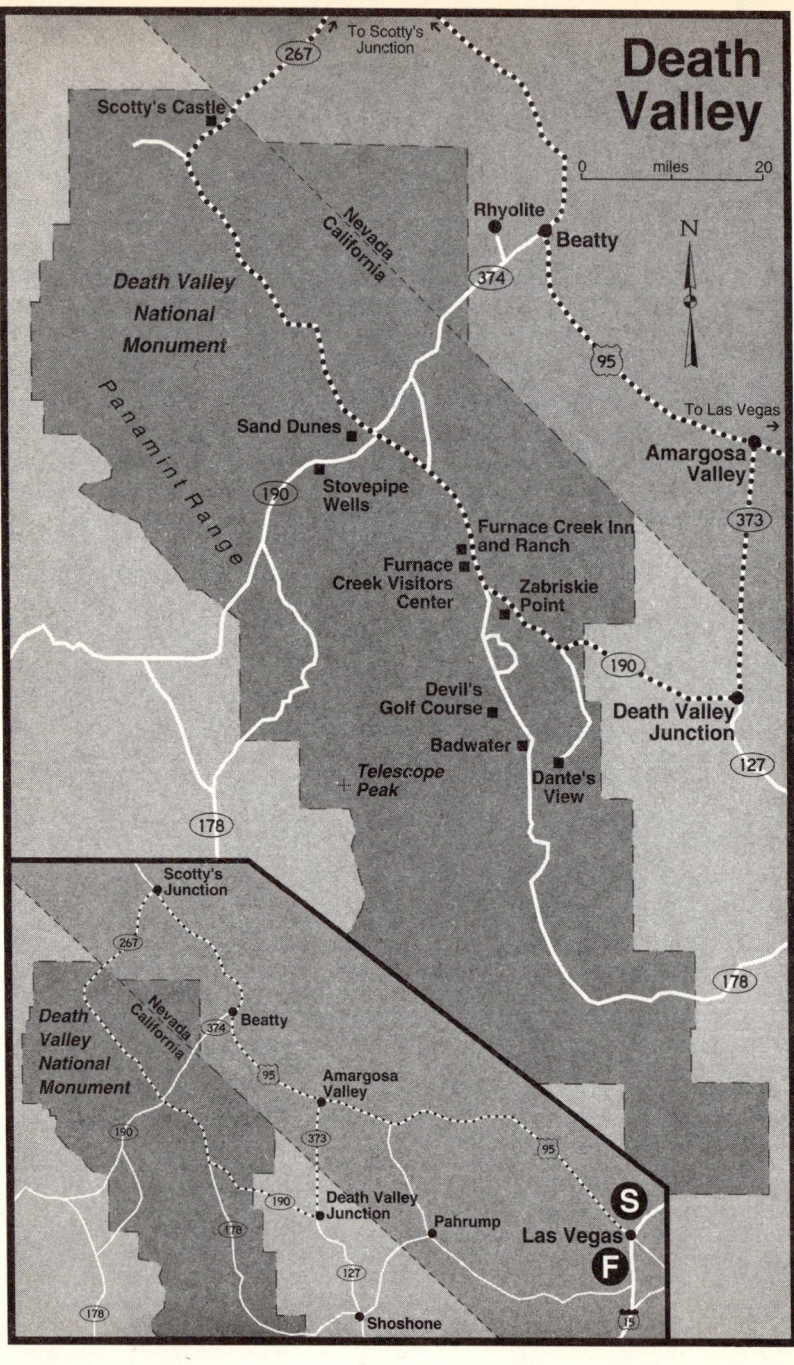

Tour 6: Death Valley National Monument, Rhyolite

Death Valley's stark visual appeal evokes a strong emotional response. While other western national parks and monuments allow visitors to view the beauty of the West, Death Valley invites you to experience something of the spirit of the Old West — the determination, drive, and sense of hope that made this part of America what it is today. The original pioneers knew that they faced the very real possibility of death as they started out across this valley. Most of them made it and went on to new lives in California; at least one lies buried beneath its sands. You can't visit Death Valley without instinctively finding yourself thinking about these settlers. It's a monument to the American zeitgeist of the time and to the spirit of the pioneers who traveled the American West.

Though times have changed since the pioneer days, the weather hasn't: Summer months in Death Valley still bring temperatures consistently above 100F (the average daily high temperature in July is 116F!). If you *do* plan to visit during this time, check to see that your car air conditioner is working, bring along a thermos of something cold, and be sure to get a copy of *Hot Weather Hints* from the visitors' center (Furnace Creek; phone: 619-786-2331). On the return trip to Las Vegas our tour stops at the fascinating ghost town of Rhyolite, a once-booming mining community that was California's third-largest.

Expect to pay more than $150 for a double room in hotels listed below as expensive; between $80 and $150 for those listed as moderate; and less than $80 for those listed as inexpensive.

En Route from Las Vegas The most direct route for the 140-mile drive to Death Valley is north via US 95 from Las Vegas. Follow US 95 through a landscape of sand, sagebrush, and dramatic, wind-swept mountains to Amargosa Valley (Lathrop Wells). Turn left (south) onto Route 373. Follow this route (which crosses into California) for 23 miles until you reach the Death Valley junction. Turn right onto Route 190, which winds for 50 miles northwest through Death Valley National Monument; most of the major sights in the valley are located along or near this route.

DEATH VALLEY NATIONAL MONUMENT: One of the largest of our national monuments, Death Valley National Monument covers 3,000 square miles,

550 of which are below sea level. According to legend, the 120-mile valley originally was called Tomesha ("ground afire") by the Indians, but was given its present name by a party of pioneers who got lost in the valley during the Gold Rush. To the '49ers and the early settlers, Death Valley was a potentially deadly obstacle to be overcome in order to reach the riches of California. Modern travelers find it an exciting, dramatic place that can be explored in relative safety.

Death Valley is part of a region of extremes. At 282 feet below sea level, it is the lowest point in the entire Western Hemisphere. Only 70 air miles away stands the highest point in the continental US — Mt. Whitney, 14,494 feet above sea level. Death Valley is also one of the hottest places on earth, with temperatures recorded as high as 134F in the shade (the all-time world record is 136F, recorded in Libya, in 1922).

Each of the canyons and mountains surrounding the lowlands of Death Valley seems to have its own special colors. Golden Canyon has bright golds and rich purples; Mustard Canyon is various shades of ocher. The Black Mountains have reds, greens, and tans. A particularly interesting attraction is Mosaic Canyon, with walls of smooth beige dolomite marble and eroded surfaces embedded with brilliantly colored pebbles.

If a scientist were to tell you he or she was going to Death Valley to study fish, you might raise an eyebrow. However, several species of fish in the streams of Death Valley do not exist anywhere else in the world. There are, in fact, more than 40 species of plant and animal life indigenous only to Death Valley. Despite its great heat and minuscule rainfall (less than 2 inches a year), Death Valley has springs and several streams that flow — or at least trickle — all year. There's even a small marsh at Saratoga Springs. During migration periods, Death Valley is visited by such unlikely guests as Canada and snow geese, herons, and ducks.

In addition to its valid claims on things that are the highest, the lowest, the oldest, and the biggest, Death Valley also might be the richest. There are many legends about the fabulous lost mines of Death Valley. They may or may not be true, but at one time it certainly had some of the nation's most lucrative mines. There were boomtowns with colorful names like Bullfrog and Skidoo, towns that died when the mines played out, although today you'll pass what remains of these once-vibrant mining centers en route to the Furnace Creek Visitors Center, where you can pick up brochures and maps explaining how to take self-guiding auto tours. There also are slide shows, nature exhibitions, and other activities run by the rangers.

Death Valley actually is the floor of what once was a large inland lake — fed by increased precipitation during the last Ice Age — in the Sierra Nevada range. With the prevailing warming trend and decreasing rainfall, the supply of new water couldn't keep up with the evaporation rate, currently 150 inches per year. Little in the way of rain makes it past the formidable barrier of the Sierras.

If there's one mineral that Death Valley is famous for, it's borax. The borax mines were established in the 1880s, when roads in Death Valley were built for the legendary 20-mule team wagons that hauled the borax out of the valley. Three of the modern roads in the valley follow the route of the old mule teams. At the Harmony Borax Works, 1½ miles north of the visitors' center, are the remains of one of the first processing plants.

One of the most famous landmarks in Death Valley is Scotty's Castle. Walter Scott (or "Death Valley Scotty," as he was known) once had been a performer in Buffalo Bill's *Wild West Show*. He claimed to have built an elaborate, lavishly furnished castle in Grapevine Canyon at the north end of Death Valley, claiming he had paid for it with gold from a secret mine. The castle, standing in an oasis on the edge of the desert, has been famous ever since it was built. The romantic tale of a secret gold mine is, unfortunately, false. The castle was actually built by Albert M. Johnson, a wealthy Chicago businessman who came to Death Valley to check on what turned out to be Scotty's nonexistent mine and later became friends with the flamboyant ex-cowboy.

Among the most spectacular sights of Death Valley are the fantastically eroded golden badlands of Zabriskie Point; the Sahara-like Sand Dunes; the Devil's Golf Course, a craggy white salt flat where the salt pinnacles are as high as 4 feet — and still growing; and Dante's View, from which you look down at Badwater, the lowest point in Death Valley, and up at Telescope Peak, the highest point at 11,046 feet. The latter especially is a must-see. Campgrounds are scattered throughout the valley, among them Furnace Creek, Mesquite Springs, and Wildrose, which are open all year. Reservations are accepted at Furnace Creek only, through *Mistix* (phone: 800-365-2267), but there's almost always plenty of room for everyone, except on holiday weekends and the second weekend in November (the annual *Death Valley '49er Encampment*). The tourist season runs from mid-fall to mid-spring, and the weather is pleasant during the winter. If you're planning to do any hiking, keep in mind at all times that Death Valley got its name for a reason. Always carry plenty of extra water.

CHECKING IN/EATING OUT: *Furnace Creek Inn* – Open from mid-October to early May, this luxurious, 68-room inn has a swimming pool, tennis, an 18-hole golf course (at 205 feet below sea level, the world's lowest), a lounge with entertainment, a fine restaurant, and palm-lined gardens. *Mailing address:* Box 1, Death Valley, CA 92328 (phone: 619-786-2345 or 800-528-6367). Expensive.

Furnace Creek Ranch – This 250-room place has more casual accommodations in cottages and motel units, with a swimming pool, access to the *Furnace Creek Inn* golf course, tennis, horseback riding, restaurant, cocktail lounge, and service station. Adjacent to trailer park and landing strip for light planes. Open all year. Next to the visitors' center on Rte. 190 (phone: 619-786-2361 or 800-528-6367). Moderate.

Stovepipe Wells – Simply furnished, this motel has 82 rooms, a heated pool, 2 restaurants, a cocktail lounge, and a landing strip. Open year-round. Twenty-five miles north of Furnace Creek on Rte. 190 (phone: 619-786-2387). Inexpensive.

En Route from Death Valley From Scotty's Castle, take Route 267 north for 21 miles to Scotty's Junction; then take I-95 south for 36 miles to Beatty. From here take Route 374 southwest for 4 miles to Rhyolite.

RHYOLITE: Way before Las Vegas eclipsed the rest of Nevada, the state was dotted with bustling mining towns that seemed to spring up as quickly as they disappeared. Fueled by the heady promise of infinite wealth that the mines held, gold- and silver-crazed prospectors set up camp in places like Rhyolite, transforming them seemingly overnight into full-fledged communities with banks, hotels, schools, churches, and, naturally, scores of saloons notorious for anything-goes lawlessness and debauchery. Rhyolite — at its height, the third-largest city in the state — stands as a relic of the raucous days of the wild west, as well as a haunting reminder of the extraordinary transience of those cities.

Following a gold strike in 1904, Rhyolite boomed, as miners poured into the area, erecting makeshift tents and shacks. A year later, the town boasted a water system, a post office, and a school; within 2 years Rhyolite's population had ballooned to as many as 10,000, and the residents enjoyed such modern conveniences as electricity, a phone system, three newspapers, a stock exchange, a hospital, a jail, hotels, 48 saloons, two churches, and even an opera house. In 1911, when the mines played out, most of Rhyolite's residents moved away, and the railroads ripped up their tracks and abandoned the town. By 1912, the last mine in the area had closed, the newspapers had folded, and the elaborate *Southern* hotel had been dismantled.

Other than some ramshackle miners' shanties, very few structures in Rhyolite have withstood the test of time. The *Bottle House,* created in 1906 by the (apparently) eccentric Tommy Kelly, is the town's major attraction. To build this oddity, Kelly used thousands (estimates range from 30,000 to 50,000) of Anheuser Busch beer bottles, stacked horizontally atop one another. The only other building still intact is the abandoned railroad depot. Remains of the town's light-peach-colored walls, standing out in stark, eerie relief against the brilliant cobalt-blue sky, call to mind ancient Roman ruins. The remnants of the once-impressive 3-story John S. Cook Bank, the old schoolhouse, and the general store are set against the purplish Bullfrog Hills. For more information about Rhyolite, write to *Friends of Rhyolite,* PO Box 85, Amargosa Valley, Nevada 89020 (no phone).

To return to Las Vegas, follow Route 374 4 miles northeast to Beatty. From there, take I-95 for 120 miles southeast back to Las Vegas.

Tour 7: Zion and Bryce Canyon

According to official Utah sources, one-seventh of all the national parks in the US lie within a 200-mile circle in southern Utah. One of the most spectacular, Zion National Park, is only 154 miles from Las Vegas, about a 3-hour drive. Believing there was a divine presence in Zion National Park, the Mormons gave it its name, which means "heavenly resting place." Indeed, even the most jaded traveler, dwarfed by the vertiginously sheer, gothic canyon walls that loom as high as 2,000 feet, cannot help but be moved by the majesty of these gorges and cliffs. Zion's canyons, carved over millennia by the Virgin River, are graced with scores of waterfalls and an environment rife with ferns, fauna, and, especially in the summer, exquisite wildflowers.

A mere (it's all relative, we admit) 90 miles farther is Bryce Canyon, whose bizarre formations rival the canyon walls of Zion, its older and more sedate geological sibling. In some places, Bryce's hallucinatory pinnacles, formed of crumbly rock, look like huge, grotesque peach- and cotton-candy-colored sand castles; in other sections, like towering yellow, ocher, and purple spires and obelisks. The park, much of it blanketed by forests of fir and spruce, exudes an almost ephemeral quality. In fact, Bryce Canyon is undergoing a constant process of erosion, as evidenced by the chunks of rock on its floor.

Those visiting Zion and Bryce from Las Vegas should plan on at least a 1-night stay. Rent a car in Vegas, drive to Zion and Bryce, and then return to Las Vegas.

All the accommodations along this route fall into roughly the same price range; for a double room in any of them, expect to pay between $70 and $90.

En Route from Las Vegas Take US 15 north for 120 miles to the small town of St. George, Utah, known for its white-steeple-topped Mormon temple; dating from 1877, it's the oldest Mormon temple in the world still in use. Unfortunately, only Mormons are permitted inside, but there is a visitors' center on the premises (440 S. 300 E.; phone: 801-673-5181). The *Seven Wives Inn* bed and breakfast establishment, built in 1873 by Utah pioneer Judge Wooley, has four-poster beds, caned rocking chairs, and lovely old prints hanging on the walls. The claw-foot bathtubs and oak washstands recall the stateliness of times long past. The place's distinctive name refers to the marital status of polygamist Benjamin Franklin Johnson, the great-grandfather of the current owners; 7 of the 13 bedrooms are named for his seven wives (217 N. 100 W.; phone: 801-628-3737). If you just want to stop for a bite, a full menu is offered at *Sil's* (939 E. St. George Blvd.; phone: 801-634-9910).

From St. George, take US 15 for 40 miles to Zion National Park.

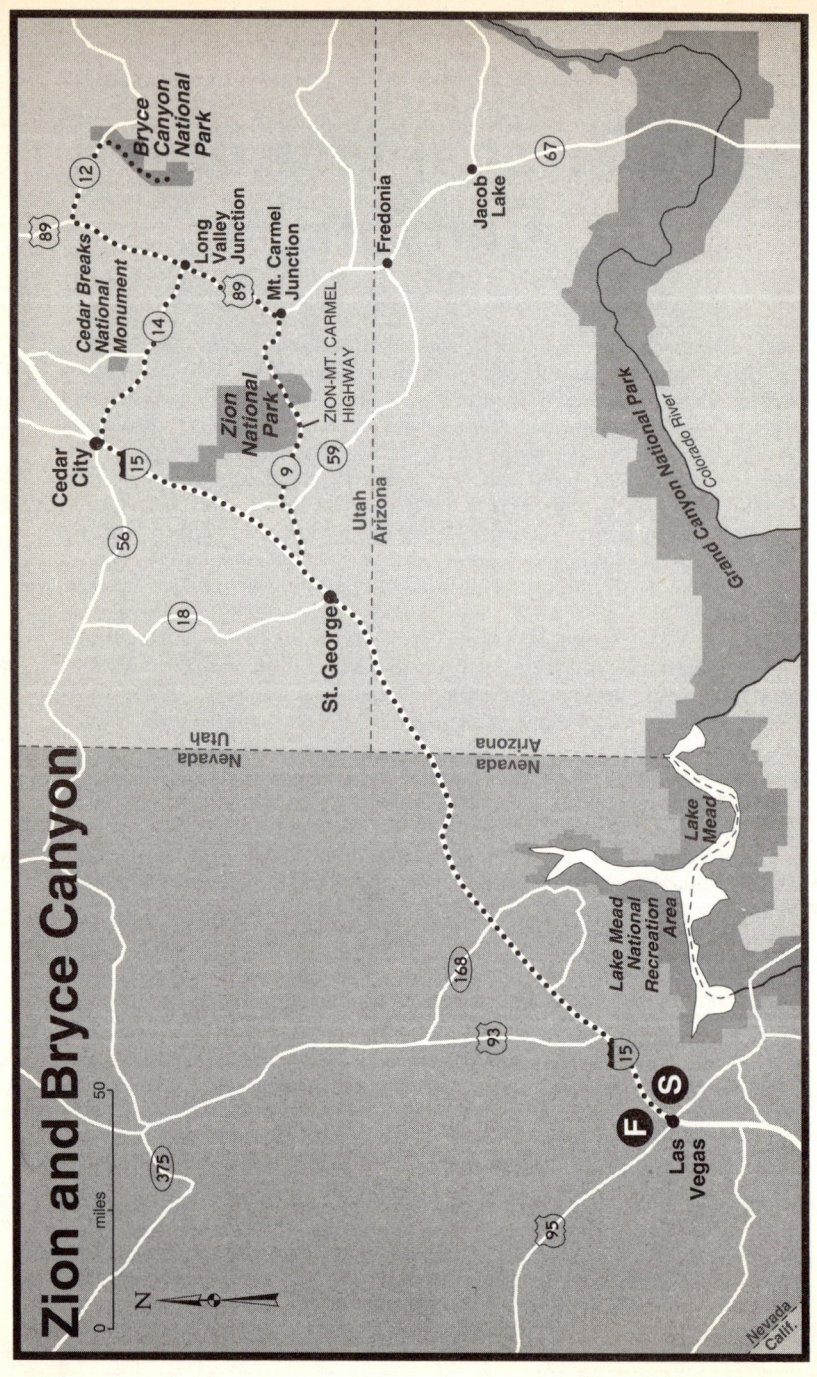

DIRECTIONS / Zion and Bryce Canyon

ZION NATIONAL PARK: A series of dramatic gorges and canyons, Zion is geologically part of the area that includes the Grand Canyon, 125 miles to the south, and Bryce Canyon, 89 miles to the northeast. From the air, the three canyons look like a series of steps, with Grand Canyon the first, Zion in the middle, and Bryce Canyon, the top. The middle sibling of this vast natural canyon-scape is younger than the Grand Canyon and older than Bryce. It dates to the Mesozoic era, a period familiar to us as the time when dinosaurs stalked the earth. (It is possible to see dinosaur footprints in the rocks at Zion if you ask at a visitors' center.) At first a sea, then a desert, Zion's layered buttes and canyons are actually the scars of incredibly harsh climatic changes. These shifts created psychedelic purple, lilac, yellow, and pink rock walls and gorges that shimmer in the clear light. When you see it, you'll know why they call this "the land of rainbow canyons." Geologists believe Zion Canyon was formed by the Virgin River, which carved a gorge out of deep layers of sediment left from the shallow seas that covered the area. We're not sure whether the river was named after explorer Thomas Virgin or the Virgin Mary; it's a moot issue among historians and geologists. The 229 square miles of Zion National Park (established in 1919) were named by a 19th-century Mormon, Isaac Behunin, and the Mormons named a number of the canyon's rock formations as well, including Angels Landing, Three Patriarchs, and Cathedral Mount.

Zion is most impressive for the intense and rugged beauty of its canyons, some of which are impassable even today, just as they were when explorers began visiting the area last century, and for the splendid incandescence of the color of its rock formations. There is a breathtaking drive on the Zion–Mt. Carmel Highway, which runs along the east section of the park, connecting with Canyon Drive, zigzagging up Pine Creek Canyon and through the 5,607-foot-long tunnel. This road, which connects US 15 and US 89, is all the more remarkable when you consider that it was completed in 1930, the year Zion and Bryce canyons were first photographed from the air. Before setting out on this road, be sure to read the tunnel information.

Any visit should begin at the Zion Canyon Visitors Center near the southern entrance, where there's a museum of geological exhibitions and an information desk (phone: 801-772-3256). The lobby affords an excellent view of multicolored Zion Canyon. Another visitors' center is to the north, at the Kolob Canyons exit off US 15. Overnight hikes on any of the 65 miles of trails require permits, which you can pick up at the visitors' centers before setting out. And be sure to check weather conditions — the trails around the canyon rim are sometimes closed due to snow. From *Zion Lodge* (see *Checking In*), you also can embark on horseback trips on Sandbench Trail. For a combined driving-hiking expedition, drive to the Temple of Sinawava, 8 miles from the south entrance of the park. Inside the amphitheater-shaped temple are the two giant pillars for which the temple got its name: the Altar and the Pulpit. Once you reach the temple, the road stops, so you'll have to get out and walk. From here, it's a mile to the beginning of the Narrows, where the Virgin River, sometimes no more than 20 feet wide, races through the giant walls of rock, where columbine and shooting star flowers grow in spring. You can join a guided nature hike during the summer or camp along the ash-, cottonwood-, and moonflower-lined banks of the river in the two designated areas. It's 2½ strenuous miles to Angels Landing at the top of the canyon, but the view is worth it. There is a 2-day backpacking trip along the 12-mile West Rim Trail. The southwestern section of Zion National Park is desert. Coalpits Wash is the home of lizards, cacti, and a small waterfall.

 CHECKING IN: *Zion Lodge* – A group of cabins with gas fireplaces and motel units with a total of 120 rooms. There are horseback riding facilities, a snack bar, and a restaurant. Park tours in an open-air tram and shuttle service are offered from *Memorial Day* to *Labor Day.* Zion National Park (phone: 801-586-7686).

En Route from Zion National Park From the east entrance of the park, follow Route 9 to the junction with US 89; take US 89 north for 44 miles and then right (east) on Route 12 for 13 miles to Bryce Canyon National Park.

BRYCE CANYON NATIONAL PARK: It is believed that the Paiute Indians called the stone formations at Bryce Canyon "tall colored rocks standing like ghosts" and thought the twisted shapes had been cast into stone by a vengeful god. Technically, Bryce's canyons are not canyons at all but breaks in the earth, tremendous pink and white limestone amphitheaters as deep as 1,000 feet. Standing at the eastern edge of the Paunsaugunt Plateau, Bryce Canyon National Park is laced by a network of tributaries (usually dry) of the Paria River. You can get a great view of the splintered rock plateau stretching to the north from the 9,105-foot-high Rainbow Point. (We recommend taking it easy at Bryce Canyon; the 8,000- to 9,000-foot altitude will tire you quickly.)

As at Zion, the best place to start your explorations of Bryce Canyon's 35,835 acres is the visitors' center (phone: 801-834-5322). Here you'll find geological, natural history, and archaeological exhibits. Guided naturalist activities are offered in the summer; horseback rides are available in the spring, summer, and fall. In the summer, there is also a park tour in a restored 1938 *White Motors* original touring limousine, which leaves from *Bryce Canyon Lodge* (see *Checking In*). There are 20 miles of driving roads along the rim of the canyon and 61 miles of hiking trails for exploring either the top or the bottom of the canyon. The most popular hiking trail is the Navajo Loop Trail, a 1- to 2-hour excursion that takes you more than 500 feet into the canyon, past Thor's Hammer and other rock formations. The trail intersects with the 3½-mile Peekaboo Loop Trail and Queen's Garden Trail. Although the Paunsaugunt Plateau was given its name because of a preponderance of beaver (its name means "home of the beaver"), there are no beavers in Bryce Canyon. You should, however, be able to spot skunks, deer, marmots, chipmunks, and squirrels without too much difficulty. Hawks, swallows, and ravens are among the more prevalent winged creatures that can be seen above Bryce Canyon. This is also one of the best places in the country for photography. Light sparkles here, illuminating the canyons so that they seem to glow with an inner fire. Dawn and dusk are the best times to take pictures. Winter activities include cross-country skiing, snowshoeing (snowshoes can usually be borrowed at the visitors' center), and winter camping. Part of one campground is open all winter. Each of the park's two campgrounds has a 14-day restriction.

 CHECKING IN: ***Best Western Ruby's Inn*** – One mile from the entrance to Bryce Canyon, this motel offers 216 units, a restaurant, conference facilities, a grocery store, and an indoor pool. Rte. 63, Bryce Canyon National Park (phone: 801-834-5341 or 800-528-1234).

Bryce Canyon Lodge – This complex comprises cabins, all with gas fireplaces, and motel units with a total of 114 rooms, 4 suites, and a restaurant in the main building. Bryce Canyon National Park (phone: 801-586-7686).

Bryce Canyon Pines – About 8 miles from the park. Facilities include a restaurant, a coffee shop, and a heated swimming pool. Some of the 50 rooms have fireplaces. Rte. 12, Bryce Canyon National Park (phone: 801-834-5441).

The quickest way back to Las Vegas is via Route 12 for 13 miles to US 89, which in another 21 miles intersects with Route 14. Take that for 41 miles to Cedar City, where you can pick up US 15 for 164 miles to Las Vegas.

INDEX

Index

Accommodations. *See* Hotels
Actor's Repertory Theater, 9, 85
Advanced Purchase Excursion (APEX) fares, 11, 12–13
Airplane travel
  cancellations due to personal and/or family emergencies, 65–66
  charter flights, 20–21
    bookings, 21–22
  with children, 54–55
  consumer protection, 26
  discounts on scheduled flights, 22–26
    bartered travel sources, 25–26
    consolidators and bucket shops, 22–24
    generic air travel, 25
    last-minute travel clubs, 24–25
    net fare sources, 22
  flight insurance, 41
  hints for handicapped travelers, 46–47
  scheduled flights, 10
    Advanced Purchase Excursion (APEX) fares, 11, 12–13
    airline clubs, 18–19
    baggage, 18
    delays and cancellations, 19–20
    fares, 10–14
    frequent flyers, 14–15
    getting bumped, 19
    low-fare airlines, 15
    meals, 17–18
    reservations, 15–16
    seating, 16–17
    smoking, 17
    taxes, 15
    tickets, 10
  transportation from the airport to city, 26–27
  trip cancellation and interruption insurance, 40
Aladdin, 89
  casinos at, 110
  shows at, 10, 86, 89
Alcoholic beverages, 66

Automatic teller machines (ATM), 59–60
Automobile insurance, 29, 41

Baccarat, 120
Baggage, 18
  insurance for personal effects and, 39
Bally's, 87, 100, 106, 142
  casinos at, 110
  shows at, 10, 85, 86, 87, 100, 101, 107–8
Bankruptcy and/or default insurance, 40–41
Banking hours, 60
Bartered travel sources, 25–26
Baseball, 83
Basketball, 83–84, 101–2
Bayley, Judy, Theatre, 9, 85
Betting, 84
  See also Casinos; Gambling
Big Falls, 150
Big Six, 116
Bingo, 117
Binion's Horseshoe, casinos at, 110
Black Canyon, 155
Blackjack, 119–20
Boats. *See* Cruises
Bonnie Springs Ranch, 145, 147
Books and bookstores, 69–70
  See also Publications
Bottle House, 166
Boulder City, 82, 153–57
  map, 152
Boulder City Museum, 154
Boulder Dam, 126
Boxing, 84
Brunch, best, 95–96, 106
Bryce Canyon, 134, 167, 170–71
Bryce Canyon National Park, 170–71
Bucket shops and consolidators, 22–24
Buses, 80
Business hours, 60
  in casinos, 102

176 INDEX

Caesars Palace, 78, 87, 141
  casinos at, 103, 109, 110
  shows at, 10
Cameras and equipment, 71
  See also Photographing
Car rental, 27–30, 80
  costs, 28–30
  hints for for handicapped travelers, 47
  insurance, 29, 41
  requirements, 28
Cash machines (ATMs), 59–60
Casinos, 108–9
  business hours in, 102
  favorites, 109–12
  games
    baccarat, 120
    big six, 116
    bingo, 117
    blackjack, 119–20
    craps, 118–19
    keno, 117
    roulette, 117–18
    slots, 115–16
  in hotels, 76–77
  in Laughlin, 160
  rules in, 112
  table manners, 114–15
  terminology in, 112–14
Cathedral Rock, 150
Charleston Heights Arts Center, 9, 85
Children, traveling with, 53–56
  accommodations, 55
  air travel, 54–55
  planning, 53–54
  publications, 53–54
Circus Circus, 102–3, 137–38
  casinos at, 78, 110
  shows at, 56, 78, 91, 138
Clark County Heritage Museum, 82
Clark County Marriage License Bureau, 121
Climate, 9, 135, 160, 163–64
Colleges and universities, 83
Colorado River, boat cruises on, 160
Combination insurance policies, 41–42
Computer services, 70
Consolidators and bucket shops, 22–24
Consumer protection, 26
Convention Center, 78, 89
Costs, calculating, 35
  for car rental, 28–30
Cottonwood Valley, 146
Country clubs, 84

Craps, 118–19
Credit cards, 58–59
  insurance offered by, 29, 39
  telephone calls with, 61
Cruises
  on Colorado River, 160
  on Lake Mead, 33–34, 130, 155
Cultural events, 9–10

Death Valley, 79, 134, 163, 165–66
  map, 162
Death Valley National Monument, 163–65
Default and/or bankruptcy insurance, 40–41
Desert Inn, 75–76, 87–88, 103–4, 138
  casinos at, 88, 104, 110
  golf tournament at, 103–4, 127
  shows at, 104
Devil's Golf Course, 79, 165
Dolphin Habitat, 56, 83, 140
Downtown, slots in, 116
Drinking, 66
Drugs
  illegal, 66–67
  prescription, 64, 80
Dunes, casinos at, 110

Echo Cliff, 150
Electricity, 62
Elephant Rock, 156
Emergency medical treatment, 63–64
  See also Health care
Entertainment, tourist information on, 80
Excalibur, 77, 89, 142–43
  casinos at, 110
  shows at, 10, 86, 89, 108, 143

Fashion Show Mall, 138–39, 140
Festivals, 10
  See also Special Events
First aid, 63
Fishing, 78, 84, 129–30, 155
Fitzgerald's, casinos at, 110–11
Fitness centers, 84
Flamingo Hilton, 75, 89, 139–40, 141–42
  shows at, 10, 85, 86, 89, 107
Flight insurance, 41
Food
  on airplanes, 17–18
  brunch, 95–96, 106
  See also Restaurants

INDEX 177

Football, 84
Frequent flyers, 14–15

Gambling, 76–77, 100–1
  sports betting, 84
  See also Casinos
Generic air travel, 25
Golden Nugget, 78, 88–89, 100, 104, 111
Golf, 84
  country clubs, 84, 127–28
  tournaments, 10, 81, 103–4, 127
Grand Canyon, air tour of, 33
Guinness World of Records Museum, 10, 56, 82, 137

Ham, Artemus W., Concert Hall, 9, 85
Handicapped travelers, hints for, 42–48
  airplane travel, 46–47
  ground transportation, 47
  package tours, 47–48
  planning, 42–46
  publications, 43–46
Harrah's, 89, 139
Health care, 62–66
  first aid, 63
  hints for older travelers, 51
  medical assistance, 63–64
  minimizing risks, 63
  pharmacies and prescription drugs, 64, 80
  planning, 62–63
  publications, 65
Hellorado Festival, 10, 81
Herigstad's Gallery, 81–82
Hiking, 150–51
Hoover Dam, 78, 133, 153, 154–55
Hoover Dam Museum, 82
Hotels, 87–91
  best in city, 102–5
  downtown, 78
  on strip, 76–78
  shows at, 85–86
  surcharges for telephone calls, 62
  tipping, 67
  See also Accommodations; *names of specific hotels*

Ice Box Canyon, 146
Imperial Palace, 139–40
  shows at, 85–86, 108
Imperial Palace Auto Collection, 10, 82
Insurance, 38–42
  automobile, 29, 41
  baggage and personal effects, 39
  combination policies, 41–42
  default and/or bankruptcy, 40–41
  flight, 41
  personal accident and sickness, 39–40
  trip cancellation and interruption, 40

Jaycees State Fair, 10, 81
Jogging, 84–85

Keno, 117
Kyle Canyon, 149–50

Lake Mead, 78, 129–30, 133, 153, 155–56
  air tour of, 33
  boat cruises, 33–34, 130, 155
Lake Mead National Recreation Area, 154
Lake Mohave, 160
Last-minute travel clubs, 24–25
Las Vegas Art Museum, 10, 82
Las Vegas Chamber Orchestra, 85
Las Vegas Hilton, 10, 89
  casinos at, 111, 137
  shows at, 10, 137
Las Vegas International Marathon, 10, 33, 81
Las Vegas Invitational Golf Tournament, 10, 81, 127
Las Vegas Natural History Museum, 10, 82
Las Vegas Senior Classic, 10, 127
Lathrop Wells, 79
Laughlin, 134, 159–61
  map, 158
Lee Canyon, 149
Legal aid, 66
Liberace Museum, 10, 82
Lied Discovery Children's Museum, 56, 82
Local services, 80–81
Lost City Museum of Archaeology, 10, 83, 133, 153, 156–57
Low-fare airlines, 15
LPGA International Golf Tournament, 10, 81

Magazines, 70
  See also Publications
Mail, 60–61, 80–81
Maps
  Boulder City, 152
  Mt. Charleston, 148

178 INDEX

Maps (*cont.*)
   Death Valley National Monument, 162
   Las Vegas, 4–5
   Laughlin, 158
   Red Rock Canyon, 144
   The Strip, 136
   Zion and Bryce Canyon, 168
Medical assistance, 63–64, 80
   See also Health care
Mesquite Flat, 79
MGM Grand, 77, 78, 109, 142, 143
Mineral Collection, 82
Minotaur Fine Arts Ltd., 82
Mirage, 77–78, 88, 100, 104–5, 109, 140–41
   casinos at, 111
   Dolphin Habitat at, 56, 83, 140
   shows at, 10, 85, 88, 104, 107
Moapa Valley, 156–57
Money
   cash machines (ATMs), 59–60
   check cashing, 80, 115
   credit cards, 58–59
   sending, 59
   See also Credit cards; Traveler's checks
Mt. Charleston, 78–79, 85, 122, 133–34, 149–51
   accommodations, 149, 150–51
   map, 148
Mouse's Tank, 156
Museum of Natural History, 10, 82–83, 122
Museums, 81–83
Music, 85

National Finals Rodeo, 10, 81
Net fare sources, 22
Nevada Dance Theatre, 85
Nevada Golf Hall of Fame, 128
Nevada Opera Theatre, 85
Nevada State Museum and Historical Society, 83
Nevada Test Site, 150
Newsletters, 70
   See also Publications
New West Stage Company, 9, 85
New Year's Eve, 10, 100
Nightclubs and nightlife, 85–86
   best shows, 101, 106–8
   tickets for, 86
   See also specific hotels

Older travelers, 50
   discounts and packages, 51–53
   health care, 51
   planning, 50–51
Old Nevada, 145, 147
Omnimax, 141

Package tours, 30–34
   for handicapped travelers, 47–48
   for older travelers, 51–53
   offered by hotels, 34
   for single travelers, 49–50
   See also Tours
Pahrump Valley Vineyards, 145, 147
Palace Station, casinos at, 111
Pawnshops, 115
Personal accident and sickness insurance, 39–40
Personal effects insurance, 39
Pharmacies and prescriptions, 64, 80
Photography, 122–26
   Bryce Canyon National Park, 170
   in casinos, 114
   equipment for, 71
Pine Creek Canyon, 146
Planning the trip, 35–37
   health care, 62–63
   hints for traveling with children, 53–54
   hints for handicapped travelers, 42–46
   hints for older travelers, 50–51
   hints for single travelers, 49–50
Plaza Hotel, 89–90
   casinos at, 111
   shows at, 86, 108
Publications
   books, 69–70
   for handicapped travelers, 43–46
   health care, 65
   magazines, 70
   newsletters, 70
   for older travelers, 51
   for single travelers, 50
   for traveling with children, 53–54, 55

Red Rock Canyon, 126, 133, 145–47
Red Rock Canyon Conservation Area, 79
Religion, 68
Repertory Theater, 85
Restaurants, 91–96, 102
   at Lake Mead, 155
   best in city, 105–6

INDEX 179

in Laughlin, 161
in Mt. Charleston, 150
in Red Rock Canyon, 147
tipping, 67
See also Food
Rhyolite, 166
Ripley's Believe It or Not Odditorium, 10, 56, 83
Riviera, 90
  casinos at, 111
  shows at, 10, 85, 86, 108, 138
Rock climbing, 79
Rodeos, 10, 81
Roulette, 117–18

Sahara, 90, 100, 137
  casinos at, 111
  shows at, 86
Sales tax, 80
Sam's, casinos at, 111
Sands, 90
  casinos at, 111
  shows at, 90, 139
Sandstone Quarry, 146
Scotty's Castle, 79, 165
Scuba diving, 130
Searchlight, 159
Searchlight Museum, 159
Senior Classic Golf Tournament, 81
Sex tease clubs, 86
Shopping, 83
  at Fashion Show Mall, 83, 138–39
  at Forum Shops, 87, 103, 141
  hours, 60
  specialty, 83
Single travelers, hints for, 49–50
  package tours, 49–50
  planning, 49
  publications, 50
Skiing, 85, 151
Ski Lee, 149, 151
Slots, 115–16
Special events, 81
Sports and fitness, 83–85, 127–30
Spring Mountain Ranch, 85, 145, 146–47
Spring Mountain State Park, 79
Stardust, 90, 100, 138
  shows at, 85
Strip
  casinos on, 76–78, 109
  hotel shows on, 85–86
  hotels on, 87–91
  photography on, 125–26
  tennis courts on, 128–29
  tour of, 135–43
    map, 136
Sunburn, 63

Taxes
  on airfare, 15
  sales, 80
Taxis, 80
Telephone, 61–62, 80
  emergency number, 62
  hotel surcharges for calls, 62
Telescope Peak, 79, 150, 165
Tennis, 85, 128–29
Theater, 85
Thomas and Mack Center, 10, 101–2
Tickets, for nightclub shows, 86
Time zone, 60
Tipping, 67–68
  in casinos, 114
Tourist information, 69–70, 79–80
Tours, 133–71
  Boulder City, Hoover Dam, Lake Mead, Valley of Fire, 153–57
    map, 152
  Death Valley National Monument, Rhyolite, 163–66
    map, 162
  of Grand Canyon, 33
  Laughlin, 159–61
    map, 158
  Mt. Charleston, 149–51
    map, 148
  Red Rock Canyon, Pahrump Winery, 145–47
    map, 144
  strip, 135–43
    map, 136
  Zion and Bryce Canyon, 167–71
    map, 168
  See also Package tours
Transportation, 80
  from the airport to the city, 26–7
  hints for handicapped travelers, 47
  local, 80
  See also Airplane travel; Buses; Car rental; Limousines; Taxis
Travel agents, how to use, 37–38

Traveler's checks, 57–58
Treasure Island, 141
Trip cancellation and interruption insurance, 40
Tropicana, 90–91, 109, 142
   shows at, 10, 85, 86, 90–91

University of Nevada at Las Vegas, 82, 83

Valley of Fire State Park, 126, 153, 156
Vegas World, 100
   casinos at, 111–12, 116

Walking tours. *See* Tours
Water, drinking, 63
Weather, 9, 135, 160, 163, 164
Weddings, 81, 120–22
   chapels, 81, 121–22
Wet 'n' Wild Theme Park, 56, 78, 137
Willow Spring, 146
Wineries, 147
World Series of Poker, 81, 112

Zabriskie Point, 165
Zion National Park, 134, 167, 169–70
Zoo. *See* Mirage